ALSO BY HAROLD BLOOM

HAROLD

The AMERICAN

The Emergence of

SIMON & SCHUSTER

BLOOM

RELIGION

the Post-Christian Nation

NEW YORK LONDON TORONTO SYDNEY TOKYO SINGAPORE

SIMON & SCHUSTER
SIMON & SCHUSTER BUILDING
ROCKEFELLER CENTER
1230 AVENUE OF THE AMERICAS
NEW YORK, NEW YORK 10020

SIMON & SCHUSTER AND COLOPHON ARE REGISTERED TRADEMARKS
OF SIMON & SCHUSTER INC.

DESIGNED BY KAROLINA HARRIS
MANUFACTURED IN THE UNITED STATES OF AMERICA

LIBRARY OF CONGRESS CATALOGING-IN-PUBLICATION DATA
BLOOM, HAROLD.
   THE AMERICAN RELIGION: THE EMERGENCE OF THE POST-CHRISTIAN NATION/HAROLD BLOOM.
      P. CM.
   INCLUDES INDEX.
   1. UNITED STATES—RELIGION. 2. CHRISTIAN SECTS—UNITED STATES. 3. GNOSTICISM. I. TITLE.
BR515.B58 1992
291'.0973—DC20   91-47559 CIP
ISBN 0-671-67997-X

Acknowledgments

I am much indebted to my editor, Robert Bender, to my copy editor, Andrew Attaway, to my literary agents, Glen Hartley and Lynn Chu, and to my research assistants: Joy Beth Lawrence, Michael Dietz, Anne Blue, David Daily, Daryl Calkins, Jennifer Wagner, Scott Gunn, and Martha Scrpas.

My largest obligation must go unacknowledged. The Southern Baptist minister who assisted me in the three chapters upon that denomination has chosen, no doubt wisely, to go unnamed in this book. My quotations from the person whom I have called the Reverend John Doe nevertheless are not of my own composition. My interpretations of his insights are my own, and are not always shared by him.

Harold Bloom
September 1, 1991

for Richard Poirier

Contents

Even now, in 1848, it certainly looks as though politics were everything; but it will be seen that the catastrophe (the Revolution) corresponds to us and is the obverse of the Reformation: then everything pointed to a religious movement and proved to be political; now everything points to a political movement, but will become religious.

—Søren Kierkegaard, *Journals*
(edited by Alexander Dru)

Invocation:
The Evening Land

FREEDOM, in the context of the American Religion, means being alone with God or with Jesus, the American God or the American Christ. In social reality, this translates as solitude, at least in the inmost sense. The soul stands apart, and something deeper than the soul, the Real Me or self or spark, thus is made free to be utterly alone with a God who is also quite separate and solitary, that is, a free God or God of freedom. What makes it possible for the self and God to commune so freely is that the self already is of God; unlike body and even soul, the American self is no part of the Creation, or of evolution through the ages. The American self is not the Adam of Genesis but is a more primordial Adam, a Man before there were men or women. Higher and earlier than the angels, this true Adam is as old as God, older than the Bible, and is free of time, unstained by mortality. Whatever the social and political consequences of this vision, its imaginative strength is extraordinary. No American pragmatically feels free if she is not alone, and no American ultimately concedes that she is part of nature.

Our war against Iraq, just completed, was a true religious war, but not one in which Islam was involved spiritually, on either side. Rather it was the war of the American Religion (and of the Amer-

ican Religion abroad, even among our Arab allies) against whatever
denies the self's status and function as the true standard of being
and of value. Democracy is not at issue here, and even private
property is not at the center. President George Bush, generally not
considered overdevout, followed President Reagan and other precursors (Nixon, Ford, Carter) by summoning Billy Graham as an
emblem of the American Religion. Appearing, Bible perpetually in
hand, at the President's side, Graham implicitly certified the war
as having biblical sanction. I will venture, in this book, that while
Judaism and traditional Christianity are not biblical religions (despite all their assertions), the American Religion indeed is biblical,
though its Bible may be confined largely to Saint Paul (the Southern Baptists) or be an American set of replacement Scriptures (the
Mormons, Seventh-day Adventists, Christian Scientists, among
others).

Sydney Ahlstrom emphasized that there was no distinctive
American theology, even though he (and Tolstoy before him) spoke
of "the American religion." If that religion had a theologian, according to Ahlstrom, it was Emerson. Of America, Emerson observed: "Great country, diminutive minds. America is formless,
has no terrible and no beautiful condensation." That was in June
1847, when the American sage was still angry about our famous
engagement in the Mexican War, Mexico being the Iraq of that
American moment. His observation remains true; we are formless.
Our imaginative literature, despite its major sequence of poets and
novelists—Hawthorne, Melville, Whitman, Dickinson, Mark
Twain, Henry James, Frost, Stevens, Eliot, Faulkner, Fitzgerald,
Hemingway, Hart Crane—gives us as yet neither a terrible nor a
beautiful condensation of our national character. These all are
strong authors, but they tend to keep their distance from the
Orphic and Gnostic abysses of the national self, lest they vanish
into it. If we are to find our frequently terrible, sometimes beautiful condensation, then I suspect we must locate it in the inner and
formless forms of our national faith, in the implicit vagaries of the
African-American religionists, the Southern Baptists, the Mormons, the Pentecostals, and the other peculiarly American varieties
of spiritual experience.

Nothing could be further from the American Religion than the
famous and beautiful remark by Spinoza in his *Ethics:* that whoever
loved God truly should not expect to be loved by God in return.

The essence of the American is the belief that God loves her or
him, a conviction shared by nearly nine out of ten of us, according
to a Gallup poll. To live in a country where the vast majority so
enjoys God's affection is deeply moving, and perhaps an entire
society can sustain being the object of so sublime a regard, which
after all was granted only to King David in the whole of the Hebrew Bible. The process of democratizing and Americanizing
Christianity, traced so powerfully by Nathan Hatch and Jon Butler, may have stemmed from the American Revolution, or con-
versely, may have helped engender the Revolution. Not being a
historian, I cannot tell. But as a religious critic I remain startled by
and obsessed with the revivalistic element in our religious experience. Revivalism, in America, tends to be the perpetual shock of
the individual discovering yet again what she and he always have
known, which is that God loves her and him on an absolutely
personal and indeed intimate basis. Spinoza's noble disinterested-
ness or intellectual love of God has been profoundly un-American,
at least since the start of our nineteenth century, here in our Eve
ning Land.

I
ORIGINS

1
What Is Religious Criticism?

THIS is an American literary critic's book about the inner spirit of our national faith, but the genre of this study is not literary criticism. Rather, I have attempted the experiment of what I call religious criticism, a mode of description, analysis, and judgment that seeks to bring us closer to the workings of the religious imagination. Literary criticism, as I have learned to practice it, relies finally upon an irreducibly *aesthetic* dimension in plays, poems, and narratives. Analogously, religious criticism must seek for the irreducibly *spiritual* dimension in religious matters or phenomena of any kind. Aesthetic values, in my vision, transcend societal and political concerns, since such concerns increasingly are better served by bad art than by good. Spiritual values similarly transcend the claims of society and politics, which now also seem to benefit more from unimaginative than from imaginative beliefs. Literature and religion are not allied enterprises, except insofar as both are conceptual orphans, stumbling about in our cosmological emptiness that stretches between the unattainable poles of meaning and of truth.

As the object of religious criticism, or this quest for a spirituality that survives every reduction, I have taken our unacknowledged national faith, which I follow Sydney Ahlstrom (and Tolstoy) in calling the American Religion. Mormons and Southern Baptists call themselves Christians, but like most Americans they are closer to ancient Gnostics than to early Christians. I have centered more upon the Mormons and the Southern Baptists than upon our other major denominations (for reasons that I will expound fully), but most American Methodists, Roman Catholics, and even Jews and Muslims are also more Gnostic than normative in their deepest and unwariest beliefs. The American Religion is pervasive and overwhelming, however it is masked, and even our secularists, indeed even our professed atheists, are more Gnostic than humanist in their ultimate presuppositions. We are a religiously mad culture, furiously searching for the spirit, but each of us is subject and object of the one quest, which must be for the original self, a spark or breath in us that we are convinced goes back to before the Creation.

A nation obsessed with religion rather desperately needs a religious criticism, whether or not it is prepared to receive any commentary whatsoever on so problematical and personal a question as the individual's relation to group persuasions: a country that regards itself as Christian hardly will welcome a kakangelist who arrives with the ill-tidings that its beliefs are not at all what they purport to be. The authority of the critic is therefore a relevant matter; just as urgent will be his declaration of interest. He is decidedly not a Christian, but is a Gnostic Jew, who has his own quarrel with normative Judaism. So "Gnostic" is for him scarcely an accusatory term, nor are Christian Gnostics more or less preferable to traditional Protestants. The standard of value in this book is the religious imagination, and the American Religion, in its fullest formulations, is judged to be an imaginative triumph. Its social and political consequences are something else, but my own emphasis sets these aside.

Most contemporary studies of religion in the United States are exercises in sociology or in history; more rarely, they invoke psychology and philosophy, and sometimes even theology. Religious criticism pragmatically follows Emerson and William James in seeking always the American difference, which for worse and for better certainly has made a difference. As for European precursors, religious criticism must cite Kierkegaard and Nietzsche, who more than Carlyle and Matthew Arnold may be said to have established the mode. Kierkegaard's critical enterprise was to understand the immense difficulty of becoming a Christian in any society ostensibly Christian:

> Just think what it means to live in a Christian state, a Christian nation, where everything is Christian, and we are all Christians, where, however a man twists and turns, he sees nothing but Christianity and Christendom, the truth and witnesses to the truth—it is not unlikely that this may have an influence upon the nobler domestic animals, and thereby in turn upon that which, according to the judgment of both the veterinary and the priest, is the most important thing, namely, the progeny.

Nietzsche, being a post-Christian, urged us to meet this dilemma by taking just one step more, and forgiving ourselves through our own grace, after which the entire drama of fall and redemption would be acted out in one's own self. "All religions are at the deepest level systems of cruelties" may be Nietzsche's darkest insight, particularly since he taught us that only pain, suffering, cruelty creates memory for human beings, as for animals. Christianity gives suffering a meaning not so much to relieve suffering as to allow meaning to get started. The suffering of Jesus gives Christianity its supposed truth and its supposed meaning, since the Christ or God-Man does not come so much that we can share God's joy, but rather that God can share our suffering. We perish of the truth, in Nietzsche, and we perish without it, in Kierkegaard. This is religious criticism, but not wholly apt for America, which may be why Emerson and William James, rather than Kierkegaard and Nietzsche, are the more pragmatic models for an American religious criticism.

The greatest document of that criticism may always be Emerson's "Divinity School Address" of 1838, with its extraordinarily American vision of Christ:

> Jesus Christ belonged to the true race of prophets. He saw with open eye the mystery of the soul. Drawn by its severe harmony, ravished with its beauty, he lived in it, and had his being there. Alone in all history he estimated the greatness of man. One man was true to what is in you and me. He saw that God incarnates himself in man, and evermore goes forth anew to take possession of his World. He said, in this jubilee of sublime emotion, "I am

divine. Through me, God acts; through me, speaks. Would you see God, see me; or see thee, when thou also thinkest as I now think." But what a distortion did his doctrine and memory suffer in the same, in the next, and the following ages! There is no doctrine of the Reason which will bear to be taught by the Understanding. The understanding caught this high chant from the poet's lips, and said, in the next age, "This was Jehovah come down out of heaven. I will kill you, if you say he was a man." The idioms of his language and the figures of his rhetoric have usurped the place of his truth; and churches are not built on his principles, but on his tropes. Christianity became a Mythus, as the poetic teaching of Greece and of Egypt, before. He spoke of miracles; for he felt that man's life was a miracle, and all that man doth, and he knew that this daily miracle shines as the character ascends. But the word Miracle, as pronounced by Christian churches, gives a false impression; it is Monster. It is not one with the blowing clover and the fallen rain.

Emerson, like William James after him, makes the American Religion beautifully overt, and after more than one hundred and fifty years this passage still has the capacity to give offence, particularly to Fundamentalists who cannot understand their own version of the American Religion. What makes Emerson's paragraph a superb model for American religious criticism is condensed into its key sentence: "The idioms of his language and the figures of his rhetoric have usurped the place of his truth; and churches are not built on his principles, but on his tropes." Substitute Freud for Jesus as the antecedent for "his" in that sentence and you receive a powerful insight into a minor but influential version of the American Religion, the Institutes for Psychoanalysis that forlornly dot our cities. The Freudian Fundamentalists (of the Ego Psychology sect) are as literal minded as the Southern Baptist Fundamentalists, and both groups believe that their sacred texts, the Standard Edition of Freud and the Holy Bible, somehow interpret themselves and are inerrant. Emerson knows that religion is imagined, and always must be reimagined, but Fundamentalists of any persuasion refuse to know that they have chosen forms of worship from poetic tales (to paraphrase William Blake rather than Emerson, who is very close here to Blake).

The next great leap in American religious criticism belongs to

William James, who as yet has found no successor. Introducing his lectures that became *The Varieties of Religious Experience* (1902), James permanently marked the American sense of religion as being almost wholly experiential:

> Religion, therefore, as I now ask you arbitrarily to take it, shall mean for us *the feelings, acts, and experiences of individual men in their solitude, so far as they apprehend themselves to stand in relation to whatever they may consider the divine.* Since the relation may be either moral, physical, or ritual, it is evident that out of religion in the sense in which we take it, theologies, philosophies, and ecclesiastical organizations may secondarily grow. In these lectures, however, as I have already said, the immediate personal experiences will amply fill our time, and we shall hardly consider theology or ecclesiasticism at all.

James's italics center the Emersonianism of his vision, and bring us closer to crucial elements that mark the American difference: solitude, individuality and the pragmatism of feelings, acts, and experiences rather than thoughts, desires, and memories. The "personal" modifies "experiences" and prepares for the American Christ of the twentieth century, who has become *a personal experience* for the American Christian, quite clearly for the Evangelicals. Less obviously, this is Christ for all who wish to call themselves Christians in the United States. Perhaps it is the Christ of all Americans, whether Mormons or Jews, Muslims or secularists, since the American Christ is more an American than he is Christ.

Awareness, centered on the self, is *faith* for an American: that may be the principal teaching of religious criticism as practiced by Emerson and by William James. *Habits of the Heart* (1985), a study by Robert Bellah and four other sociologists, philosophers, and theologians, may take us as far into the dilemmas of religious self-awareness in contemporary America as sociology ever can take us. In their chapter on religion, Bellah and his colleagues present us with "Sheilaism," named for a young nurse they call Sheila Larson. "Sheilaism" urges us to love ourselves and be gentle with ourselves, a benign doctrine surely. Bellah's group rather gently chides this benignity, since Sheilaism would make us a nation of two hundred and fifty million sects:

In any case, the influence of the sects on American society has been enormous. They are a major source of our individualism and of the pervasive American idea that all social groups are fragile and in need of constant energetic effort to maintain them.

The American self or sect, and the American social group, alike are fragile: this persuasion is certainly rampant among us, and is the central insight of *Habits of the Heart*. Is it a *religious* insight, product of religious criticism? I think not, which suggests a crucial limit in the sociology of religion. Is an American sect somehow at once self and social group? Is there not a Mormon or Southern Baptist self that is intrinsically at odds with Mormon or Southern Baptist gatherings? The fragility of a self or of a sect of one is very different from the fragility of the Southern Baptist Convention. Walt Whitman is our Hermetic national poet, our celebrant of the American self, but he sings two selves at once. One is Walt Whitman, an American, one of the roughs, endlessly merging into groups, but the other is "the real me" or "me myself," absolutely fragile, always standing apart. Two American selves (at the least) would be the amendment that American poetry and literary criticism, and religious criticism, would offer to the sociology of religion.

Bellah and his colleagues have the ardent aim of reconstituting our social world, so that individualism would clash less with commitment in American life. The endeavor is doubtless admirable, but a keener mode of religious criticism might show that our partly hidden national religion teaches a purely inner freedom. *Habits of the Heart* makes a useful contrast with a fierce polemical work, Philip J. Lee's *Against the Protestant Gnostics* (1987). Lee, raised as an American Southern Presbyterian, is now a Presbyterian parish minister in Canada, and writes from a traditionally Protestant perspective against what he accurately judges to be a pervasive Gnosticism in American Protestantism. He sees what I see, the American Religion, but what fascinates me moves him to dread and wrath, whether he encounters it among liberal or Fundamentalist Protestants. His indictment seems to me misdirected, because what is so profoundly American clearly does suit the religious genius of our nation, and cannot be extirpated. But Lee deserves all praise for seeing clearly what is indeed there to be seen, though concealed in the multiple masks of supposed Protestantism.

Much of my next chapter will be given to a presentation of historical Gnosticism, so that I wish to give only a minimal account of it here, enough to explain Lee's *Against the Protestant Gnostics* and its uncanny relation to Bellah's *Habits of the Heart*. Lee regards ancient Gnosticism as a Christian heresy, but such a judgment is highly disputable. I myself believe that Gnosticism, like Christianity itself, began as a Jewish heresy, just as Islam rose as a kind of Jewish Christian restoration movement, Muhammad's attempt to return to what he took to be the faith of Abraham, and of Abraham's son, Ishmael, traditional ancestor of the Arabs. But *the* Gnostics, in a narrow sense, were a proto-Christian sect of the second century of the Common Era, whose broad beliefs centered in two absolute convictions: the Creation, of the world and of mankind in its present form, was the same event as the Fall of the world and of man, but humankind has in it a spark or breath of the uncreated, of God, and that spark can find its way back to the uncreated, unfallen world, in a solitary act of knowledge.

What Lee protests in American Protestantism is the exaltation of the elite self as against community, a protest pragmatically parallel to the feeling of Bellah and his associates that society is sacrificed in the individualism of American spiritual life. Against Lee and Bellah, I surmise that the spiritual life of our contemporary America is overdetermined, and that what is working through our spirituality are tendencies now nearly two centuries old. Urging the need for community upon American religionists is a vain enterprise; the experiential encounter with Jesus or God is too overwhelming for memories of community to abide, and the believer returns from the abyss of ecstasy with the self enhanced and otherness devalued. Even in Mormonism, where the family, not the individual, is the exalted unity, the Mormon as priest, being always a male, hardly regards his wife and children as being wholly other than himself. How are we to understand, and judge, an American spirituality that, to be authentic, seems always fated to make the believer, ultimately, a worse citizen, despite all the blatherings of our ideology?

II

The genre of this book, as I have stated, is what I call "religious criticism." In literary criticism, there must be a final reliance upon an irreducibly aesthetic element in one's experience of what is being studied. Without the aesthetic, we are not reading a poem, play, story, or novel, but something else. There must be a similarly irreducible element when we study religion; our experience is prior to analysis, whether we call what we experience "the divine" or "the transcendental" or simply "the spiritual." Yet the work of literary criticism is done upon texts, or the relations between texts, or the relations between texts and authors. Though I study texts in this book, from the Bible to the *Supreme Wisdom* of Elijah Muhammad, I do not think that texts can give us the essence of the American Religion. Nor do relations between texts, or even between texts and believers, take us very far into our weirdly pervasive national faith. So creedless is the American Religion that it needs to be tracked by particles rather than by principles.

To write this book I have read and reread everything that remotely could be considered to be an American religious text, and I have read also every historical and interpretative study of religion in America that I could find. But I am not a historian or a sociologist or a psychologist of religion, let alone a theologian. And manifestly I am not myself a religious visionary or prophet. As a literary critic, I have followed Walter Pater in writing what he called "appreciations," and as a religious critic I aspire to write the same. I am not a Christian by faith, nor a Protestant by sensibility, and so I am hardly disconcerted to discover that the American Religion is post-Christian, despite its protestations, and even that it has begun to abandon Protestant modes of thought and feeling. If we are Americans, then to some degree we share in the American Religion, however unknowingly or unwillingly. The religious critic sets forth to appreciate the varieties of the American religious experience, following in this the founders of our religious criticism: Emerson and William James.

Broadly speaking, there are two main forms of the American Religion: imported and domestic. It is definitive of the American Religion that this difference recedes rapidly once we begin reflecting upon our beliefs. The Southern Baptist Convention, being Baptist, lineally derives from the Old World, and yet is as profoundly indigenous as are the Mormons, who owe nothing to Europe. What makes the American Religion so American is that the Christianizing of the American people, in the generation after the

Revolution, persuasively redefined what Christianizing meant, by returning history to origins and to essentials.

The inaugural question for religious criticism should be: What is the essence of religion? Freud said it was the longing for the father. Others have called it desire for the mother, or for transcendence, or for reality, or for an occult self before or beyond experience. I fear that all these are idealizations, and I offer as evidence the suggestion that they would vanish from us if we did not know that we must die. Religion, whether it be shamanism or Protestantism, rises from our apprehension of death. To give a meaning to meaninglessness is the endless quest of religion. Nietzsche told us that we possessed art lest we perish of the truth. I don't think that Shakespeare would have agreed. Clearly we possess religion, if we want to, precisely to obscure the truth of our perishing. The tragedy of truth is the story of Hamlet or of Lear, and those are not religious stories. When the J Writer began to tell the stories of what we now call the Bible, those stories were art and not religion. Death is no concern or burden for J, and not much more of a burden for Shakespeare. When death becomes the center, then religion begins.

I am not suggesting that religion is mere thanatology, or even that—like its rivals, psychoanalysis and Marxism—it is condemned always to move between the poles of sexuality and death. Compared to Freud and Marx, religion is "more numerous of windows, superior of doors," which is how Emily Dickinson rated possibility over prose. But possibility is more at home with art than with religion, at least since religion ceased to be a pure shamanism. It did not take Durkheim and Weber to make religion into a branch of sociology. When religion abandoned magic, it sociologized itself. Sociological study of postshamanistic religion tends to be redundant, even narcissistic: the sociologist holds up the mirror to herself. Since our universities are driving towards the multicultural, they should replace their sociology departments by an importation of authentic Siberian shamans. Levitations and transformations would teach us what sociology of religion cannot: the place of death in our lives and of religious yearning in our deaths.

By what authority can an unbeliever read Saint Paul or Joseph Smith or Mary Baker Eddy or Ellen Harmon White and make a critical judgment upon them? How can an unbeliever examine the workings of Southern Baptist religious experience and achieve an insight into it, or analyze Jehovah's Witnesses' accounts of Armageddon and estimate the spiritual value thereof? If the unbeliever is neither sociologist nor anthropologist, neither historian nor theologian, what empowers him to make distinctions as he wanders among the bewilderments of our sects and denominations? I myself am an unbelieving Jew of strong Gnostic tendencies, and a literary critic by profession. Obsession with the American varieties of Orphism and Gnosticism, of Enthusiasm and Antinomianism, seems to be the driving principle of my concern with what I call the American Religion. No Western nation is as religion-soaked as ours, where nine out of ten of us love God and are loved by him in return. That mutual passion centers our society and demands some understanding, if our doom-eager society is to be understood at all.

As Americans, we are obsessed also with information, and we regard religion as the most vital aspect of information. I reflect that Gnosticism was (and is) a kind of information theory. Matter and energy are rejected, or at least placed under the sign of negation. Information becomes the emblem of salvation; the false Creation-Fall concerned matter and energy, but the Pleroma, or Fullness, the original Abyss, is all information. Americans always have had a tendency to quest for the unfindable primitive Christian Church. What they actually seek to restore is not the church of the first Christians, but the primal Abyss, named by the ancient Gnostics as both our foremother and our forefather. Our national millenarianism, so pervasive in the nineteenth century and still tempestuous among Fundamentalists and Pentecostals, associates itself with the books of Daniel and of Revelation and leads to our crusading wars, and to unwholesome fantasies like George Bush's New World Order. Only a Gnostic reading of the Bible can make us into the land of the Promise. The new irony of American history is that we fight now to make the world safe for Gnosticism, our sense of religion.

But what is religion? A universal obsessional neurosis, according to Sigmund Freud, would be the answer, which is reductive but indisputably suggestive. Even more suggestive is the notorious Marxist assertion that religion is the opiate of the common folk. Both judgments depend upon the sense that religion is a belief, or at least a trusting, and so the Freudian and Marxist reductions have their apparent relevance for Christianity or Islam or Judaism. That they seem to me inappropriate for considering the American Religion tells me something about our unofficial but pervasive national faith. It does not believe or trust, it *knows*, though it wants always to know yet more. The American Religion manifests itself as an information anxiety, but that seems to me a better definition of nearly all religion than the attempts to see faith as a compulsive neurosis or as a drug. It is neither obsessive nor intoxicating to ask, "Where were we?" and "Where are we journeying?", or best of all, "What makes us free?" The American Religion always has asked "What makes us free?"; but political freedom has little to do with that question. What is it that makes us free of the presence of other selves? What leaves us alone, not with the created world, but with what preceded the outward creation? Something in the American self is persuaded that it also preceded the created world. An abyss within the self finds itself at peace when it is alone with an abyss that preceded the world God made. The freedom assured by the American Religion is not what Protestants once called Christian Liberty, but is a solitude in which the inner loneliness is at home in an outer loneliness.

The authentic American Religion rarely proclaims its full knowledge, or its knowledge of the Fullness. And since the American Religion was syncretic, from the start, it can establish itself within nearly any available outward form. Of all the exotic sects indigenous to the United States, only five have become indelible strands of the American Religion: Mormonism, Christian Science, Seventh-day Adventism, Jehovah's Witnesses, Pentecostalism. Their strong survival, despite their startling doctrines, essentially stems from their self-concealed core of the American Religion: Orphic, Gnostic, millenarian. Other religions have promised us Eternity; only the American Religion promises what Freud tells us we cannot have: "an improved infancy," as Hart Crane called it.

It is an old surmise among students of religion, following van der Leeuw, that the gods (and God) are belated in questions of religion. At the origin, there is the manifestation of the sacred as power, and there is the human experience as object of that power. The power can be an indifferent destiny rather than a God or gods, or it can be a force that intervenes, whether benignly or malevolently, but still without a consciousness or personality of its own. Whatever it is, to be surprised by it is to be avoided, if possible. Awareness and observation are necessary in regard to it, and probably preceded worship or reverence as the proper human stance towards a more-than-human power.

I argue in this book that the American Religion, which is so prevalent among us, masks itself as Protestant Christianity yet has ceased to be Christian. It has kept the figure of Jesus, a very solitary and personal American Jesus, who is also the resurrected Jesus rather than the crucified Jesus or the Jesus who ascended again to the Father. I do not think that the Christian God has been retained by us, though he is invoked endlessly by our leaders, and by our flag-waving President in particular, with especial fervor in the context of war. But this invoked force appears to be the American destiny, the God of our national faith. The most Gnostic element in the American Religion is an astonishing reversal of ancient Gnosticism: we worship the Demiurge as God, more often than not under the name of manifest Necessity. As for the alien God of the Gnostics, he has vanished, except for his fragments or sparks scattered among our few elitists of the spirit, or for his shadow in the solitary figure of the American Jesus.

As a religious critic, I find two characteristics invariably present in every authentic version of the American Religion, whether it be Pentecostal or Southern Baptist or Mormon or whatever (since this study knows its limits, and cannot meditate upon every variety of our religious experience as we approach the twenty-first century). The American finds God in herself or himself, but only after finding the freedom to know God by experiencing a total inward solitude. Freedom, in a very special sense, is the preparation without which God will not allow himself to be revealed in the self. And this freedom is in itself double; the spark or spirit must know itself to be free both of other selves and of the created world. In perfect solitude, the American spirit learns again its absolute isolation as a spark of God floating in a sea of space. What is around it has been created by God, but the spirit is as old as God is, and so is no part of God's creation. What was created fell away from the spirit, a fall that was creation. God or Jesus will find the spirit, because there is something in the spirit that already is God or Jesus, but the divine shall seek out each spirit only in total isolation.

Salvation, for the American, cannot come through the community or the congregation, but is a one-on-one act of confrontation. Though a Protestant heritage, this confrontation is Americanized in the Evening Land. Even in traditional Protestantism, revivalism gradually fostered a very un-Calvinistic sense of conversion within the self, unaided by any larger context. Philip Greven's *The Protestant Temperament* (1977) distinguishes three Protestant stances towards the self in seventeenth- and eighteenth-century America: Evangelical, Moderate, and Genteel; or respectively, the Self Suppressed, the Self Controlled, the Self Asserted. By the early nineteenth century, when the American Religion proper is born at Cane Ridge, the joint projects of Democratizing and Re-Christianizing America, as traced respectively by Nathan Hatch and Jon Butler, had performed the most remarkable of all American tricklings-down. The Genteel mode of the Self Asserted ran wild at Cane Ridge among mountain men and women, establishing a spirituality that has been with us since. All of the unique qualities convincingly ascribed by Greven to Genteel Self-Assertion are now the common emotions of our contemporary Pentecostals and rural Baptists, giving the glory at once to God and to their own magical or occult selves.

Greven presumably would not accept my broadening of his argument, but part of his book's power is its tracing of the diffusions, across time, of a sense of self in America more assertive and finally universal than European society ever had sustained. Perry Miller, in his studies of the New England mind, had identified American Puritan religion with its theology. Greven's emphasis is upon religious experience, which is a question of temperament rather than of intellectual acceptance. Temperament, and not theology, determines the self's stance in religion. What was genteel temperament in pre-Revolutionary America became popularized with the apocalyptic turn into the nineteenth century. Nathan A. Hatch's *The Democratization of American Christianity* (1989) still holds on to the interpretive fiction of a Second Great Awakening at the century's turn, but Hatch's awareness far transcends that worn-out shibboleth of scholars:

In the aftermath of the Second Great Awakening, many Americans divorced religious leadership from social position, completing a separation that had been building for a century. They ascribed authority to preachers ill qualified to stand for public office. In a new nation, premised on equality and struggling to free itself from the past, people were ready to see the hand of God upon a Lorenzo Dow, a Joseph Smith, or a William Miller.

They could rejoice that, at last, the weak were confounding the mighty, the last becoming first. (p. 226)

A step beyond Hatch's argument is taken in Jon Butler's *Awash in a Sea of Faith* (1990), where Great Awakenings are rightly viewed as retrospective fictions, and where the "unique spiritual hothouse" aspect of America in the first half of the nineteenth century is vividly emphasized. Hatch and Butler are religious historians; my own concern, as a religious critic, is to suggest the outlines of the emergent American Religion, though I attempt a brief history of it, from Cane Ridge through Billy Graham, in my third chapter. Here I return to the American self, to note again that its loneliness and its unsponsored freedom (as no part of the Creation) were the central attributes that made the American Religion not only possible but inevitable. Early nineteenth-century America inaugurated a sense of solitude in space, of the spirit sublimely aware of itself against the background of a cosmological emptiness that did not, and could not, know the spirit.

III

Freud's *The Future of an Illusion* (1927) can be accounted as one of the great failures of religious criticism. Simply, he underestimated his opponent, and is therefore about as convincing against religion as T. S. Eliot was against psychoanalysis. One can learn a great deal about how *not* to write religious criticism by reading Freud, who manages just on this one matter to be sublimely beside the point, as here:

> If . . . we turn again to religious doctrines, we may reiterate that they are all illusions, they do not admit of proof, and no one can be compelled to consider them as true or to believe in them. Some of them are so improbable, so very incompatible with everything we have laboriously discovered about the reality of the world . . . that we may compare them to delusions.

Freud startles us, just this once, by a kind of innocence. If you term the Resurrection an illusion or a delusion, what have you accomplished against Christianity? Psychoanalysis is an interpretation of the world, and of human nature. So, rather massively, is

Christianity. After a lifetime of reading Freud, I am perfectly willing to substitute the word "psychoanalytic" for the word "religious" in that passage of *The Future of an Illusion*. After all, as we have discovered, psychoanalytic doctrines certainly do not admit of proof, and are either illusions or delusions if we literalize them. We no more possess libido than we would possess *destrudo*, had Freud gone ahead with a rejected notion that would have fueled the death drive with its own separate, negative energy. And the death drive, while wonderfully suggestive, is either an illusion or a delusion, as is the unconscious or any other major Freudian trope. But nothing is accomplished against psychoanalysis by listing its illusions and delusions.

Religious criticism can begin therefore by dispensing with any ambition to dismiss illusions or delusions. Its function, like that of all criticism, is to build bridges across gaps, to explain in particular the very curious relations that generally prevail between theology and actual religious experience, in whatever faith. Where threads move across denominational lines, as in the American Religion, then the function of religious criticism becomes more complex. Theologics will fall away, and the varieties of religious experience will begin to suggest subtler demarcations, keener sounds than earlier could have been apprehended. One of my central arguments in this book is that the Southern Baptists and the Mormons, who violently oppose one another, betray remarkably parallel configurations in spiritual temperament and in what might be called the sensibility of belief. In my analysis, they are different varieties of the American Religion, and they actually share far more than they dispute in their Gnostic, Enthusiastic, and Orphic affinities. There is a shape darkly emergent in much American Protestantism, the outline of a religion not yet fully evident among us but stretching like a long shadow beyond us. Aspects of it are evident in the overtly indigenous faiths, of which Mormonism is the most impressive, as well as in the Southern Baptist Convention, itself an original American formulation even though it proclaims its continuities with earlier Baptist tradition. Religious criticism, confronted by indigenous American visions, is compelled to become a national criticism, aware that we are a dangerously religion-soaked, even religion-mad, society. That cultural condition is the largest given for American religious criticism, and the most urgent challenge. How can it be that nearly nine out of ten of us are passionately convinced that God loves her or him on a personal and individual basis? Why is it that the American Religion exports so well abroad, not just in Asia and Africa and Latin America but in Western and Eastern Europe as well? Jehovah's Witnesses, Pentecostals, Seventh-day Adventists, as well as the Mormons and the Southern Baptists, convert many millions of people to their idiosyncratic American visions of God, death, and judgment, and yet these are people who more often than not do not speak English, American or otherwise, and know of the United States only what television and the missionaries have brought them. What is the appeal of the American Religion abroad?

I emphasized earlier my own sense that religious criticism, in at least one respect, has to take literary criticism as its analogue and model, substituting an irreducibly spiritual element for the irreducible effect of the aesthetic. History, sociology, anthropology, and psychology, working together, almost invariably reduce religion in much the same way that they reduce imaginative literature. A poem, whatever its uses to historians or social scientists, is only secondarily a political or societal document. What it seeks is a validation as a source of value in itself, though the motives of the author doubtless always extend into communal spheres. Religious doctrines and experiences alike share with poems a stance against dying, or to put this most simply, the category of the "religious" is set against death even as the "poetic" seeks a triumph over time. Criticism, as I conceive it, seeks the poetic in poetry, and should seek the religious in religion.

What again is the proper discipline for the study of religion? I have not found "the human sciences" or any historicism or politics or philosophy to be of much use for studying what is poetic about poetry. I begin to understand that only religion can study religion. Poetic criticism, the study of the hidden roads that lead from poem to poem, has its analogue in religious criticism, which uncovers the winding paths that link together faiths as antithetical to one another as the Mormons and the Southern Baptists. Like poetry, religion is a culmination of the growing inner self, but religion is the poetry, not the opiate, of the masses. The inner structures of the imagination prevail in religion as they do in poetry, but they are harder to trace, because religion builds its temples in the outward world. There is also the problem of offence. Only a score or two of handfuls of people (besides the poets) care about poetry, but in the United States nearly everyone is quick to be outraged if their sense of the sacred suffers trespass. Unlike most countries, we have no overt national religion, but a partly concealed one has been developing among us for some two centuries now. It is almost purely experiential, and despite its insistences, it is scarcely Christian in any traditional way. A religion of the self burgeons, under many names, and seeks to know its own inwardness, in isolation. What the American self has found, since about 1800, is its own freedom —from the world, from time, from other selves. But this freedom is a very expensive torso, because of what it is obliged to leave out: society, temporality, the other. What remains, for it, is solitude and the abyss.

The United States of America is a religion-mad country. It has been inflamed in this regard for about two centuries now. *The People's Religion* by George Gallup, Jr., and Jim Castelli (1989) polls the nation and discovers that 88 percent among us believe that God loves them, 9 percent are uncertain, while only 3 percent say that the Lord's affection for them is nonexistent. But then 94 percent of us believe in God, and 90 percent pray. These astonishing figures contrast remarkably to Western European convictions about the Supreme Being, let alone to European prayer performances. It is scarcely credible to assert that we are a more Christian people than the Western Europeans, despite our polled pieties. This book proposes a rather different explanation: we think we are Christian, but we are not. The issue is not religion in America but rather what I call the American Religion. We can speak of religion in Western Europe, but hardly of the European Religion. They are Christians, or they are not. There are indeed millions of Christians in the United States, but most Americans who think that they are Christians truly are something else, intensely religious but devout in the American Religion, a faith that is old among us, and that comes in many guises and disguises, and that overdetermines much of our national life.

Though this book to some extent adopts a chronological organization, it is hardly a history of the American Religion, and is not at all a history of religion in America. I am neither a historian nor what is called a cultural critic, and I write both to blame and to praise the American Religion. My concern is to identify our national faith, to interpret its mode of spirituality, and to prophesy its future. I conceive this book as religious criticism rather than as religious history or as an essay in the sociology of religion. Criticism, whether it be of belief or poetry, necessarily must share in the nature of what is being studied, if only because the proper work of criticism is contamination. Criticism contaminates, but itself has begun in a state of contamination. What I seek to describe in this book contaminated me long ago and lingers in me now. Any American who studies a large aspect of her country's culture, such as its imaginative literature, has been influenced by our national religion, which is as pervasive as it is unofficial. An involuntary believer in the American Religion, I myself need to know better what envelops us all.

Religious criticism, like literary criticism, is a mode of interpretation, but unlike the critic of imaginative literature, the critic of religion, as I conceive her, is not primarily an interpreter of texts. A critic's function is to compare and judge perceptions and sensations, the perceptions and sensations not only represented by imaginative literature or by religion, but themselves the product of poetry or of belief. While a literary critic must protect literature against belief, whether societal or transcendental, a religious critic cannot protect belief, whether from society or from rival modes such as psychoanalysis, philosophy, science, and art. The function of criticism is to purge us not of selfhood (upon which the American Religion centers and relies) but of self-righteousness, of all the deadly moral virtues, of what William Blake called "the selfish virtues of the natural heart."

In offering *The American Religion* as a work of religious criticism, I remind myself that this interpretive mode, in its later phases, has been practiced by prophetic figures: Emerson, Nietzsche, Freud. Religious criticism and prophecy are two names for the same activity of the spirit. If one is an American and has a religious temperament, however eccentric or even esoteric, then one necessarily has some relation to the American Religion. The central argument of this book is that we all of us are affected by the consequences of our national faith, and that one variety or another of it frequently is the actual substance of what we confront in what at first seem secular phenomena in the United States. The central fact about American life, as we enter the final decade of the twentieth century, is that our religiosity is everywhere. Even our erotic relationships of the more sustained sort, marriage included, have acquired many of the stigmata of our religious intensities. Religious novelists like the Protestant John Updike and the Catholic Walker Percy not only portray a displacement of religious needs and obligations into the erotic realm, but themselves sometimes fall into the same confusion. Experiential religion cannot be confined, and there is little evidence that the American Religion wishes any limitation; witness the Mormon Church and the now Fundamentalist-dominated Southern Baptist Convention, let alone such other American originals as Jehovah's Witnesses and the Assemblies of God. The American difference in religion produces the irony that Roman Catholicism, in the United States, is a relatively restrained mode of faith.

The relationship of American Baptists to European Christian tradition is not radically different from that of the Mormons or other American originals to their more remote English and Continental antecedents. The power of *religious desire* seems to have become greatly magnified in the United States, in a kind of parallel to the magnification of creative desire in Melville, Whitman, and Dickinson. Perhaps this parallel is clearest in William and Henry James, where the exaltation of the desire to believe, the will to know spirit, so dominant in William, has so many analogues in the patterns of creative desire in his brother's novels. American romance is a bewildering enough literary genre, but its cousin is the yet more baffling romance dimension of the American Religion. Where there is overwhelming religious desire, there must also be religious anxiety, for which the pragmatic name is Fundamentalism, the great curse of all American religion, and of all religion in this American century. Fundamentalism, strictly considered, is an attempt to overcome the terror of death by a crude literalization of the Christian intimation of immortality. One of the uses of religious criticism is that it is the appropriate instrument for dissecting, understanding, and perhaps someday destroying Fundamentalism, which is the shadow side of what is most spiritual and valuable in the American Religion.

One of the great insights made available by parallel elements in literary criticism and in religious criticism is that creative desire and religious desire have more in common with one another than either has with Eros. The poetic character, as I understand it, begins in a rebellion against death, and so in a conviction that its origins are not natural, that they go back to an abyss preceding the coming into being of the world. Something very like this is the origin of the American religious character. Even if one accepted Schopenhauer's morose myth of the relation between sexual desire and the Will to Live, one would be a very long way from both poetry and prophecy, since neither finds the object of desire in mere nature. American religion, like American imaginative literature, is a severely internalized quest romance, in which some version of immortality serves as the object of desire. Compare the Roman Catholic crucifix with the cross of all Baptist churches, as well as of most other American Protestant denominations. The Catholics worship Christ crucified, but the Baptists salute the empty cross, from which Jesus already has risen. Resurrection is the entire concern of the American Religion, which gets Christ off the cross as quickly as Milton removed him, in just a line and a half of *Paradise Lost*.

One of the grand myths of the American Religion is the restoration of the Primitive Church, which probably never existed. The Southern Baptists in some sense take as their paradigm an interval about which the New Testament tells us almost nothing, the forty days the Disciples went about in the company of Jesus after his resurrection. I think that not only the Baptists but all adherents of the American Religion, whatever their denomination, quest for that condition. When they speak, sing, pray about walking with Jesus, they mean neither the man on the road to eventual crucifixion nor the ascended God, but rather the Jesus who walked and lived with his Disciples again for forty days and forty nights. Those days, for the Mormons, include Christ's sojourn in America, where Joseph Smith envisioned him coming soon after the Resurrection, in the greatest single imaginative breakthrough of the Book of Mormon. The largest heresy among all those that constitute the American Religion is this most implicit and profoundly poetic of all heresies: the American walks alone with Jesus in a perpetually expanded interval founded upon the forty days' sojourn of the risen Son of Man. American Gnosticism escapes from time by entering into the life upon earth already enjoyed by the Man who died and then conquered death.

Religious criticism needs to enter that area, which lies between theology and spiritual experience, an area akin to what early Christians, Gnostics included, would have called the Pleroma, the Fullness, both of space and of time. What the great Southern Baptist sage E. Y. Mullins called *"soul competency"* would appear to be the gift that comes from having walked with the resurrected Jesus, and not as part of a crowd of disciples, but absolutely *alone with Jesus.* Testimony founded on this solitary companionship frequently mentions a third shadowy presence, sometimes identified with the Holy Spirit and sometimes with the chastised, overcome figure of death himself or herself. One can recall American poetry's two remarkable visions of such shadowy companionship, Walt Whitman's and T. S. Eliot's, in *"When Lilacs Last in the Dooryard Bloom'd"* and *"The Waste Land,"* respectively. Both of these are American romance visions, and complexly akin to the Baptist hymnody that celebrates the experience of walking with the resurrected Christ.

IV

D. H. Lawrence, meditating upon Fenimore Cooper's Natty Bumppo, saw that Cooper's reversal of his hero's career (composed backwards, from old age to youth) reflected the history of American consciousness. America had started European and venerable, and then grew back to become new and youthful. Lawrence's judgment applies also to religion in America, which began as European Protestantism and from the turn into the nineteenth century on had become a new mode, still developing among us. Seeking to explain to myself, as an emergent religious critic, exactly how I felt towards the American Religion, I recalled the observations concerning Emerson written down by Henry James, Senior, in 1884, two years after the sage's death. James, whose exasperation with his beloved Emerson was memorably expressed in a famous exclamation—"O you man without a handle!"—tried this time to grasp hold of the handle he called "innocence":

He was . . . fundamentally treacherous to civilization, without being at all aware himself of the fact . . . He appeared to me utterly unconscious of himself as either good or evil. He had no conscience, in fact, and lived by perception, which is an altogether lower or less spiritual faculty. The more universalized a man is by genius or natural birth, the less is he spiritually individualized, making up in breadth of endowment what he lacks in depth. This was remarkably the case with Emerson. In his books or public capacity he was constantly electrifying you by sayings full of divine inspiration . . . No man could look at him speaking (or when he was silent either, for that matter) without having a vision of the divinest beauty . . . He was nothing else than a show-figure of almighty power in our nature . . .

Incontestably the main thing about him, however, as I have already said, was that he unconsciously brought you face to face with the infinite in humanity . . . This was Emerson's incontestable virtue to every one who appreciated him, that he recognized no God outside of himself and his interlocutor, and recognized him there only as the *liaison* between the two, taking care that all their intercourse should be holy with a holiness undreamed of before by man or angel. For it is not a holiness taught by books or the example of tiresome, diseased, self-conscious saints, but simply by one's redeemed flesh and blood. In short, the only holiness which Emerson recognized, and for which he consistently lived, was innocence.

This is a very American innocence, and the whole passage by the senior James reminds me of Sydney Ahlstrom's observation that "Emerson is in fact the theologian of something we may almost term 'the American religion.' " In Emerson, the Swedenborgian James recognized many of the stigmata that persuade me of the presence of the American Religion: freedom from mere conscience; reliance upon experiential perception; a sense of power; the presence of the God within; the innocence of "one's redeemed flesh and blood." What Freud would call our discomfort with culture, or civilization with its discontents, is far away. And so, all unaware, Emerson was "fundamentally treacherous to civilization," for what was civilization except European age.

Religious criticism, confronted by authentic American spirituality, is at first disarmed, for Kierkegaard and Nietzsche are not wholly relevant to the American Newness. Kierkegaard's emphasis upon the dialectical difficulties of becoming a Christian in an ostensibly Christian nation does not meet the American situation, where those truly driven towards faith are not moving towards anything that much resembles historical Christianity. And Nietzsche's critique of asceticism scarcely touches the ardors of American spiri-

tuality, where next to nothing is surrendered for the self. I find
also that I am not aided by the stance for religious criticism taken
up by the late Northrop Frye in his final book, *The Double Vision*
(1991), subtitled "Language and Meaning in Religion." Frye attempts a move from his critical approach to literature on to one
towards religion, but it seems impossible to distinguish his percep-
tiveness from his piety, as here:

> In religion, too, we must keep a critical attitude that never uncon-
> ditionally accepts any socially established form of revelation.
> Otherwise, we are back to idolatry again, this time a self-idolatry
> rather than an idolatry of nature, where devotion to God is re-
> placed by the deifying of our own present understanding of God.
> Paul tells us that we are God's temples: if so, we should be able
> to see the folly of what was proposed by the Emperor Caligula
> for the Jerusalem temple, of putting a statue of ourselves in its
> holy place.

I find that very moving, but it is religious writing rather than
religious criticism, and would take one nowhere in regard to the
Mormons or the Southern Baptists or African-American religion.
What Frye, following tradition, calls "idolatry" is, in its form of
"self-idolatry," precisely what Emerson named as "self-reliance,"
the fundamental premise of the American Religion. Frye, who
lived and died a minister of the United Church of Canada, says in
The Double Vision that "it would be absurd to see the New Testament as only a work of literature." Doubtless, from a clergyman's
perspective, that is so, but the view there is not that of a literary
critic as such. "Self-idolatry" cannot be a religious critic's working
term. Just as a literary critic does not recognize the emphasis of
"*only* a work of literature," as though one could speak of "mere"
literature, so the moral judgment in the notion of "idolatry" does
not belong to the work of religious criticism. Moral criticism, political criticism, social criticism have now usurped the place of the
aesthetic in what passes for literary criticism in our academies. The
function of religious criticism at the present time is to keep the
spiritual in religion from following the aesthetic in literature into
the discard trays of the politically correct School of Resentment.
Anti-intellectualism pervades American political, social, and moral
life, and its answering chorus is the political correctness of the

academic pseudo-Left. Fundamentalism is the parodistic curse of the American Religion, and the political, social, moral, and even economic consequences of its anti-intellectualism are quite vicious. But such consequences cannot be the concern of religious criticism. Instead, it is the total obliteration of the spiritual in and by Fundamentalism that religious criticism needs to uncover and to analyze.

2
Enthusiasm, Gnosticism, American Orphism

PRESIDENT George Bush, whatever other eminence awaits him, is already bound to be memorable as the American leader most deeply attached to linked emblems of our national religion: the flag and the fetus, our Cross and our Divine Child. The flag and the fetus together symbolize the American Religion, the partly concealed but scarcely repressed national faith. Defining religion is always difficult, particularly since civil belief and its pragmatic consequences are radically different when compared to historical and traditional creeds. Religion, in the ostensibly Protestant United States, is something subtly other than Christianity, though to say that we are a post-Christian country is misleading. Rather, we are post-Protestant, and we live a persuasive redefinition of Christianity. It is so persuasive that we refuse to admit that we *have* revised the traditional religion into a faith that better fits our national temperament, aspirations, and anxieties. A blend of ancient heresies and nineteenth-century stresses, the American Religion moves towards the twenty-first century with an unrestrained triumphalism, easily convertible into our political vagaries.

Somewhere George Santayana remarked that religion has to be as particular as language. You speak one language at a time, and you cannot practice religion in general. A living religion, he went

on, had to be idiosyncratic; its power came from some precise
swerve or bias. Except for the orange squash called the New Age,
every religion discussed in this book is idiosyncratic almost beyond
belief. I would not call all of them alive beyond belief, but they are
(almost all of them) dangerously interesting, when compared to
what now thrives as the mainline Protestant denominations in the
United States. What is spiritually alive in the mainline groupings
is rarely a restored intensity of historical and doctrinal Protestantism. More often, it is another outcropping of Enthusiasm or Gnosticism, another variety of the American Religion. For the impulses
that created the Mormons or the authentic Southern Baptists or
the crucial African-American beliefs are as central to us as is the
American language itself. Our spirituality is another of our idioms.
Creeds do not suit the American spirit. The freedom we go on
associating with solitude and with wildness does not easily assimi-
late to the otherness of historical doctrines.

Since this is a study in religious criticism, I will center upon
what I judge to be the two most American of our faiths, those of
the Mormons and the Southern Baptist Convention. I approach
both of these, in the pragmatic spirit of William James, as varieties
of religious *experience*, and will emphasize equally questions of irreducible spirituality and of the temperament of the believer in her
or his encounter with God. The Mormons rightly stress their indubitable status as an American original, with a precise genesis in
the visions granted to their prophet, seer, and revelator, Joseph
Smith. The Baptists, true to the American grain (as are the Mormons), trace their origin in a great American myth, the primitive
Christian Church of ancient Israel. I follow religious historians in
relocating Southern Baptist origins in early nineteenth-century
America, but I break with those historians in finding the true and
belated father of Southern Baptism to have been Edgar Young
Mullins (1860–1928), who redefined the faith in his great manifesto
of 1908, *The Axioms of Religion*. So far as I can tell, Mullins invented
the term "soul competency" for the most crucial Baptist freedom,
when he insisted that "the doctrine of the soul's competency in
religion under God is the historical significance of the Baptists."
Mullins prevailed in that judgment until the current takeover of the
Southern Baptist Convention by Know-Nothings masking as Fundamentalists. Ironically, much of the Mullinsesque or Moderate
Southern Baptist heritage now so severely jeopardized by the sup-

posed Fundamentalists may well have been of African–American Baptist origin, as I will show much later in this book. That makes it all the more appropriate that Texas Know-Nothings are destroying the Southern Baptist Convention, and so are obliterating the last organized stand of a religion of the Inner Light in the United States. The priesthood of the believer is being replaced by a hierarchy that will be at once more dogmatic and less intellectualized than the structure of authority in the Roman Catholic Church. A highly individualized, even eccentric religion of Enthusiastic experience will dwindle down into a vapidity.

The American Religion is, in many respects, a continuation into the nineteenth and twentieth centuries of what was termed Enthusiasm in Europe, particularly during the seventeenth and eighteenth centuries, when the term tended to be used in disapproval. In its literal sense, Enthusiasm suggests divine inspiration or even possession, but genteel Christians of the Enlightenment gave the term its figurative force of emotionalism and even fanaticism. I myself recognize now that the origin of this book on *The American Religion* goes back to my purchasing and reading Monsignor Ronald Knox's *Enthusiasm* in 1960 (it was first published in 1950). Catholic chaplain at Oxford University from 1926 to 1939, the urbane Knox had translated the Bible into the prose of George Moore, but found his true achievement in his *Enthusiasm: A Chapter in the History of Religion*. Knox's *Enthusiasm*, which I have just read again after thirty years, remains a superb study of heresies and revivalisms, narrated with a verve worthy of the book's dedicatee, Evelyn Waugh, whose comic genius owed something to the gentler ironies of his spiritual mentor, Knox.

Enthusiasm's protagonists include the entire sequence of grand eccentrics from Montanus of Phrygia in the second century down through Anabaptists, Quakers, Jansenists, and Quietists on to John Wesley and his followers in the mid-eighteenth century. Of his Enthusiasts (whom he both adores and strenuously disapproves), Knox stresses that all of them were spiritual elitists, "ultrasupernaturalists," for whom "grace has destroyed nature, and replaced it," rather than corrected it. Therefore they lust for theocracy, or the rule of the Saints, and in the interim are given to revivalism and ecstasy while they wait for Jesus, whose Second Coming is all but hourly expected. The great time for Enthusiasm was the seventeenth century: George Fox and the Quakers, Pascal and the

Catholic Jansenists in France, and the French Quietist mystics of
the turn into the eighteenth century, led by Madame Guyon and
Fénelon. But none of these, not even Fox, were precursors of the
American Religion. That distinction belongs rather to John Wesley, who received a supreme experience of conversion on May 24,
1738. Conversion is so much the fundamental experience of what
will come to be the American Religion that a brief meditation upon
its generic nature seems quite necessary at this point.

Conversion by A. D. Nock (1933) is the classical study of this
peculiar subject; even though it confines itself to the period from
Alexander the Great to Saint Augustine, it nevertheless provides
unsurpassed insights into the psychology of religious conversion,
insights professedly based upon William James's profound sur-
mises. James emphasized that "the sense of our present wrongness"
counted in consciousness far more than any ideal towards which
the sinner could strive. Conversion therefore was always more a
struggle "away from" than an onward drive. Nock gives as his
formula: "renunciation and a new start." But this is to underestimate Enthusiastic revival, which from early on became the American mode of conversion until it culminated at Cane Ridge,
Kentucky, in a mode that is the subject of my next chapter. Knox
attributes "the religion of experience" with its conversions that *must
be felt* to Wesley, who was to that extent a precursor of the American Religion. I myself suspect that the paradigm came from the
earliest black Baptists in America, but Knox is vivid in describing
the Wesleyan innovation, which nevertheless he admits was not
consistent, whether in the great founder of Methodism or in his
followers:

Was the New Birth always and necessarily an *experience?* In order
to be a Christian, as opposed to an almost Christian, must you
have *felt*, at some time or another, that your sins were forgiven,
or was a change in your outward behaviour sufficient evidence of
that fact? . . . It looks as if Wesley had thought out for himself,
very early, that identification of "grace" with spiritual consola-
tions, against which devout authors are constantly warning us.
At the very outset of his evangelistic career you find him expecting adult baptism to be accompanied by the *consciousness* of a New
Birth, and disappointed when it turns out otherwise . . . So con-

vinced an experimentalist is he that he expects the sense of pardon to be, not merely felt, but manifested. (pp. 538–39)

What is so tentative here has become consistent, fierce, even raging in the Enthusiasm of the American Religion, where Southern Baptist or Pentecostal conversion invariably is felt, manifested, and exuberantly communicated. Wesley, in the American perspective, must now be seen as a bridging figure between a more restrained English mode of Enthusiasm and the violence, both internal and external, of the American Religion. Experiential faith, largely divorced from doctrine, would have left an emptiness in America but for something more vibrant that replaced doctrine, a timeless *knowing* that in itself saves. Wesley still believed that God had performed in history, but the American knowing cancels history, even the history of God before he discovered America. Gnosticism, ancient and American, has gotten a bad name, from Saint Irenaeus down to Tom Wolfe, but here I dissent. President Eisenhower is notorious for remarking that the United States was and had to be a religious nation, and that he didn't care what religion it had, as long as it had one. I take a sadder view; we are, alas, the most religious of countries, and only varieties of the American Religion finally will flourish among us, whether its devotees call it Mormonism, Protestantism, Catholicism, Islam, Judaism, or what-you-will. And the American Religion, for its two centuries of existence, seems to me irretrievably Gnostic. It is a knowing, by and of an uncreated self, or self-within-the-self, and the knowledge leads to freedom, a dangerous and doom-eager freedom: from nature, time, history, community, other selves. I shake my head in unhappy wonderment at the politically correct younger intellectuals, who hope to subvert what they cannot begin to understand, an obsessed society wholly in the grip of a dominant Gnosticism.

If you have a religious temperament, or a yearning for religion, and yet you cannot accept Jewish, Catholic, Protestant, or Muslim explanations as to why an omnipotent God permits the perpetual victory of evil and misfortune, then you may be tempted by Gnosticism, even if you never quite know just what Gnosticism is, or was. Personal experience and meditation upon history alike make me impatient with all attempts at justifying the ways of God to man. The God of Moses, Jesus, and Muhammad seems equally indulgent towards schizophrenia and the Holocaust. There is also the God of the Gnostic speculator Valentinus of Alexandria, and of the Kabbalist rabbi Isaac Luria of Safed, and that God is estranged or withdrawn from our world of hallucinations and death camps. The Alien God of Gnostic vision can be regarded as the projection of an ancient heresy, if you wish, or as a living reality, though one to whom no churches or temples are overtly dedicated. Gnosticism, to me, seems less of a fossil than are our organized, socially accepted mainline religions, but I scarcely intend this book to be either a Gnostic manifesto or a treatise upon conversion.

Bentley Layton's *The Gnostic Scriptures* (1984) is the most useful collection of authentic Gnostic texts of the first three centuries of the Common Era yet made available in any language. With its persuasive introductions, this volume constitutes an inevitable starting point for anyone who wishes to be guided through the mazes of ancient Gnosticism, whether considered as a historical phenomenon or as the founding outline of a timeless religious stance. Layton's imagination holds in a single complex image the extraordinary intricacies of what Hans Jonas calls the Gnostic myth: a vast cosmological emptiness, the *kenoma*, where we wander and weep, tyrannized by the Archons, who are lords of misrule, headed by the Demiurge, a deity who created the cosmos, and our bodies and souls, in one blundering act that was also a Fall. An act of creation that in itself constituted a catastrophic fall is hardly the vision of creation in normative Judaism or in any of the branches of Christianity. Sun and earth, Adam and Eve, all begin as disasters in some versions of Gnostic myth, which has nothing good to say about nature, and which has no hope either for our bodies or our outward souls, no hope indeed for anything confined within the limits of space and time. Yet Gnosticism, if we are to consider it a religion, or at least a spiritual stance, is anything but nihilistic or hopeless, which may be why it is now, and always has been, the hidden religion of the United States, the American Religion proper. Peculiar as this must sound, all any among us need do to begin to understand Gnosticism is to ask ourselves: What do I actually regard my innermost self as being? In that secret place, Ronald Reagan and the characters of Thomas Pynchon's fiction blend together. Though I will cite a number of American and contemporary versions of Gnosticism before I am done, any useful account of Gnosticism needs to commence with the history of a magic or occult self, "spark" or *pneuma* as the Gnostics called it, rather than the soul or psyche, and such a history begins long before the Gnostics, who flourished most (if they flourished at all) in the Hellenistic world of the second century of the Common Era.

Gnosticism takes its origins in a strong reaction against or creative misreading of an overwhelming precursor, the Hebrew Bible. The arch villain for the Gnostics was the Demiurge, a creator god whose name parodied the Demiurge of Plato's *Timaeus*, where he is portrayed as an artisan, "world-maker," who does the best he can at imitating the true Forms of Eternity. But for the Gnostics, the Demiurge is the Yahweh (and Elohim), the Hebraic vision of the creator god in Genesis, a god taken by the Gnostics to be at best a botcher or ignoramus, or at worst a spirit of malevolence. The high god of the Hebrews is not the alien or true God of the Gnostics, who indeed was identified by many Gnostics with the primordial Abyss, the void and deep from which the Hebrew god or Demiurge stole or displaced the stuff for his false creation.

The biblical Hebrews, so far as we can tell, did not believe in a magic or occult self as compared to a soul. Such an ontological self appears to have started as a shamanistic idea, which migrated south from Scythia and Thrace into Greece during the fifth century before the Common Era. Pythagoras and Empedocles presumably were the first to domesticate this self-within-the-soul in Greece. Our modern authority here is E. R. Dodds, in his masterly *The Greeks and the Irrational* (1951), which traces the fortunes of the occult self or *daemon*:

> It is significant that Empedocles, on whom our knowledge of early Greek puritanism chiefly depends, avoids applying the term *psyche* to the indestructible self. He appears to have thought of the *psyche* as being the vital warmth which at death is reabsorbed in the fiery element from which it came . . . The occult self which persisted through successive incarnations he called, not "*psyche*," but "*daemon*." This *daemon* has, apparently, nothing to do with perception or thought, which Empedocles held to be mechanically determined; the function of the daemon is to be the carrier of man's potential divinity and actual guilt. It is nearer in some ways to the indwelling spirit which the shaman inherits from other shamans than it is to the rational "soul" in which Socrates believed; but it has been moralised as a guilt-carrier, and the

world of the senses has become the Hades in which it suffers torment. (p. 153)

This shamanistic magical self is very close to the Pauline and Gnostic *pneuma*, the spark or transcendental self that is free of the fallen or created world. Hans Jonas, the most illuminating modern expositor of Gnosticism, fascinatingly parallels Dodds's distinction in *The Gnostic Religion* (1958):

In the New Testament, especially in St. Paul, this transcendent principle in the human soul is called the "spirit" (*pneuma*), "the spirit in us," "the inner man," eschatologically also called "the new man." It is remarkable that Paul, writing in Greek and certainly not ignorant of Greek terminological traditions, never uses in this connection the term *"psyche,"* which since the Orphics and Plato had denoted the divine principle in us. On the contrary, he *opposes*, as did the Greek-writing Gnostics after him, "soul" and "spirit," and "psychic man" and "pneumatic man." Obviously the Greek meaning of *psyche*, with all its dignity, did not suffice to express the new conception of a principle transcending all natural and cosmic associations that adhered to the Greek concept. The term *pneuma* serves in Greek Gnosticism generally as the equivalent of the expressions for the spiritual "self," for which Greek, unlike some oriental languages, lacked an indigenous word. . . . In some of the Christian Gnostics it is called also the "spark" and the "seed of light." (p. 124)

The indigenous word appears to have been *"daemon,"* since Dodds and Jonas discuss the same distinction, fundamentally between self (*pneuma* or *daemon*) and soul (*psyche*). This distinction, I suspect, entered America via two very different sources, the African-American inheritance of "the little me within the big me," and the broad Orphic influence that flowed through Emerson and, more popularly, through the folk tradition. American Orphism makes the third in a triad with Enthusiasm and Gnosticism, all fusing together in the fusion of the American Religion. Orphism was an esoteric mystery cult whose central teaching was the potential divinity of the elitist self. A religion of quasi-shamanistic ecstasy, it preached the extraordinary idea that the redeemed or resurrected human life would be an eternal intoxication. We will see several versions of the Americanization of this notion in the chapters ahead, but here I will focus upon the Orphism of Emerson, hardly a representative man, but certainly our elitist seer.

Ralph Waldo Emerson, visiting Mormon country in Salt Lake City in 1871, dismissed the Latter-day Saints as "an after-clap of Puritanism." Born just two years before the Mormon prophet Joseph Smith, Emerson survived his fellow New Englander by some thirty eight years. As contemporaries, they possessed nothing in common, and scarcely could have been further apart in moral character, personality, social class, education, intellectual sophistication, indeed in intellect itself. Their largest difference is an immemorial one: between sage and prophet. Emerson, sage of Concord, remains our national oracle of cultural wisdom. Smith, prophet of Kirtland and Nauvoo, remains the religion-making founder of what began as a scandalous heresy and now is an eminently respectable established church, wealthy, vaguely Christian, and mostly right-wing Republican.

Had they met in their lifetimes, the Transcendental sage and the Mormon prophet could not have talked to one another. Smith's visions and prophecies were remarkably literal; the subtle Emerson, master of figurative language, knew that all visions are metaphors, and that all prophecies are rhetorical. And yet Emerson and Joseph Smith alike pioneered in creating the American Religion, the faith of and in the American self.

In his popular *A History of Christianity* (1976), Paul Johnson remarks that "America's most typical churches tended to leap straight from the nineteenth century to the age of the New Testament, and to seek to combine both" (p. 429). That leap is paralleled by the leap of nineteenth-century American literature, not to New Testament times, but to Adamic origins. Ralph Waldo Emerson is the crucial link between our literature and the American Religion, each in full development before him, but each revised by him into forms that recur even at our moment. If you are of the American Religion, then you never cease to yearn for the pure or primitive Church, for the faith of and in a perpetual earliness. An American now is convinced that God loves her or him (88 percent affirm this) or perhaps has that affection (9 percent) and only a few (3 percent) believe that they are not the beloved of Eternity. If one reflects that two out of three Evangelicals (31 percent of Americans) believe that God speaks to them directly, then one has the sense that American awareness of God, and of the relation between God and the self, is very different from that of European Christianity, and perhaps from that of any Christianity the world has yet seen.

Awareness, centered on the self, is *faith* for the American Religion. Emerson, writing in his journal in 1831, gave his nation one of its prime statements of its spiritual peculiarities:

> Remember then, were not the words that made your blood run cold, that brought the blood to your cheeks, that made you tremble or delighted you—did they not sound to you as old as yourself? Was it not truth that you knew before, or do you ever expect to be moved from the pulpit or from man by anything but plain truth? Never. It is God in you that responds to God without, or affirms his own words trembling on the lips of another.

Did they not sound to you as old as yourself? The self is the truth, and there is a spark at its center that is best and oldest, being the God within. Is this Christianity? Jon Butler, in his groundbreaking *Awash in a Sea of Faith: Christianizing the American People* (1990), sensibly urges us to abandon the notion that Puritanism was the crucial force in shaping American religion, that the origin of the American self was Puritan. In Butler's view, the eighteenth century, not the seventeenth, was of prime importance for our spiritual development. Enthusiasm, not a Calvinist concept, is at the heart of the American Religion. Butler emphasizes how complex and heterogeneous American Christianization becomes after 1700. That seems exactly right to me, but I ask again: was it Christianization, or was it something quite different, calling itself Christianity, that imposed itself? Is Southern Baptism in the United States today a version of Christianity? It has no theology of a traditional Protestant sort, in the European sense, and is purely a religion of experience. Yet the American Christ almost always has been *a personal experience* for the American Christian. When a contemporary Southern Baptist hears the call of Jesus to the self, what self is it that is thus addressed? Is the twice-born self part of the Creation, or is it already a part of God? And if it is as old as what calls to it, then what are the consequences of that shared earliness? Are you a Christian, in a traditional, European sense, if what is best and oldest in you was not made by God, but is God? I offer these as open questions, and I am aware that they mingle what appear to be two rival strains of the American Religion, the "positive thinking" aspect of our optimism, and the Gnostic despair of society that is our even more persistent pessimism. What is the link between these strains?

Donald Meyer, in his fine study *The Positive Thinkers* (1965, revised 1988), charts American popular religious psychology from Mrs. Eddy to President Reagan. His conclusion usefully reminds us that our current religious Right derives much of its force from its authentic place in American tradition:

The grasp for political power by the religious Right quite naturally provoked opposition, but rejection of its right to do so misconstrued American history. Separation of church and state never had meant seclusion of religion to purely private life. More decisively, separation of church and state, with its ban on any establishment of religion, had carried the positive meaning that Americans were free to invent new theologies, new churches, new religions. This fertility of invention was not some principle laid down in the Constitution but a fact of American life. (p. 388)

Meyer's shrewdest insight is to link religious Right Fundamentalism to the Harmonial tradition and its Positive Thinking:

But the relevance of the religious Right to the emergent new economic issues depended finally on theology. The 1983 tract *Power for Living,* while reaching out to claim economic rewards for its evangel, was not really a mind-cure tract. It intended instead to harness personal success to its standard fundamentalist thesis. In the process it revealed not so much differences from positive thinking as what positive thinking had repressed. The heart of fundamentalism was of course its attitude towards authority. It granted complete authority over the mind to an outside power. So did positive thinking. Fundamentalism's outside authority was the Bible, inerrant, complete, all-sufficient for all human need. Positive thinking's was a psychology of automanipulation. Neither could abide a relationship of self to outer reality in which the self remained a project, in process, engaged in unfinishable evolution. Both recoiled from opening the self to new life not already guaranteed to fit neatly in the old. Inevitably, this meant a mystified idea of God. (pp. 391–92)

The tract *Power for Living* (1983) came out of the Arthur DeMoss Foundation in Georgia, one of the conservative covens of the Reaganite alliance of Positive Thinking and Know-Nothing Fundamentalism, just another instance of the peculiar merging of parodistic American Religion, and a Republican Party converted to stances at once against evolution and against abortion. I would suggest that we need to alter our understanding of just what it is that most deeply motivates Fundamentalists in their ongoing crusade against post-Darwinian accounts of evolution. American Fundamentalists passionately defend Creationism, and impose its teaching (wherever they can), supposedly because of their bedrock conviction of Biblical Inerrancy. It seems indeed that for them the great "Monkey Trial" at Dayton, Tennessee, in the summer of 1925 has never ended, and that William Jennings Bryan has never died. The devastation of Bryan by Clarence Darrow's cross-examination, which so entertains the rest of us, somehow goes on not touching them, even here, on the date of Noah's flood:

> DARROW: But what do you think that the Bible itself says? Don't you know how it was arrived at?
> BRYAN: I never made a calculation.
> DARROW: A calculation from what?
> BRYAN: I could not say.
> DARROW: From the generations of man?
> BRYAN: I would not want to say that.
> DARROW: What do you think?
> BRYAN: I do not think about things I don't think about.
> DARROW: Do you think about things you do think about?
> BRYAN: Well, sometimes.

This is serious fun, as much now as it was then, even if we lack a Mencken to be inspired by it. "They are everywhere where learning is too heavy a burden for mortal minds to carry" was Mencken's observation on the Fundamentalists, and certainly their psychic violence against intellect and scholarship continues, but the issue remains a clash between different senses of knowledge. Fundamentalism, as I intimate throughout this book, is a parody of the American Religion, but its defensive anxieties and its wounded aggressivities stem nevertheless from what is most authentic in the American Gnosis. The true issue is by no means Biblical Inerrancy, because the Fundamentalists, as unwitting Gnostics, do not believe anyway that God made *them*. Their deepest knowledge is that they were no part of the Creation, but existed as spirits before it, and so are as old as God himself. To be told that they evolved from a common ancestor both of themselves and of apes is no better or worse for them than to be assured that they all descend from a single African woman. What wounds them unforgivingly is not the idea of evolution (in whatever version) but the demonstration that they were never God, or part of God. Their sense of their freedom depends ultimately upon being free not only of time and of nature but, more secretively, being free of the very Creationism they urge upon all the rest of us.

That ultimate Fundamentalist freedom returns me to President Bush's principled stance in defense of his linked emblems of the American Religion, the flag and the fetus, both equally dear to Fundamentalists, and to their allies. Defenders of a woman's right to abortion frequently are embittered by the evidently greater concern of President Bush and the Fundamentalists for the fetus than for the infant. The fetus must not be aborted, but whether the infant starves or not seems, for Bush and his spiritual instructors, a very secondary matter. Let us cast this bitterness away; as American Religionists, the President and his pneumatic supporters are palpably and devoutly sincere. Being Gnostics (however confusedly), they value the unborn over the born, because the Creation and the Fall truly were the same event. The fetus is innocent, but the new-born babe is sadly fallen away from freedom. One sees why the fetus and the flag are one; the baby is not alone, and will drain the pious taxpayer, but the fetus can wave over the land of the free, whose Fundamentalists will remain solitary and godlike, poised always *before* the Creation. As a religious critic, I cannot deny the admirable spiritual consistency of Bushian Gnosticism.

Nietzsche taught us that cause-and-effect is a fiction, a figuration compelled by our grammar. Sociological, political, economic, even anthropological reductions of religion are mere fictions (though sometimes useful ones) but so are spiritual explanations of a society and its politics. I find this a comfort, since I am religiously moved by American Gnosticism but politically appalled by what may be some of its consequences. Since the Reagan-Bush national Republicans have become one with the American Religion, my fear is that we will never again see a Democrat in the Presidency during my lifetime. The religion of the spark or pneumatic self consistently leads to a denial of communal concern, and so perhaps to an exploitation of the helpless by the elite. I want to believe that last sentence of cause-and-effect to be a fiction also, but it is a persuasive fiction, and makes me very unhappy. What I have called American Orphism has led on to what is most distinctive in our cultural and aesthetic achievement, but it may have had a miserable fallout upon our political morality. The Church triumphed over ancient Gnosticism because of its greater social efficacy. American Gnosticism, now indistinguishable from our national triumphalism, continues to rejoice in its social inutility.

3
Cane Ridge through Billy Graham

WHAT this book terms the American Religion will not end until the nation ends, and yet did not come into full existence for nearly a generation after the nation began. I remember, in the summer of 1969, brooding on the Woodstock rock festival, and finding in it many of the stigmata of the great camp meetings of American revival tradition. The first Woodstock, and the most extraordinary camp meeting ever, took place at Cane Ridge, Kentucky, starting on August 6, 1801, and going on for a week afterwards. Perhaps as many as twenty-five thousand people experienced the ecstasies of Cane Ridge, a number more than comparable to the Woodstock throngs of half a million, given the enormous difference in population across a century and two-thirds.

The backwoodsmen and their families, like the young Americans at Woodstock, underwent the singular experience of blending into an Orphic unison, in which denominational differences dissolved. Presbyterians, Baptists, Methodists at once became American Religionists, rapt by ecstasy. Barton Stone, then a Presbyterian minister, came out of Cane Ridge as an incipient Restorationist, searching again for the Primitive Church. His quest was to lead, in time, to the formation of such denominations as the Disciples of Christ and the Churches of Christ, and so his legacy is with us still. Yet Stone preached at Cane Ridge not as a prophet of future denominations, nor as a conscious founder of the American Religion, but primarily as a fugitive from Calvinism. In his memoirs, he prefaces his account of Cane Ridge with a fierce denunciation of Calvinism:

> Calvinism is among the heaviest clogs on Christianity in the world. It is a dark mountain between heaven and earth, and is amongst the most discouraging hindrances to sinners from seeking the kingdom of God, and engenders bondage and gloominess to the saints. Its influence is felt throughout the Christian world, even where it is least suspected. Its first link is total depravity. Yet are there thousands of precious saints in this system. (*Voices from Cane Ridge*, ed. Rhodes Thompson [1954], p. 63)

To save those saints, the Maryland-born Stone came into Kentucky in the spring of 1801, drawn by the religious excitement of a New Birth ministered to by James McGready and other Presbyterian preachers abandoning Calvinism. Stone describes the first camp meeting at which he assisted with a full sense of the uncanny breaking forth:

> There, on the edge of a prairie in Logan county, Kentucky, the multitudes came together, and continued a number of days and nights encamped on the ground; during which time worship was carried on in some part of the encampment. The scene to me was new and passing strange. It baffled description. Many, very many fell down, as men slain in battle, and continued for hours together in an apparently breathless and motionless state—sometimes for a few moments reviving, and exhibiting symptoms of life by a deep groan, or piercing shriek, or by a prayer for mercy most fervently uttered. After lying thus for hours, they obtained deliverance. The gloomy cloud, which had covered their faces, seemed gradually and visibly to disappear, and hope in smiles brightened into joy—they would rise shouting deliverance. (pp. 64–65)

At Cane Ridge in August, the climactic camp meeting occurred, with Methodist and Baptist preachers joining Stone and the other soon-to-be-ex-Presbyterians: "We all engaged in singing the same songs of praise—all united in prayer—all preached the same things —free salvation urged upon all by faith and repentance." No one present had ever seen so many people in one place before, since a crowd of about twenty-five thousand would be radically startling to Kentuckians, being more than twelve times as numerous as their largest city at that time. Particularly since so many of these were frontier people, living in relative isolation, the effect had to be a unique experience for them. Sydney Ahlstrom reminded us that these were rough people, profane, heavy drinkers, violent, and that they had never attended night meetings before. Conversions and lovemaking intermingled, while Stone memorably recorded a major outbreak of Enthusiasm, with all its strenuous peculiarities:

The bodily agitations or exercises, attending the excitement in the beginning of this century, were various, and called by various names;—as, the falling exercise—the jerks—the dancing exercise —the barking exercise—the laughing and singing exercise, &c. —The falling exercise was very common among all classes, the saints and sinners of every age and of every grade, from the philosopher to the clown. The subject of this exercise would, generally, with a piercing scream, fall like a log on the floor, earth, or mud, and appear as dead. . . .

The jerks cannot be so easily described. Sometimes the subject of the jerks would be affected in some one member of the body, and sometimes in the whole system. When the head alone was affected, it would be jerked backward and forward, or from side to side, so quickly that the features of the face could not be distinguished. When the whole system was affected, I have seen the person stand in one place, and jerk backward and forward in quick succession, their head nearly touching the floor behind and before. All classes, saints and sinners, the strong as well as the weak, were thus affected. I have inquired of those thus affected. They could not account for it; but some have told me that those were among the happiest seasons of their lives. I have seen some wicked persons thus affected, and all the time cursing the jerks, while they were thrown to the earth with violence. Though so awful to behold, I do not remember that any one of the thousands I have seen ever sustained an injury in body. This was as strange as the exercise itself.

The dancing exercise. This generally began with the jerks, and was peculiar to professors of religion. The subject, after jerking awhile, began to dance, and then the jerks would cease. Such dancing was indeed heavenly to the spectators; there was nothing in it like levity, nor calculated to excite levity in the beholders. The smile of heaven shone on the countenance of the subject, and assimilated to angels appeared the whole person. Sometimes the motion was quick and sometimes slow. Thus they continued to move forward and backward in the same track or alley till nature seemed exhausted, and they would fall prostrate on the flow or earth, unless caught by those standing by. While thus exercised, I have heard their solemn praises and prayers ascending to God.

The barking exercise, (as opposers contemptuously called it,) was nothing but the jerks. A person affected with the jerks, especially in his head, would often make a grunt, or bark, if you please, from the suddenness of the jerk. This name of barking seems to have had its origin from an old Presbyterian preacher of East Tennessee. He had gone into the woods for private devotion, and was seized with the jerks. Standing near a sapling, he caught hold of it, to prevent his falling, and as his head jerked back, he uttered a grunt or kind of noise similar to a bark, his face being turned upwards. Some wag discovered him in this position, and reported that he found him barking up a tree.

The laughing exercise was frequent, confined solely with the religious. It was a loud, hearty laughter, but one *sui generis;* it excited laughter in none else. The subject appeared rapturously solemn, and his laughter excited solemnity in saints and sinners. It is truly indescribable.

The running exercise was nothing more than, that persons feeling something of these bodily agitations, through fear, attempted to run away, and thus escape from them; but it commonly happened that they ran not far, before they fell, or became so greatly agitated that they could proceed no farther . . .

I shall close this chapter with the singing exercise. This is more unaccountable than any thing else I ever saw. The subject in a very happy state of mind would sing most melodiously, not from the mouth or nose, but entirely in the breast, the sounds issuing thence. Such music silenced every thing, and attracted the attention of all. It was most heavenly. None could ever be tired of hearing it. Doctor J. P. Campbell and myself were together at a meeting, and were attending to a pious lady thus exercised, and concluded it to be something surpassing any thing we had known in nature.

I cite this only partly for the fun of it; Barton Stone clearly was persuaded of the sincerity and authenticity of these seizures, and they retain a grotesque power. More substantively, they carry us all the way back to the more exuberant of Ronald Knox's Enthusiasts: the Montanists of ancient Phrygia; the Ranters and many early Quakers; the French Camisards at the turn into the eighteenth century; the convulsionaries of Saint-Medard in the early 1730s who embarrassed the Jansenists; the Moravians, only a few years later; the Wesleyan outbursts of the eighteenth century; the Shakers and Irvingites in the nineteenth, whose outbursts go on well after Cane Ridge. What Stone so soberly describes is endemic in the history of Enthusiasm, and is featured in Pentecostal and other revivals down to this moment. Knox, regarding the Saint-Medard convulsions with Roman Catholic–Oxonian disdain, quite accurately identifies the sadomasochistic sexuality strongly present in these phenomena. However you cleanse or dress up Revivalism, the outbursts of Enthusiasm truly are their norm and not their aberration. There was something frightening as well as grotesque in the Cane Ridge peculiarities, and one sees why the Presbyterian Church turned against Cane Ridge.

As I write these pages (in July 1991), those unfrocked but active Assemblies of God Pentecostal televangelists, Jimmy Swaggart and Marvin Gorman, continue with their litigation and their incessant publicizing of one another's sexual misadventures. All this is sublimely beside the point, since there is no way to disentangle the sexual drive from Pentecostalism any more than we can excise it from the Enthusiastic revival at Cane Ridge. What was born as Barton Stone and his fellow preachers chanted on was a fundamental but scarcely ever avowed principle of the American Religion: creedlessness, or the *doctrine of experience*, as oxymoronic a phrase as even I can imagine. The drunk, sexually aroused communicants at Cane Ridge, like their drugged and aroused Woodstockian descendants a century and a half later, participated in a kind of orgiastic individualism, in which all the holy rolling was the outward mark of an inward grace that traumatically put away frontier loneliness and instead put on the doctrine of experience that exalted such loneliness into a being-alone-with-Jesus. A solitude that only the two could share pragmatically is no different from the perpetual American loneliness, but spiritually it became an absolute difference. Most simply, the American Jesus was born at Cane Ridge, and is with us still, in Nashville and Salt Lake City, in New Orleans and in East Harlem storefronts. He is a Jesus who barely was crucified, and whose forty days of Resurrection upon earth never have ended. Or if he ascended, he has come back and keeps coming back in the pouring out of Spirit. He cannot be known in or through a church, but only one on one, and then indeed he is known, with far more immediacy evidently than even heightened sexual experience can provide, more even than frontier violence can provide. American revivalism, with its endless Great Awakenings, is as recurrent a phenomenon as American violence. We don't have crime waves any more than we have Great Awakenings; violent crime and religious revivalism are constant throughout our history. Crime waves are journalistic fictions, Great Awakenings are scholarly fictions, and both conceal the troubling near identity between the religion of violence and the violence of religion. Cane Ridge set the pattern of addiction in which Americans bear away the Kingdom of Heaven by violence.

Whether the Cane Ridge camp meeting ecstasies arose from a kind of self-hypnosis, as some scholars have speculated, or were psychosexual in nature, as I tend to suppose, makes only a little difference in judging the event after two centuries. Either way, the entire South was soon awash in the sea of faith, to employ Jon Butler's ironic version of Matthew Arnold's "Dover Beach." All over the region the heretofore rival Presbyterian, Methodist, and Baptist preachers banded together, in what became virtually an immense series of repetitions of Cane Ridge, complete with throngs of repentant sinners and all the spasmodic exercises of the Spirit breaking forth in the flesh. A complex, probably unconscious influence of the Black Baptist churches was at work, but I will defer a consideration of this until my discussion of African-American religion in Chapter 15. What I find crucial here is the emergence of a pragmatic, experiential faith that called itself Christianity while possessing features very unlike European or earlier American doctrinal formulations. The most notorious of all our clichés, rugged individualism, finds one of the few contexts that can restore it to freshness in the atmosphere of Cane Ridge and subsequent revivals. Most scholars of American religion find the origins of Southern spirituality in the post-Revolutionary swerve away from the unpatriotic Anglican Church. Yet something very close to Evangelical personalism was prevalent among slave Baptists a generation before the Revolution, and a peculiar inwardness pervaded the South almost from the start. Aside from the invisible influence of the African-Americans, with their memories of ancestral images of "little me," a magical or occult self, within the larger me, there was a Southern reliance upon experiential religion of the Orphic sort. The conversion from death to life was purely emotional and individual; it seemed always to exclude a social dimension. One might almost say that the Southern Jesus came to set the pattern for what is now the American Jesus: the resurrected friend, walking and talking one-on-one, with the repentant sinner. And this Jesus came to one, of his own will, and not the sinner's; he chose one. Preachers could prepare the sinner's heart, but only Jesus truly could begin the process of salvation. What was missing in all this quite private luminosity was simply most of historic Christianity. I hasten to add that I am celebrating, not deploring, when I make that observation. So far as I can tell, the Southern Jesus, which is to say the American Jesus, is not so much an agent of redemption as he is an imparter of knowledge, which returns us to the analysis of an American Gnosis in my previous chapter. Jesus is not so much an event in history for the American Religionist as he is a knower of the secrets of God who in return can be known by the individual. Hidden in this process is a sense that depravity is only a lack of saving knowledge. Salvation, through knowing the knowing Jesus, is a reversal wholly experiential in nature, an internalization of a self already internalized. Jesus is not a first-century Jew, but a nineteenth- or twentieth-century American, whose principal difference from other Americans is that he already has risen from the dead. Having mastered this knowledge, he teaches it to whom he will. Whatever this is (and I am not unmoved by it), we would be inaccurate to regard such a faith as historic Christianity.

The South was and is a special case, spiritually speaking, as California also is in this century. The California of the nineteenth century, weirdly enough, in religious zeal and inventiveness was the western reserve of New York State, out of which so many American originals emerged, of which the most remarkable and permanent was Mormonism. Revivalism, which we now tend to associate with California, the South, and the Midwest, was a perpetual flame in the "Burned-over District" between the Adirondacks and the shores of Lake Ontario. My own favorite study of American religion is the marvelous book by Whitney R. Cross, *The Burned-over District: The Social and Intellectual History of Enthusiastic Religion in Western New York, 1800–1850* (1950). Cross chronicled the wildness of American spiritual freedom among a population self-exiled from New England in search of economic opportunity (many were younger sons) and of a religious vitalism that had dimmed with the decline of Congregationalism. Cane Ridge and the following Southern camp meetings were more spectacular manifestations than the individual revivalist events of the Burned-over District, but the Southerners were far surpassed in Gnostic intensity and Enthusiastic zeal for millennial innovation by the transplanted children of the Puritan tradition.

Millennial movements in the Burned-over region started with the Shakers, themselves transplanted from old England and finding their true abode in western New York State. Their founder, Ann Lee, began as a desperate, lower-class English wife, who had gone through four painful births, lost all four infants, joined a band of Shaking Quakers (in dissent from the main body of Quakers), and was imprisoned for disturbing the peace in Manchester during the summer of 1770. With waking eyes, she beheld Adam and Eve in the initial act of human sexuality and suddenly understood that lovemaking itself constituted the Fall from Paradise. By 1774, Ann Lee had removed herself and her followers to America. She died in 1784, only about forty-eight years old, leaving her movement as one of the oddest spiritual legacies in our troubled religious history. There are no Shakers today, but they lasted nearly two centuries, an astonishing span for an absolutely celibate sect that could only survive through adoptions and conversions. All that people of general education (particularly those who have visited a beautifully preserved Shaker village) remember now are the Shakers' skills at handicrafts and furniture, their reputation for eccentric dancing, and their rigorous aversion from sexual life. But there is a small but illuminating contribution of Shakerism to the spiritual composite I call the American Religion, if only by the Shaker highlighting of the sexual component in American millenarianism.

As I understand our American Gnosis, it tends to exclude a sense of the communal. Ann Lee's vision of God essentially was Gnostic, and followed the ancient concept that God was both our foremother and our forefather, both female and male. In America, the Shaker founder went further, and soon was regarded by her followers as a female Jesus, and became known as Mother Ann Lee, in a relation both divine and maternal. Though all Shakers, and not just Mother Ann, incarnated the Spirit, they became in effect an extended family, all of them her children. The gifts of the Spirit were thus both singular and familial, and an odd blend of individualism and communalism had been created. Ronald Knox, with his customarily genial Roman disapproval for "bad faith," made clear that he preferred the Shakers to the Mormons, a delightful preference when you consider that the former are now extinct, and the latter crowd the headquarters of the FBI, CIA, and allied agencies, something Knox could not have foreseen forty years ago:

> It would have been tempting to say something in this book about the Mormons, but who can feel certain that the founders of the movement were at any time in good faith? . . . There was more fun to be had, you feel, in the cloistered shades of Mount Lebanon. The Shakers for us! (p. 558)

As a celibate himself, Knox quite naturally preferred Mother Ann to the healthily sensual Prophet Joseph, but his elegy for his Shakers makes clear why they have vanished, and the Mormons have become permanent, and may yet become multitudes, though Knox in *this* passage certainly did not have the Mormons in mind:

> Enthusiasm does not maintain itself at fever heat; dance as you will, flap your hands as you will, you cannot conjure up the old days when people rolled on the floor in agonies of convincement, and talked in strange sounds which might, for all they knew, be the language of the Hotmatots. Meanwhile, the fundamental theology of the Shakers, like that of the Quakers from whom they descended, was largely a negative thing; they revolted from the theologizing of the older sects, and failed to provide themselves with such a corpus of doctrine as should resist, in more sophisticated days, the encroachments of rationalism. (p. 565)

Despite my forty years' passion for Knox's *Enthusiasm* as an indubitably great book, I think that this is quite wrong, and needs to be very strongly misread if it is to be of use. The Southern Baptists' theology (as I will show later) is also largely a negative thing, whether in Moderates or in Fundamentalists, but the denomination never stops growing, even though soon enough it will be even more in schism than it already is. Creedlessness is a positive asset for any version or variety of the American Religion, and Mormon theology is so jerry-built that no one can hope to get it straight (as I will also show later). At their most numerous, there may have been five thousand or so Shakers; American Religionists are as lustful as they are violent, and why should they not be? The Shakers are gone not because rationalism encroached; our wretched land groans under the press of Know-Nothing Fundamentalists, and rationalism cannot nick them. No, the Shakers are gone because they were not American enough, though they lasted longer here than they would have done had Ann Lee gone anywhere else. As the Roman Catholic Church in the United States keeps refusing to learn, celibacy is less and less an American option.

Ann Lee is important because she became an American extreme, like Mary Baker Eddy after her. More typical of Burned-over District spirituality were the Perfectionists, high-spirited young women and young men who sought what they charmingly called "perfect sanctification," which tradition used to call "antinomianism." About 1834 or so, the Burned-over Perfectionists achieved their apotheosis, described by Whitney R. Cross in not only the best passages in his book, but in what I would nominate as the high point of American religious history writing. As an added charm, Cross features the splendid Lucina Umphreville, surely the authentic heroine of the American Religion:

It was in the spring of 1835 that Lucina Umphreville took up the idea "that carnal union was not to be tolerated even in marriage, while spiritual union whether in or out of marriage represented a high state of attainment." Practically simultaneously, at Brimfield, Massachusetts, Maria Brown decided to demonstrate that her piety could overcome lowly desires, by proving that she could sleep chastely with her minister . . .

When news of the "Brimfield Bundling" reached central New York, the saints in this region also reacted in horror . . .

During the summer of 1836, changes in both doctrine and practice came about almost simultaneously. At the Chapman homestead on the south shore of Oneida Lake, Maria Brown was

visiting Mrs. Chapman and the "fascinating" Lucina Umphreville
. . . Soon Jarvis Rider and Charles Lovett joined the party . . .

The New Yorkers only tried to prove to Maria that they could
succeed where she had failed, in the same kind of test of their
highly spiritual unions . . .

Both couples, Rider and Lucina, and Lovett and Mrs. Chapman, felt guilty rather than proud when Mr. Chapman came
home. Chapman went after Lovett with a horsewhip but was
struck blind in the act. This "act of God" probably put the stamp
of authority on the doctrine of security from sin and led to its
spread through the cults about central New York. (pp. 243–4)

Cross just here seems a heroic precursor of Edward Gorey, who
alone could illustrate this appropriately. The quotation marks
above refer to an account by John Humphrey Noyes, an even
grander Perfectionist, who tells us that he broke off his Brimfield
visit to walk home all the way to Putney, Vermont, so as not to be
associated with the self-wounding of Maria Brown's name. Noyes
chose a better way, in his famous experiment in "Complex Marriage," the Oneida Community, which does not trouble our imaginations enough, despite Lawrence Foster's fine book, *Religion and
Sexuality* (1981), which studies it in conjunction with the early
Shakers and with the more notorious Mormon doctrine of Plural
or Celestial Marriage. Noyes was an astonishingly able founder
and leader of Perfectionist communities, first at Putney and then
at Oneida, from 1838 (when he was twenty-seven) on to 1881, five
years before his death. His Perfectionism stemmed from being
refused ordination (after studying divinity at Yale) on the understandable grounds that he had reduced the gospel to sinlessness.
There could be no other belief for him, since he insisted that the
fall of Jerusalem and the Temple to the Romans in the year 70 of
the Common Era had ended the biblical ordinances because the
Second Coming of Jesus Christ had taken place then also. If Ann
Lee had preached what the Church Fathers would have called an
ascetic Gnosticism, then Noyes, like Joseph Smith, would have
been regarded by them as a libertine Gnostic. Joseph Smith certainly did not lack a large share of the joy of life, but John Noyes
was no libertine. Because the biblical dispensation was ended, the
saints were to live for perfection alone, and so a purely individual
relation to the Spirit now had to yield to a communal good, which

alone could secure sinlessness. Possessive sexual intercourse was to be set aside for the higher good of eugenics and more serene social kinship. "Male continence" or *coitus reservatus* (charmingly called *karezza* in an approving essay by Aldous Huxley) was prescribed as the proper means of birth control, to be avoided only in particular cases of prescribed eugenics. This worked quite well, as Foster indicates:

> Undoubtedly, that low birth rate can be traced to the practise of having women past menopause induct young men into male continence and having older, more experienced men induct young women. (p. 95)

Foster and other scholars do not seek to link the details of Noyes's sexual program to his theology, but only the link truly belongs to my subject. If there is a new dispensation, then the ideas of marriage in the old dispensation are no longer valid. Mother Ann Lee, a second if female Jesus, proclaimed celibacy. Joseph Smith, prophet and king of the Kingdom of God, proclaimed Celestial Marriage, or the plurality of wives. John Noyes, neither redeemer nor prophet but a religious reformer, announced Complex Marriage and male continence. For all, the old times were ended, but one sees why only Smith's way could have been a pragmatic success in the long run. The Shakers died; Noyes and his followers held out for decades, but yielded finally to societal disapproval and to the psychology of private enterprise, both in sexual and in commercial realms. Brigham Young maintained Joseph's system in Utah until he died, but by 1890 it was clear that statehood would be withheld unless polygamy was abolished. Even then, the Mormons shrewdly intended the Manifesto of 1890 to be an outward mask only, and polygamous marriages were tacitly permitted, but gradually middle-class respectability, as G. B. Shaw called it, came into play, and the Manifesto was used to push the polygamous out of the community. But until that happened, Smith's major purpose certainly was accomplished, and the Mormons were confirmed as a chosen people, set aside from all others.

Dispensationalism accompanies millenarianism; it was fitting and inevitable that the crucial American outburst of nineteenth-century millenarianism should have broken out in the Burned-over District, and it adds piquancy that its prophet should have been

William Miller, giving rise to many scholarly slogans of "Millerism and Millenarianism." Except for historians of American religion, no one now remembers William Miller, a fate he shares with his namesake, a New York State congressman who would have been our Vice President had Barry Goldwater been elected President. The first William Miller deserves recall, if only because his effect upon our religious history has been so consequential. Both Seventh-day Adventism and (less directly) Jehovah's Witnesses ultimately originate in the Great Disappointment, which was the reaction of the Millerite movement to the world's failure to reach its end in 1843. The end was redated to October 22, 1844, but the universe again would not oblige, since Jesus Christ had not come, despite William Miller's prophecy. Some scholars assert that there were ten thousand Millerites; other estimates range up to a million, presumably including momentary fellow travelers.

The prophet Daniel had proclaimed that the sanctuary would be cleansed after two thousand three hundred days (Daniel 8:14), which William Miller, Baptist lay preacher and New York State Yankee farmer, calculated would take everyone to the year 1843, at which time Jesus certainly would come again. For about a decade before the promised end, Miller went about and lectured, presenting his mystical mathematics to increasingly large audiences. Essentially a Northeastern phenomenon, Millerism nevertheless reached out to the Middle West and to Canada. But it went no farther south than Washington D.C., and tended to be dismissed by the Southerners as Yankee madness. Sometimes the Millerite movement seems to me the weirdest religious phenomenon in nineteenth-century America, since even if there were only forty thousand intense Millerites, which seems a rational estimate, that was an extraordinary number a hundred and fifty years ago. Despite the vagaries of current American Fundamentalists, with their occasional expectations of being taken up to heaven in the Rapture, I am skeptical that a new Millerism could sweep the nation now. As this decade wears on, my skepticism may recede, for in what spirit will a religion-mad country apprehend the approach of the year 2000?

Like many Americans of all periods, Miller studied his Bible with incessant zeal and became a premillennialist, expecting Christ's Advent to come before the thousand years of peace on earth. Miller differed in that his calculations became fiercely precise. For a long time, he placed the Advent about 1843, and then he yielded to various stimuli, outer and inner, and located it exactly on October 22, 1844. His palpable sincerity (and bad judgment) was manifested by the exactitude of his prophecy; if one goes into that business, clearly one should be as oracular and indefinite as possible. But Miller persuaded himself, with increasing zeal, and became a Baptist clergyman, and then proceeded to institutionalize his growing audience. Ministers and Perfectionists rallied to him, and Adventism began to hover somewhere between a movement and a denomination, though one without any particular doctrine except for the exactitude of the end time. The summer of 1844 necessarily was the grand period for the Millerites. Zeal continued unabated through October 22 in the certainty that there would be no October 23, but it dawned nevertheless.

Miller and his principal supporters led a number of followers into what became the Advent Christians; their arithmetic had been bad, but they would go on waiting for the End, until gradually they did trail off. The authentic American Religionists among the Millerites could not accept such a stance; either they went over to other organized Enthusiasts (some even became Shakers), or else they insisted that, in the Spirit, Christ indeed had entered the sanctuary on October 22. These latter ultimately organized themselves as the Seventh-day Adventists, and will be considered in a later chapter, but they were certainly no comfort to Miller himself, though they were to be his only lasting legacy. He died in 1849, after a few frustrating years ministering to a small Vermont congregation of Advent Christians, since the infuriated Baptists had expelled him. Yet he seems now to have been the overdetermined victim of Burned-over creedlessness and Perfectionism. Enthusiastic religion has few resources for protecting itself from itself. Nothing could have been more doom-eager than Millerism, but it differed only in degree, not in kind, from more lasting and self-sustaining varieties of the American Religion. An exemplary comparison can be made between the blighted William Miller and the brilliantly successful Charles Grandison Finney, the major evangelist of the era of the Burned-over District. Finney is universally regarded as the paragon of modern Evangelical revivalism, the precursor of such eminent unrest-inducers as Dwight Lyman Moody, William Ashley Sunday, and William Franklin Graham, our reigning figure. In Finney's career, better even than Graham's, one can see how American creedlessness learned to make gestures to the End, while taking care not to fall into the Millerite abyss.

Finney was ostensibly Presbyterian, as Graham is formally Southern Baptist, but both men rapidly transcended denominational limitations. A pragmatic exploiter of his own charisma, Finney had the insight to know that only a purely personal, violently emotional, totally experiential mode of salvation was appropriate for the Burned-over sinner. What had been spontaneous at Cane Ridge was systematized into a technique by Finney two generations later. A Finney revival could go on for ten nights in sequence, because this most ambitious of preachers did not seek merely to convert. Perfectionism became, in Finney's campaigns, a practical approach to whole masses of souls, each of which was assured it could cleanse itself forever of all human sin en route to the goal of "entire sanctification." Near-converts who shivered upon the "anxious bench" (Finney's own marvelous invention) were so prayed over in public by the almost dreadfully outspoken evangelist that they were delighted to collapse into his sanctification. By the time Finney went out to become president of Oberlin College, in 1851, he had created a new American form, at once religious revival, popular spectacle, and serious social crusade. Unlike those who came after him, culminating in Billy Graham, Finney demanded good works of his converts, particularly in behalf of the antislavery movement.

I have traced this brief history of the gathering tendency I have been calling the American Religion from the tumultuous revival at Cane Ridge through the sectarian explosion of the early decades of the nineteenth century, and later in this book I will reflect upon the rise of African-American and Southern Baptist churches after the Civil War. The story leads on through Protestant Fundamentalism and its revivalism, but here I wish to conclude by centering upon the curiously representative figure of Billy Graham, who has become something like the archetypal minister of this parody of the American Religion. Born in 1918, Graham achieved celebrity with his Los Angeles revival of 1949, carried out as he turned thirty-one. In the next decade, Graham pretty much expressed what he had to say, and for more than thirty years now he has been a mere repetition of his early zeal. The best study of Graham remains William G. McLoughlin's *Billy Graham: Revivalist in a Secular Age* (1960), as thirty years after, very little needs to be added.

Graham has mellowed; he has been nationally and internationally institutionalized; and he looks better than ever on television, whether in the company of the President of the United States or addressing a moderately aroused audience waiting to be revived by him. Graham goes well with Bush, because Graham is a kinder, gentler Fundamentalist than his major precursors, but he remains as much a Fundamentalist as Bush remains a Big Business Republican. Inspired by McLoughlin, I have read through Graham's *Peace with God* (1953), still his central manifesto. Clearly expressed despite its vapidity, *Peace with God* is an unremarkable exposition of the usual Fundamentalist doctrine. Yet, interestingly enough, it does not read today as a 1950s period piece, and in its own placid way is quite timeless. Graham himself has remained a fifties period piece, bound to that decade's vision of a prosperous, well-scrubbed America. For someone like myself, who divides his time between New York City and New Haven, Connecticut, the truly jarring moment in early Graham comes when he tells us that

> in India tonight over 100,000,000 people will go to bed hungry, if they have a bed to go to. And when they drive the trucks down the streets of Calcutta tomorrow morning they will pick up people that have died of starvation, as I have seen them in India.

This comes from a peroration where Graham salutes America for its affluence, and reminds us that the Bible says it is all right to be rich. There is no point ever in disputing the Bible with a Fundamentalist, but as I write (May 1991), there are over two million homeless in the United States, at least five million children (and countless adults) go to bed hungry in Graham's land, and New York City is widely apprehended as the new Calcutta. Graham indeed is a strange figure to have become the center of a national, really an official, cult of admiration. From at least 1957 on, Graham had been advising us that Communism was literally the work of the Devil, but then as far back as 1950, he anticipated Armageddon and the Second Coming as being imminent. Now, in 1991, the Devil seems to have abandoned Russia, and a more seasoned Graham ceases to prophesy the end, but Christianity and patriotism remain one, and Graham may yet gaze round and find us another nation performing the labor of the Devil.

None of this would matter except for Graham's evidently permanent position as a national icon. For more than forty years he has been the Pope of Protestant America, and will maintain that position until he dies. He does little harm; he does little good; and in his proper person he is religiously quite meaningless. Since he belongs to popular culture, he is not much more the concern of religious criticism than Frank Sinatra is, or George Bush. Parodies of spirituality, though, have their own interest, and their own uses, and Graham remains highly instructive. He is in no way original as an entertainer on the Revivalist circuit; McLoughlin, with agile inerrancy, charts Graham's descent from Dwight Moody in particular. To Moody belong all of Graham's characteristic methods and refinements of organization: advertising, advance men, publicity campaigns, specially trained staff (including counselors, prayer leaders, singers, ushers), committees of major financiers and churchmen, published audited accounts of donations, collections, and expenses. Even the idea of a solo singer originated with Moody, whose Ira Sankey was the precursor of mellifluous George Beverly Shea. Moody, like Finney before him, did not abound with theological ideas, but either seems more substantive now than the rhetorical Graham. His diffuseness, and his technique, allowed him to become a kind of Pope of the American Religion abroad, but with the final irony, reported in the press even as I conclude this chapter, that many in his Russian audiences mutter how much better they know the text of the Bible than Graham does.

II

AMERICAN ORIGINAL: THE MORMONS

4

A Religion Becomes a People: The Kingdom of God

A major American poet, perhaps one called a Gentile by the Latter-day Saints, some time in the future will write their early story as the epic it was. Nothing else in all of American history strikes me as *materia poetica* equal to the early Mormons, to Joseph Smith, Brigham Young, Parley and Orson Pratt, and the men and women who were their followers and friends. John Greenleaf Whittier, Quaker poet and Abolitionist, attended a Mormon service in Lowell, Massachusetts, in 1847, and came away deeply moved:

> In listening to these modern prophets, I discovered, as I think, the great secret of their success in making converts. They speak to a common feeling; they minister to a universal want. They contrast strongly the miraculous power of the gospel in the apostolic time with the present state of our nominal Christianity. They ask for the signs of divine power; the faith, overcoming all things, which opened the prison doors of the apostles, gave them power over the elements, which rebuked disease and death itself, and made visible to all the presence of the living God. They ask for any declaration in the Scriptures that this miraculous power of faith was to be confined to the first confessors of Christianity. (William Muldur and A. Russell Mortensen, eds., *Among the Mormons* [1958], pp. 157–58)

It is difficult to recapture Whittier's precise emotion, but without something like it early Mormonism cannot be comprehended. Fawn Brodie, still Joseph Smith's great biographer despite Mormon anger at her work, began her book *No Man Knows My History: The Life of Joseph Smith the Mormon Prophet* (1945; 2d ed., 1971) by shrewdly noting that "Joseph Smith dared to found a new religion in the age of printing." But Smith's writings cannot explain away the pathos that Whittier felt, or that even I feel, one hundred and fifty years later and believing as I do that all religion is a kind of spilled poetry, bad and good. There was something in Smith and his vision that remains central to our country and its spirituality. Mrs. Brodie, by no means unmoved by a post-Mormon pathos, summed up the prophet's spiritual achievement a touch too harshly:

> Joseph had a ranging fancy, a revolutionary vigor, and a genius for improvisation, and what he could mold with these he made well. With them he created a book and a religion, but he could not create a truly spiritual content for that religion. He could canalize aspirations formed elsewhere into a new structure and provide the ritualistic shell of new observances. But within the dogma of the church there is no new Sermon on the Mount, no new saga of redemption, nothing for which Joseph himself might stand. His martyrdom was a chance event, wholly incidental to the creed that he created. (p. 403)

That is religious criticism, by the tenets worked out in my first chapter, and as such it is inadequate, though not wrong. Starting with the Sermon on the Mount as criterion is to set a standard for "a truly spiritual content" parallel to setting *Macbeth* or *Paradise Lost* as a criterion for American poetry's aesthetic achievement. Here my analogy between literary and religious criticism necessarily touches a limit, since to a Mormon the Pearl of Great Price is as canonical as the New Testament. But only a handful or two of Mormons, past or present, have been authentic religious critics of their own faith, and most of those have been expelled by the church (like Mrs. Brodie) or departed on their own.

Joseph Smith was a religious genius, though only a mixed orator and an indifferent writer. His followers, for at least a century now, have backtracked from his radical newness to a public stance some-

times difficult to distinguish from Protestantism, but Smith himself
was in no traditional sense a Protestant, or indeed even a Christian.
Mrs. Brodie saw the truth when she beheld the religion of her
ancestors as having the same relation to Christianity that Christianity had to Judaism, or that Islam had to both the religion of the
Book and the religion of the Son of Man. The two crucial branches
of the American Religion, in my judgment, are the Mormons and
the Southern Baptists, violent opponents of one another, yet each
American to the core and neither having anything accurately in
common with what historically has been considered Christianity.
Both insist otherwise, but so does nearly every other American sect
and denomination, every American variety of our pragmatic and
experiential religion. To myself, culturally an American Jewish
intellectual but not an adherent of normative Judaism, nothing
about our country seems so marvelously strange, so terrible and so
wonderful, as its weird identification with ancient Israelite religion
and with the primitive Christian Church that supposedly came out
of it. The largest paradox concerning the American Religion is that
it is truly a biblical religion, whereas Judaism and Christianity
never were that, despite all their passionate protestations. Normative Judaism is the religion of the Oral Law, the strong interpretation of the Bible set forth by the great rabbis of the second century
of the Common Era. Christianity is the religion of the Church
Fathers and of the Protestant theologians who broke with the
Church, and Catholics and Protestants alike joined the rabbinical
sages in offering definitive interpretations that displaced Scripture.
The American Religion, unlike Judaism and Christianity, is actually biblical, even when it offers and exalts alternative texts as
well.

Joseph Smith's alternative texts—the Book of Mormon, the Pearl
of Great Price (itself made up of several rather distinct works), and
the Doctrine and Covenants—are all stunted stepchildren of the
Bible. I need to say something like "stunted" because what we now
call the Bible is the result of a complex process of canonization for
which the criteria were surprisingly aesthetic, or at least reconcilable with the aesthetic. The Song of Songs is in the Bible because it
had enchanted the great Rabbi Akiba, and something in that en-
chantment was not altogether different from my bewitchment by
our Song of Songs, Walt Whitman's "When Lilacs Last in the
Dooryard Bloom'd." But all of Mormon Scripture is the work of

Joseph Smith, and his life, personality, and visions far transcended his talents at the composition of divine texts. Mormonism no longer *is* Joseph Smith, but it was from 1830 to 1890, the sixty years of its spiritual greatness, punctuated by the martyrdom of its prophet in 1844. A good introduction to Smith's career, down to March 1, 1842, is a letter sent by the Prophet Joseph to John Wentworth, a Chicago newspaper editor. Thirty-seven years old, not foreseeing his death only two years and a few months later, Smith wrote from where he reigned, the Mormon city of Nauvoo, Illinois, at the height of his self-confidence and authority. Because these are the best pages of prose that he ever composed, and since they conclude with thirteen points that have become a creed for Mormons, I want to analyze them very closely, in order to begin to understand the revelation of Joseph Smith.

The Wentworth letter, which prints up as six pages, is marked by the dignity of a simple eloquence, and by the self-possession of a religious innovator who is so secure in the truth of his doctrine that he can state its pith with an almost miraculous economy. It is a good beginning for the religious critic of Smith, because it raises immediately the crucial question of the Mormon seer's achievement. Whatever his lapses, Smith was an authentic religious genius, unique in our national history. The Wentworth letter starts with the prophet's birth, in Sharon, Vermont, on December 23, 1805, and passes rapidly to his first visions, which rightly now are considered far more vital to the Mormons than the Book of Mormon itself, largely superseded as that was by Smith's later writings and pronouncements. The general public associates Mormonism primarily with the Book of Mormon, a curious return after a century and a half to the origins of the religion. But the centrality of the Book of Mormon actually vanished during Smith's major phase, the final five years before his murder by the Illinois militia. Ezra Taft Benson, a survivor of Eisenhower's first Cabinet, remains the Prophet, Seer, and Revelator today, at least in the pure good of theory, and Benson has devoted himself to publicizing the Book of Mormon, even though it has only a very limited relationship to the doctrines of the Latter-day Saints Church. Benson is now ninety-three; next in line is Howard W. Hunter, eighty-three, and then Gordon B. Hinckley, eighty. Behind them is the powerful Thomas S. Monson, only sixty-two. When President Monson becomes Prophet, Seer, and Revelator, there may be less reliance upon the Book of Mormon as the royal road into the Mormon religion.

The first visions, in the Wentworth letter, came to a boy of fourteen whose family already had repudiated the Puritan religious heritage of most people in New England. Joseph Smith, Sr., joined no church until his son grew up to found a new faith for the family. By then, they lived in the notorious "spiritual hothouse" of western New York, where visions were not uncommon. Though the Prophet Joseph's several accounts of his First Vision vary widely, they all emphasize what the Wentworth letter shows was unique:

> I retired to a secret place in a grove and began to call upon the Lord. While fervently engaged in supplication my mind was taken away from the objects with which I was surrounded, and I was enwrapped in a heavenly vision and saw two glorious personages who exactly resembled each other in features, and likeness, surrounded with a brilliant light which eclipsed the sun at noonday. They told me that all religious denominations were believing in incorrect doctrines, and that none of them was acknowledged of God as his church and kingdom. And I was expressly commanded to "go not after them," at the same time receiving a promise that the fulness of the gospel should at some future time be made known unto me.

It does not matter how retrospective and revised a First Vision this is; all religion necessarily is revisionary in regard to its own sacred origins. What moves me, here and elsewhere in Smith, is the sureness of his instincts, his uncanny *knowing* precisely what is needful for the inauguration of a new faith. Like Saint Paul (whose theology is almost totally cast out by the Mormons), Smith implicitly understood not only his own aims but the pragmatics of religion making, or what would *work* in matters of the spirit. For that remains the center of his achievement: the Mormons have continued for over a hundred and sixty years; they change, but they do not die. There are now about as many Mormons in our nation and the world as there are Jews, and as I remarked earlier, the Mormons, like the Jews before them, are a religion that became a people. That, I have come to understand, always was Joseph Smith's pragmatic goal, for he had the genius to see that only by becoming a people could the Mormons survive. The Wentworth letter is a religious document that celebrates the organization of a people on the basis of a spiritual idea. Smith's insight could have come only from a remarkably apt reading of the Bible, and there I would locate the secret of his religious genius. He was anything but a great writer, but he was a great reader, or creative misreader, of the Bible. Mormonism is a wonderfully strong misprision, or creative misreading, of the early history of the Jews. So strong was this act of reading that it broke through all the orthodoxies—Protestant, Catholic, Judaic—and found its way back to elements that Smith rightly intuited had been censored out of the stories of the archaic Jewish religion. Smith's radical sense of theomorphic patriarchs and anthropomorphic gods is an authentic return to J, or the Yahwist, the Bible's first author. This pragmatic distrust of the redacted text of the Bible manifests itself in some of Smith's creedal declarations towards the close of the Wentworth letter:

> We believe the Bible to be the word of God as far as it is translated correctly; we also believe the *Book of Mormon* to be the word of God.
> We believe all that God has revealed, all that he does now reveal, and we believe that he will yet reveal many great and important things pertaining to the kingdom of God.
> We believe in the literal gathering of Israel and in the restoration of the Ten Tribes. That Zion will be built upon this continent. That Christ will reign personally upon the earth, and that the earth will be renewed and receive its paradisiac glory. (William Muldur and A Russell Mortensen, eds., *Among the Mormons* [1958] pp. 16–17)

The Book of Mormon's very American link between the Indians and the lost Ten Tribes is partly behind that "literal gathering of Israel," but the "literal" actually applies to the Mormons' own gatherings—at Kirtland, in Missouri, at Nauvoo, and after Joseph's martyrdom, at what would be Salt Lake City. In this summer of 1991, as I write, Smith's vision is no more fantastic than is reality. The last of the Falashas (who may very well be the lost tribe of Dan) have been gathered literally into Israel, in the midst of a stream of arriving Russian and Georgian Jews. The Lubavitcher Hasidim strongly hint in full-page advertisements in the *New York Times* that Rabbi Menachem M. Schneerson is the Messiah, and that the time for my redemption has arrived. The Temple will be rebuilt, the Messiah will stand upon its roof and cry out, and the Messianic Era will be upon us. Of course, if the Temple were to be rebuilt upon the Dome of the Rock, then there doubtless would be an Islamic worldwide Holy War upon Israel, with Israeli nuclear retaliation, but this the Lubavitcher advertisement neglects to tell us. I cite all this only because the advertisement is truly American, rather than Judaic, and is as American as Joseph Smith and the other prophets of the American Religion. The Lubavitcher ecstasy attributes itself to the "victorious" Gulf War, to the gathering of Zion, to Rabbi Schneerson's ninetieth birthday, but its authentic cause is America. One sees again why Joseph Smith had to be an American, and why America may yet be largely Mormon, or perhaps an uneasy alliance of the Mormons, the Fundamentalist Southern Baptists, the Pentecostals, and other Evangelicals. Perhaps one can see also why the Book of Mormon made its initial appeal, and why its American ethos keeps it alive today.

With the Book of Mormon, we arrive at the center of Joseph Smith's prophetic mission, but hardly at any center of Mormonism, because of Smith's extraordinary capacity for speculative development in the fourteen years that remained to him after its publication. The Book of Mormon was not only his first work; it is the portrait of a self-educated, powerful mind at the untried age of twenty-four. It has bravura, but beyond question it is wholly tendentious and frequently tedious. If one compares it closely to Smith's imaginings in the Pearl of Great Price and Doctrine and Covenants, it seems the work of some other writer, and I don't mean Mormon or Moroni. The ordeal of prophecy, perpetually embattled both inside and outside his movement, transmogrified the ardent idealist who composed the Book of Mormon. Smith matters permanently, to America and the world, because of the fierce alchemy he underwent from 1832 through 1844. Reading any complete account of his life, one is moved to murmur, with the Christopher Smart of the *Jubilate Agno*, that "the Furnace is come up at last," a reference to Abraham's cutting of a covenant with Yahweh. If the Jews, Christians, and Muslims are the children of Abraham, then all of the Mormons past, present, and future—are the children of the American Joseph, another charming prophetic dreamer endlessly resourceful and favored by God, though with a terrible end. Abraham and Joseph both died old, and at peace; the American Joseph was murdered at thirty-eight years and six months.

I remarked in the Invocation to this book that it has only two heroes: the flamboyant Joseph Smith and the quiet twentieth-century Southern Baptist religious writer Edgar Young Mullins. Though I do not lack respect for the Mormon religion, and possess a healthy fear of its immense future, as a religious critic I judge Smith to be greater and more interesting than the current faith of the people that he created. Partly this is because he died much too soon, with a considerable portion of his innovative prophecy left incomplete. Partly this is because there has been a falling-away from his teaching and his example in the Mormon Church and people of the last century or so. An enormous religious imagination has been compromised (though not betrayed) by its descendants, even if one gets very little sense of any Mormon consciousness of that departure from Smith during a visit to Salt Lake City.

What is a contemporary non-Mormon, interested in American religion, to do with the Book of Mormon? I cannot recommend that the book be read either fully or closely, because it scarcely sustains such reading. Summaries of it are easily available, and I will not add another here. Instead, I want to note only those few aspects of the book that survive in the more mature spiritual speculations of Joseph Smith. Of course, if you believe that he "translated" ancient inscriptions upon subsequently vanishing golden plates, then all aspects of this work are equally relevant. But the genesis of the Book of Mormon is not my concern (though I assume that magical trance-states were involved, so that we can dismiss the literalism both of golden plates and of conscious charlatanry). Like many another American of his generation, Smith had drowned in the Bible, and came up from it in a state of near identification with the ancient Hebrews. And like many other Americans, Smith found the descent of the American Indians from the lost tribes of Israel to be a plausible identity, rather than a fantastic fiction. His fundamental hypothesis in the Book of Mormon is that America had experienced a thousand years of a Hebraic culture from 600 B.C. through A.D. 400. These Hebraic peoples, the fair-skinned Nephites and the dark-skinned Lamanites (direct ancestors of our Indians), were Christians (in some sense) before Christ, and Mormons (in some sense) before Joseph Smith. But for two centuries, they were also Christians after Christ, because the resurrected Jesus manifested himself to them in America (where he thoughtfully chose to repeat his Sermon on the Mount). Unfortunately, the good effect of this repetition wore off after those two centuries, and the dark skins massacred the light skins, and then in turn forgot their heritage.

Of all this, only the identity of Hebraic and American origins and the epiphany of the resurrected Christ in America were crucial to the development of Joseph Smith's religion, for out of them came his program for the new Chosen People, whose pragmatic Jerusalem is Salt Lake City. The stages of transmutation by which a new religion became a new people (thus assuring the permanent survival of the religion) can be cataloged, roughly but accurately, in this sequence:

1. Spring, 1820: The vision in which Joseph Smith beheld the Father and the Son.
2. March, 1830: The Book of Mormon goes on sale.
3. April 6, 1830: The Church organized in Fayette, New York.
4. 1830–31: Movement of Smith and his people to Kirtland, Ohio.
5. March 24, 1832: Joseph Smith tarred and feathered by a mob in Hiram, Ohio.
6. April 3, 1836: Climax of the dedication of the Kirtland temple, with visions of Jesus, Moses, Elijah.
7. 1838: Exodus of the Mormons from Kirtland to Far West, Missouri.
8. 1838–39: The Missouri-Mormon wars, ending with the exodus of Smith and his people and their founding of Nauvoo, Illinois.
9. 1839–44: The Nauvoo years, the great phase of Joseph Smith and early Mormonism, featuring the movement's growth to about 30,000 persons and the development of plural marriage, but ending in the slaughter of Joseph Smith and his brother Hyrum by the Illinois militia in the jail at Carthage on June 27, 1844.
10. 1846–47: The great Exodus of the Mormons from Nauvoo to the valley of the Great Salt Lake, under the strenuous leadership of Brigham Young, the second Prophet, Seer, and Revelator.

This is manifestly a catalog of persecution and exodus, and its contour shaped a peculiar and self-reliant people, whose characteristics are not altogether different one hundred and fifty years later, despite the determined march by the Mormons into the American Establishment in the last century. R. Laurence Moore, in his *Religious Outsiders and the Making of Americans* (1986), makes a remarkable attempt to handle all the paradoxes of Mormonism in one dialectical summary:

We come back to Tolstoy. He knew what he was talking about. Mormons taught *the* American religion, or at least a vital aspect of it, but not because their doctrines somehow sprouted naturally out of the American frontier and provided a domestic alternative to faiths imported from Europe. Mormons followed a lesson, already by their time well established in American experience, that one way of becoming American was to invent oneself out of a sense of opposition. This was perhaps the most useful consequence of America's voluntary system of church formation. The American mainstream, certainly its religious mainstream, never meant anything except what competing parties chose to make of it. It was not anything fixed. It was an area of conflict. In defining themselves as being apart from the mainstream, Mormons were in fact laying their claim to it. By declaring themselves outsiders, they were moving to the center. (pp. 45–46)

This cannot be wholly persuasive, or perhaps Moore's dialectic held until a generation ago, but is now outworn by the authentic consolidation of an American mainstream, particularly a religious mainstream. It is weirdly true, in 1991, that the Mormons are as mainstream as you are, whoever you are, at least in terms of the religion of politics, and the politics of religion. Pragmatically, the Mormons are allied in warlike patriotism, opposition to abortion, and refusal to seek economic and social justice to their doctrinal enemies: Southern Baptist Fundamentalists, Assemblies of God Pentecostals, Evangelicals of every denomination. And the current Mormon rhetoric in invoking Jesus Christ does serve as a perhaps deliberate veil behind which a post-Christian religion continues its complex development.

Joseph Smith's subtlest insight was an exercise in repetition; he absorbed the Bible, and he understood implicitly the burden of Jewish history: the religion preceded, and produced, the peculiar or set-apart people. Archaic Yahwism became biblical religion, out of which Judaism developed, and from Judaism emerged the Chosen People. The entire burden of Joseph Smith's prophecy was that the Kingdom of God was destined to be set up in America, and that only a Chosen People could rely upon themselves enough to be able to organize the Kingdom. Of all Joseph Smith's titles and functions, of all his ambitions and aspirations, only one ultimately was overwhelming. Shortly before his death in 1844, Smith was crowned king of the Kingdom of God in a secret ceremony. A third of a century later, just before his own death, Brigham Young may have undergone the same esoteric ritual, as did John Taylor after him. The Mormon Church denies these contentions, and perhaps the ten subsequent Prophets, Seers, Revelators, and First Presidents have not had the audacity to emulate Joseph Smith, Brigham Young, and John Taylor, at least down to the present moment. Still, none of the ten remotely resembled the charismatic Joseph, the grandly theocratic Brigham, or the heroic John Taylor. As precursors, these set standards impossible to achieve again.

One gets the impression that the present Mormon leadership is very patient; they believe that much of the future is theirs, particularly in America. We have not yet had a Mormon President of the United States, and perhaps we never will, but our Presidents are increasingly responsive to Mormon sensibilities, rather more than might be expected for a religious movement representing just two percent of our population. All that concerns a religious critic ought to be the spiritual question of what it is that Mormons might mean by the Kingdom of God, whether in the United States or elsewhere. Certainly, by 1843, Joseph Smith meant becoming a god, by the assumption of kingly powers, and thus presiding over the angels. On March 10, 1844, the Prophet Joseph spoke on "priesthood" and associated the Kingdom with Malachi's prophecy of Elijah's return. The Kingdom, in all of Smith's later pronouncements, became a symbol for the entire Nauvoo vision of men as gods, and so it became a synecdoche also for American destiny, a kind of Theocratic Sublime. Precisely how the Kingdom could exist without plural marriage is not clear. Fiercely as the Mormon Church now opposes its polygamist Fundamentalists, it remains true that the Church never has repudiated plural marriage *as a principle*. Joseph Smith linked both pluralities—of wives and of gods—and an imaginative separation between the two principles hardly seems possible. So one returns again to a purely speculative question: What would the Mormons wish to do if the United States ever has so large a Mormon population, and so wealthy a consolidation of Mormon economic power, that governing our democracy became impossible without Mormon cooperation? What seems like science fiction now will not seem so in 2020, if the Mormons are then one American out of eight.

Orson Pratt in 1860 presumably followed the Prophet Joseph in his frightening interpretation of the "great image" of Nebuchadnezzar's dream in the second chapter of Daniel. There the image of a huge man, made of different metals, but "his feet part of iron and part of clay," is struck upon the feet by a stone. The image falls apart, "and the stone that smote the image became a great mountain, and filled the whole earth." The prophecy of Daniel interprets the destiny of that great mountain:

> And in the days of these kings shall the God of heaven set up a kingdom, which shall never be destroyed: and the kingdom shall not be left to other people, but it shall break in pieces and consume all these kingdoms, and it shall stand for ever.
>
> Forasmuch as thou sawest that the stone was cut out of the mountain without hands, and that it brake in pieces the iron, the brass, the clay, the silver, and the gold; the great God hath made known to the king what shall come to pass hereafter: and the dream is certain, and the interpretation thereof sure. (Daniel 2:44–45)

For Joseph Smith the dream indeed was certain, and the interpretation sure: the mountain was the Mormon Kingdom of God, Joseph the prophetic stone, and the great image to be broken was the United States of America, to be followed in time by all the sinful kingdoms of the world, that is to say, every government everywhere. This is not the current, official Mormon interpretation, but we approach the central paradoxes of the Mormon people. In the judgments of President Reagan and of President Bush, of the FBI and the CIA (both replete with Mormons), of our armed forces (with many Mormon high officers), there are no more patriotic Americans than the people called Mormons. Pragmatically, this is beyond reasonable dispute, even as no American grouping is currently more dedicated to monogamy, or more strenuously insists upon itself as being Christian. Yet the Mormons, if they are at all faithful to the most crucial teachings of Joseph Smith and Brigham Young, no more believe in American democracy than they do in historical Christianity or in Western monogamy. Smith, Young, and their followers believed in theocracy, or the inspired rule of the Saints, and they looked forward to each prophet in turn ruling over the Kingdom of God, as king, first here and then every- where. As for Christianity, no one need take the Latter-day Saints Church literally upon that insistence: the Mormons after all are not even monotheists, and they take Jesus only as another name for the God of this world. And even as they continue to work towards what they call the Kingdom of God, they have not denied and indeed cannot deny the vision of a plurality of gods, or the princi- ple of a plurality of wives. None of this seems an irony to me, nor would I urge any of this as an indictment of the Mormons. They are a *total* system of belief and behavior, dedicated to particular hopes, dreams, and interpretations. Only the question of the King- dom seems to me a potential vexation for most other Americans, and even that will not be an overwhelming problem for perhaps another third of a century or so. Yet the problem *will* come, and it will be very real. On that basis, I will devote the remainder of this chapter to the Mormon vision of the Kingdom of God.

Daniel 2:44, quoted earlier, inspired Joseph Smith to a grand declaration on May 12, 1844:

I calculate to be one of the instruments of setting up the kingdom of Daniel by the word of the Lord, and I intend to lay a founda- tion that will revolutionize the whole world.

That foundation was the Council of Fifty, set up early in 1844, a year in which Smith rather quixotically declared himself a can- didate for the Presidency of the United States, and also the year of his martyrdom. There are several reasons why 1844 so far has been the crucial year in the history of Mormonism, to be superseded only sometime in the twenty-first century, when there could be the establishment of a Mormon Kingdom of God in some substan- tial part, if not all, of the United States. For everything that Joseph Smith had come to prophesy gathers itself together in his vision of kingship over the Kingdom of God. Nauvoo was not Geneva, and the joyous Prophet Joseph was anything but a repressed or repressive personality. His sense of the Kingdom was not metaphorical, though modern Mormonism, for understandable reasons, has attempted to interpret it only figuratively, at least to Gentiles. And yet the Mormon Church doubtless knows better, because it understands the Prophet's vision, and was taught by him the interpenetration of matter and spirit. The Augustinian insistence that Christ's ascension into heaven, after the forty days of Resurrection, actually had inaugurated the Kingdom of God, was explicitly and wisely repudiated by Joseph Smith. The millennium was still to come, and the function of the Mormons was to build up the Kingdom first, because Jesus would come again before the millennium began, the familiar early nineteenth-century American belief that I outlined in my third chapter.

The fullest study of Mormon millenarianism is Klaus J. Hansen's *Quest for Empire* (1967), which traces the career of the Council of Fifty that Joseph Smith organized in order to bring about a political Kingdom of God. Here and in a subsequent work, *Mormonism and the American Experience* (1981), Hansen took a rather elegiac stance towards the fierceness of early Mormonism. After a decade, the prefatory remarks to the second book seem inappropriate to the surge of Mormon power that is incessant as I write in 1991:

> By the turn of the century it had become clear that there was no place for a traditional, antipluralist Mormon kingdom in the pluralistic society of twentieth-century America. To the degree that Mormons have made their peace with modern America—and vice versa—they have become just one more tolerated and finally highly respectable minority.

As we move towards the turn of another century, one blinks at the Mormons being termed "just one more tolerated and finally highly respectable minority." Who would dare to "tolerate" Mormon economic power and political influence? The true question, to transpose Hansen, is what will be the place of the Mormon Kingdom of God in the unpredictable society of twentieth-first-century America? To answer with a prophetic guess, I turn back to the traditional, antipluralistic Mormonism of Joseph Smith. Hansen, in *Quest for Empire*, quotes Orson Pratt's notorious assertion of the priority of the Mormon Kingdom of God:

The Kingdom of God is an order of government established by divine authority. It is the only legal government that can exist in any part of the universe. All other governments are illegal and unauthorized. God, having made all beings and worlds, has the supreme right to govern them by His own laws, and by officers of His own appointment. Any people attempting to govern themselves by laws of their own making, and by officers of their own appointment, are in direct rebellion against the Kingdom of God. (pp. 184–85)

As a Mormon theologian, Orson Pratt should have written that God "organized" rather than "made" all beings and worlds, but otherwise this is sound doctrine, true to Joseph Smith and Brigham Young, and true also to the present leaders of the Church, though not the sort of thing they care to say to Gentiles. There are no references in Mormon scriptures to the formation of the Council of Fifty in the spring of 1844, and no record of the Council's proceedings in the official *History of the Church*. Mormon memoirs and traditions are reticent on Joseph Smith's secret teachings to the Council, including the coronation of Joseph Smith as king. Undoubtedly the teachings included the laws for regulating polygamy and for blood atonement, but we do not know much about those laws, as all documents relating to the Council of Fifty have been kept secret by the Church until this day. Presumably they would include instances of what the United States would have had to regard as treason: negotiations with then independent Texas, with Mexico, with France, with Great Britain, all on questions of Mormon movement to the West and the possibilities of diplomatic recognition of Mormon independence. Perhaps there are darker matters even in the secret records of the Council of Fifty, if they still exist or ever existed. But none of this ever will be known except by the innermost circles of the Mormon hierarchy.

Such details might be enchanting, but are scarcely necessary to aid us in meditating upon the Mormon dream of their Kingdom of God. If one stands back from contemporary Mormonism in order to achieve perspective upon it, the most singular impression has to be the Mormon drive for increasing the population of the Church by procreation and by strenuously pursued programs of conversion, both here and abroad. Missionary zeal is not uncommon among American sects and denominations, but the Mormons abound in it to a unique degree. Yet my concern is rather with the gradual, subtle growth of the Mormon Kingdom of God in America, by which I do not mean their annual six percent increase in numbers, but their daily augmentation in power. Again I stress that this is not a viewing-with-alarm, since I am wholly sympathetic to the achievement of Joseph Smith, and am not particularly exercised by politics. For religious criticism, the Mormon Kingdom of God is a spiritual hypostasis of the highest interest, since it raises again the issue of just how Mormonism should be regarded in the panoply of original quests for the American Religion. The cross, for the Southern Baptists as for other American Protestants, is the empty cross of the Resurrection. For the Mormons, there is no cross; you never see one in their buildings. Their regard is for the Jesus who will rule during the millennium, an altogether American Jesus. The Kingdom of God will provide that King Jesus with all the organization he will need for his rule. Triumphal beyond triumphalism and so demanding victory, the Latter-day Saints void all history that is neither ancient Israel's nor their own. Their being is original, and their destiny is godhood. What lies in between is the Kingdom of God, whose kings they crown. For a century now, the Saints have had to compromise aspects of this vision, but as their strength grows in proportion to the rest of the nation, I suspect that they may consider repealing their compromises.

Two aspects of the Saints' vision seem starkly central to me; no other American religious movement is so ambitious, and no rival even remotely approaches the spiritual audacity that drives endlessly towards accomplishing a titanic design. The Mormons fully intend to convert the nation and the world; to go from some ten million souls to six billion. This is sublimely insane, not merely because of the stunning numbers, but primarily because it means going up against such worldwide antagonists as the Roman Catholic Church and Islam, as well as such endlessly subtle formulations as Buddhism and Hinduism. Yet the Mormons will not falter; they will take the entire twentieth-first century as their span, if need be, and surely it will be. Though popular writers on the Mormons are enthralled by the array of canned goods and other supplies gathered in Salt Lake City basements against the possibility of marvelous millennial catastrophes in the year 2000, I am optimistic enough to project that hundreds of millions of Mormons will hoard similar goods against the year 3000. I do not qualify to pass on the rest of the Mormon creed, but I also do not find it possible to doubt that Joseph Smith was an authentic prophet. Where in all of American history can we find his match? The Prophet Joseph has proved again that economic and social forces do not determine human destiny. Religious history, like literary or any cultural history, is made by genius, by the mystery of rare human personalities. I am not persuaded by sociological and anthropological studies of Mormon history. Mormon history is Joseph Smith, and his continued effect upon his Saints. In proportion to his importance and his complexity, he remains the least-studied personage, of an undiminished vitality, in our entire national saga.

In April 1844, a little more than two months before his martyrdom, the Prophet Joseph Smith delivered a funeral sermon for Elder King Follett, whose violent death had been accidental. Though "the King Follett discourse" is not canonical, and survives only in the longhand report taken down by four followers, it is the effective end of Smith's career, and sometimes rises to an authentic eloquence. It is certainly one of the truly remarkable sermons ever preached in America, and boldly concerns itself with the character of God:

> God himself was once as we are now, and is an exalted man, and sits enthroned in yonder heavens! That is the great secret . . .
> I might with boldness proclaim from the house-tops that God never had the power to create the spirit of man at all. God himself could not create himself . . .
> I rejoice in hearing the testimony of my aged friends. You don't know me; you never knew my heart. No man knows my history. I cannot tell it. I don't blame anyone for not believing my history; if I had not experienced what I have, I could not believe it myself.

It was his epitaph for himself, as he neared the end of his history. He had created a religion, which already had become a people. What was the total form of an imagination capable of making a new religion and a new people, and of crowning a king for the Kingdom of God?

5

The Religion-Making Imagination of Joseph Smith

IT has become something of a commonplace to observe that modern Mormonism tends to reduce itself to another Protestant sect, another Christian heresy, while the religion of Joseph Smith, Brigham Young, Parley and Orson Pratt, and other leading early Mormons was a far more radical swerve away from Protestant tradition. Nineteenth-century Mormonism, in its deepest implications, had the same relation to Christianity that early Christianity had to Judaism. Such an assertion, made by many scholars of Mormonism, is unassailable, but I do not desire to explore its complexities here. Instead, I want to return to the imaginative origins of the Mormon religion, to the visions and conceptions of God experienced and thought by Joseph Smith. As a Jewish Gnostic, I am in no position to judge Joseph Smith as a revelator, but as a student of the American imagination I observe that his achievement as national prophet and seer is clearly unique in our history. Ralph Waldo Emerson and Walt Whitman were great writers, Jonathan Edwards and Horace Bushnell major theologians, William James a superb psychologist, and all these are crucial figures in the spiritual history of our country. Joseph Smith did not excel as a writer or as a theologian, let alone as psychologist and philosopher. But he was an authentic religious genius, and surpassed all Americans, before or since, in the possession and expression of what could be called the religion-making imagination. Even the force of Brigham Young's genius for leadership and the heroic intensity of the early Mormon people could not have assured the survival of the new religion. There had to be an immense power of the myth-making imagination at work to sustain so astonishing an innovation. That power, when it appears, invariably manifests itself in the phenomenon that Max Weber taught us to call charisma.

To ponder Smith's imagination, we need to begin by considering the charismatic element in his personality, the singular aura that attended him. We have debased the word "glamour," as we have the word "charm," and so we fall back upon charisma, in English a rather odd blend of theology and sociology, when we need a term for the element that marks a prophet and seer, the element in which the marvelously gifted Joseph Smith lived and moved and had his being, until at last and inevitably he was martyred, not so much for having offended American democracy or our national sexual morality, but for having been rather too dangerously charismatic. In that one respect, Smith resembled Aaron Burr, a purely political charismatic, whose vision of a western empire in America paralleled the dream of power that Brigham Young only barely failed to make actual. But Burr is now part of the American Picturesque, a kind of novelistic shadow hovering in our remote past. Joseph Smith is a vital part of the American Sublime, very much here in the Mormon present, even if his believers for now have chosen their own kind of patient version of what we might call the Japanese option, deferring the imperial dream in favor of economic triumph. If there is already in place any authentic version of the American Religion then, as Tolstoy surmised, it must be Mormonism, whose future as yet may prove decisive for the nation, and for more than this nation alone. But that again returns us to the charismatic personality of Joseph Smith, and to the religion-making genius that was his imagination, and that gave his followers the design for their quest.

Max Weber defined charisma as a supernatural or divine power that a prophet manifested in miracles, basing the word upon its early Christian meaning of a gift or grace that healed or else spoke in tongues. Camille Paglia, in her recent masterwork, *Sexual Personae*, questions Weber's reliance upon external deeds, and sees charisma as a pre-Christian glamour, citing Kenneth Burke's point

that "glamour" originally was a Scottish word meaning a magical
haze in the air around a favored person. Here is Paglia's shrewd
and alarming sexual definition of charisma:

> Charisma is the numinous aura around a narcissistic personality.
> It flows outward from a simplicity or unity of being and a com-
> posure and controlled vitality. There is gracious accommodation,
> yet commanding impersonality. Charisma is the radiance pro-
> duced by the interaction of male and female elements in a gifted
> personality. The charismatic woman has a masculine force and
> severity. The charismatic man has an entrancing female beauty.
> Both are hot and cold, glowing with presexual self-love.

The powerful sexual reductiveness of this definition necessarily
produces distortions when applied to the personality of any
prophet whosoever. Yet no one can study the portraits of Joseph
Smith or read descriptions of him by his contemporaries and avoid
the sense of his mysterious charm. Whatever account of charisma
is accepted, the Mormon prophet possessed that quality to a degree
unsurpassed in American history. Despite his lack of formal education, this fierce autodidact might have achieved a considerable
political career, and be remembered now as we remember his contemporary Stephen Douglas, had his genius not discovered itself in
the problematical realm of religion making. Other Americans have
been religion makers, down to Elijah Muhammad in the time just
past. Smith's difference was not a question of success as such; we
are, after all, surrounded still by Jehovah's Witnesses, Seventh-day
Adventists, and Christian Scientists, as well as by Black Muslims,
New Age Enthusiasts, and such curiosities as Theosophists, Scien-
tologists, and Moonies. One studies these beliefs, and seeks to
comprehend their appeal to those to whom they appeal. But none
of them has the imaginative vitality of Joseph Smith's revelation, a
judgment one makes on the authority of a lifetime spent in apprehending the visions of great poets and original speculators.

Researchers have not yet established, to my satisfaction, precisely how much the Prophet Joseph knew about Jewish esoteric
tradition or Kabbalah, or about the Christian Gnostic heresies.
One wants to know also just what Brigham Young had absorbed
from these sources, since some of Young's speculations about God
and Adam, and on the ascent of the soul after death, are strikingly

akin to ancient suggestions. What is clear is that Smith and his apostles restated what Moshe Idel, our great living scholar of Kabbalah, persuades me was the archaic or original Jewish religion, a Judaism that preceded even the Yahwist, the author of the earliest stories in what we now call the Five Books of Moses. To make such an assertion is to express no judgment, one way or the other, upon the authenticity of the Book of Mormon or of the Pearl of Great Price. But my observation certainly does find enormous validity in Smith's imaginative recapture of crucial elements in the archaic Jewish religion, elements evaded by normative Judaism and by the Church after it. The God of Joseph Smith is a daring revival of the God of some of the Kabbalists and Gnostics, prophetic sages who, like Smith himself, asserted that they had returned to the true religion of Yahweh or Jehovah. If Smith was mistaken, then so were they, but I hardly know just what it could mean to say that the Kabbalists or Joseph Smith were mistaken. The God of normative Judaism and of the mainline churches, at this time, is rather more remote from the God of the earliest or Yahwist portions of the Bible than is the initially surprising God of Joseph Smith.

Theology plays no part in the Hebrew Bible, but was invented by Philo and other Alexandrian Jews in order to explain away the supposed anthropomorphism of God's depiction in the early Yahwist vision. Anthropomorphism, or the idea that God could be human-all-too-human, is a poor notion anyway, as Joseph Smith implicitly understood. We are men and women, and not trees; presumably the God of trees is dendromorphic. What theologians deprecate as an anthropomorphic Yahweh is the necessary correlative of the Hebrew Bible's vision of theomorphic men and women: Abraham, Jacob, Joseph, Tamar, David. The religion-making genius of Joseph Smith, profoundly American, uniquely restored the Bible's sense of the theomorphic, a restoration that inevitably led the prophet into his most audacious restoration, patriarchal plural marriage.

That audacity I will defer for now, since its complex realization was deferred in Smith's career until its religious basis was thoroughly established, and we are only starting to recover Smith's full vision of God. Smith was haunted by the figure of Enoch, who in ancient Jewish texts was transmogrified into the angel Metatron, sometimes called the lesser Yahweh. A giant in size, radiant with light, this patriarch-angel was renowned for his total knowledge of the secrets of God. If the distinction between God and man wavers anywhere in Kabbalah, that wavering is most incessant in the fused figure of Enoch-Metatron. Enoch, who walked with God, is taken up by God and so does not die. The Kabbalists interpreted Enoch's ascent as the restoration of the state of Adam, not Adam in the Garden but a preexistent cosmic anthropos, at once God, angel, and man.

It is a crucial commonplace of Mormonism that Joseph Smith nullified the distinction between Old Testament and New Testament, and cast out all of church history that intervened between the biblical texts and himself. To apply a strictly rhetorical and literary term to the prophet's religion-making career, we can say that Smith accomplished a transumption, by joining his Latter-day Saints to the ever-earliness of the great patriarchs, and to Enoch in particular. In a transumption, earliness and lateness change places, while everything that comes in between is voided. Whether Smith had read a version of the apocalyptic Book of Enoch is uncertain, but I hardly think that written sources were necessary for many of Smith's imaginings. Enoch chose Joseph Smith because esoteric traditions always had exalted Enoch as the archetype of man-become-angel, and even become God.

The revelation of Enoch was made to the Prophet Joseph precisely as it was made to the Kabbalists, to grant unto us a more human God and a more divine man. But the Enoch of Kabbalah was a solitary figure, who went up into heaven to become Metatron, a version of the archangel Michael. It is characteristic of Joseph Smith that his Enoch founded a city, Zion, and gathered a people together there, and then took city and people up to heaven with him. In the fullness of time, Joseph prophesied, Enoch and his city would descend, to be fused into Joseph Smith's Zion, the Mormon New Jerusalem that shall gather in all the Latter-day Saints throughout the globe. The fulfillment of this prophecy would clarify the precise relation, perhaps the virtual identity, of Enoch and of Joseph. Since Joseph's religion is sacred history, in which word, event, and thing again are one, as they were for the ancient Hebrews, then the actual life of Joseph Smith must take on the pattern of Enoch's. Secular American history remembers Smith, just as it remembers Brigham Young, as a founder of cities. But Latter-day Saints differ pragmatically from Gentiles primarily because their history *is* sacred, and that returns us again to Enoch's choice of the Prophet Joseph.

Smith's religious genius always manifested itself through what might be termed his charismatic accuracy, his sure sense of relevance that governed biblical and Mormon parallels. I can only attribute to his genius or daemon his uncanny recovery of elements in ancient Jewish theurgy that had ceased to be available either to normative Judaism or to Christianity, and that had survived only in esoteric traditions unlikely to have touched Smith directly. Theurgy consists of operations designed to influence God, whether in his own dynamic nature or in relation to men. Joseph Smith's God, as the Mormon theologians rightly tell us, is finite, being subject both to space and to time, as is necessary for a material being, indeed for a passionate and dynamic being. As such a person, Smith's God is hedged in by limitations and badly needs intelligences besides his own. Smith never described the theurgical labors performed for God by the other gods or by the angels or by Mormon believers, but his vision of God suggests the outlines of such a theurgy. Smith's God, after all, began as a man, and struggled heroically in and with time and space, rather after the pattern of colonial and revolutionary Americans. Exalted now into the heavens, God necessarily is still subject to the contingencies of time and space. I think transumptively of the Prophet Joseph's God when I read the text of the Yahwist, or J Writer, author of the earliest tales of the Pentateuch. The Yahweh who closes Noah's ark with his own hands, descends to make on-the-ground inspections of Babel and Sodom, and who picnics with two angels under Abram's terebinth trees at Mamre is very close, in personality and dynamic passion, to the God of Joseph Smith, far closer than to the Platonic-Aristotelian divinity of Saint Augustine and Moses Maimonides.

Smith's God would not maintain that he will be present wherever and whenever he chooses to be present, even though he is hardly the absent numinosity of the negative theologians. The God of the American prophet simply cannot be everywhere at once, even though his own powers, like ours, are progressive. Nowhere is Joseph's genius so American as when he declares that God organized us and our world, but did not create either, since we are as early and original as he is. Emerson shrewdly anticipated David

Brion Davis in finding Mormonism to be the last expression of Puritanism, the final extension of the line of Abraham. Smith's difference from his Puritan and Judaic ancestors centered precisely where a younger Emerson ought to have felt imaginative sympathy, that is, upon envisioning a God within us whose best efforts were needed to reinforce the exalted Man in the heavens. What Whitman sang, Joseph Smith actually embodied: to be Adam early in the morning, confronting a God who had not created him, and who needed him to become a god himself.

We approach the mystery of Smith's religious genius when we seek to intuit how he came to discover the foreboding of his own charisma in Enoch. D. Michael Quinn, in his remarkable *Early Mormonism and the Magic World View* (1987), relates Joseph Smith's priesthood revelation of 1832 to esoteric rather than to traditional Christian traditions, and then goes on to the crucial instructions that Smith gave from 1842 through 1844, establishing the temple endowment. Whether or not Smith relied upon William Warburton and George S. Faber, or more likely reimagined ancient mysteries for himself, he evidently was highly conscious of restoring ancient mysteries associated with Enoch. Somehow, in an insight of genius, the Prophet Joseph recovered what Moshe Idel describes as a central mystery of Kabbalah, generally expressed in the cryptic formula: "Enoch is Metatron," an identification that makes the ascent of Enoch also a return to the original Adam, hardly to be distinguished from Yahweh himself. Only Mormons are in a position to define the essence of their own religion, but to this outsider nothing in Smith's revelations was more central than the prophet's own identification with the Kabbalistic Enoch. The union of patriarch and angel in Enoch is one of the prime tropes in Kabbalah for the ecstasy of union with the divine principle, for the actual fusion of God and man. I think that Joseph Smith would have understood immediately the grand statement of the early Kabbalist Rabbi Isaac of Acre, which was that "Enoch is Metatron" could be translated also as "a fire devouring fire." Metatron, sometimes called by Kabbalists the prince of this world, was once a man who walked this earth, Enoch, and Enoch in effect was taken by Joseph Smith as a paradigm for his finite God, who had progressed from Adam to Jehovah, from humanity to exaltation.

What I call the American Religion is a far larger and more diffuse phenomenon than is the Church of Jesus Christ of Latter-day

Saints, and as such seems to me to have three fundamental principles. The first is that what is best and oldest in us goes back well
before Creation, and so is no part of the Creation. The second is
that what makes us free is knowledge, a history of facts and events,
rather than a belief founded upon mere assent. The third is that
this freedom has a solitary element in it, an element imbued by the
loneliness of belated American time, and the American experience
of the abyss of space. What holds these principles together is the
American persuasion, however muted or obscured, that we are
mortal gods, destined to find ourselves again in worlds as yet un-
discovered. None of the three principles is quite or altogether Mormon, nor is that dangerous and beautiful persuasion, and yet
principles and persuasion alike have much to do with the charismatic personality of the Prophet Joseph Smith.

David Brion Davis, the American historian who greatly illuminates Mormonism for me, remarked that the most important fact
in our early religious history was the American tendency away
from the concept of a national church. In the Burned-over District
of upstate New York, the swarm of revivalists left transplanted
New Englanders, like the Smiths, restless and tormented, confronting a mad mix of doctrines and preachers, while longing for a
church in legitimate descent from ancient authority. A personal
God, a history of providences, a theocracy of saints: these were
Puritan inheritances. As a kind of Puritan anachronism, two centuries late, the Mormons became furious monists and perhaps the
most work-addicted culture in religious history. As Davis remarks,
their gospel of work was communal rather than individual, and
they took out to the frontier with them an organization and an
outlook that was guaranteed to alienate the selfish and violent in-
dividualists who were to surround them. If you followed a new
Enoch west in order to build a new Zion, then you were engaged
in nation building of a kind very different from your neighbors'
mode of enlarging the republic. Granted Mormon group loyalty
and self-discipline, then your economic and political potential became something substantial enough to alarm others. But if your
new Enoch, as Prophet, Seer, and Revelator, also restored patriarchal marriage customs, then indeed your capacity for disturbing
the conventional became extraordinary.

Joseph Smith's most remarkable innovation or restoration, plural
marriage, had to be abandoned by the Latter-day Saints a century

ago, as Utah's price of admission into the federal union. Sometimes it is said that the Mormons in time would have abolished polygamy on their own, but no one who has read accounts of the underground heroism of President John Taylor and other Saints, martyred by the federal law for keeping faith with Joseph Smith, will easily believe such assertions. Smith's genius for restoration exceeded that of Muhammad, and the religious necessity and sincerity of Smith's vision are beyond doubt. We can find the central formulations of Smith's religion-making imagination in the extraordinary sequence of the Doctrine and Covenants that begins with baptism for the dead in Sections 127 and 128, proceeds then to the resurrection of the body in 129 and to the tangibility of the bodies of the Father and the Son in 130. Directly after this, in Section 131, the new and everlasting covenant of marriage is stated, to be followed by the most remarkable of all the prophet's revelations, the famous Section 132, where the essentials for the attainment of godhood lead on directly to a plurality of wives. Historians, both Mormon and Gentile, have traced the long and subtle evolution of the prophet's concept of plural marriage from 1831 through the dictation of Section 132 on July 12, 1843. This evolution contains within it Joseph Smith's most original speculation, which even he dared not formulate overtly. If Smith's God was an exalted man of flesh and bone, and the literal father of Jesus, and the begetter of intelligences in many spheres, then was this God not also a polygamist? The problem is not so much one of distinguishing the Mormon God from Adam (a distinction not quite made by Brigham Young) but rather that of distinguishing God from what a theomorphic leader like Young might yet progress to be. It is the audacity of Smith's genius that he would never quite make that distinction. There is a peculiar intensity, indeed a mystical ecstasy, conveyed throughout Section 132 by the fire of Smith's rhetoric, as in Section 37:

> Abraham received concubines and they bore him children; and it was accounted unto him for righteousness, because they were given unto him, and he abode in my law; as Isaac also and Jacob did none other things than that which they were commanded, they have entered into their exaltation, according to the promises, and sit upon thrones, and are not angels but are gods.

Joseph's implication is quite plain; the function of receiving con-
cubines is to transcend the angelic state and become a god. If the
entire quest of Joseph's life was to restore archaic religion, in which
spirit and matter, God and man, were to differ only in degree, not
in kind, then the culmination of that quest had to be plural marriage. One can go further: Joseph's design indeed was as radical as
the history of religion affords. His prophetic aim was nothing less
than to change the whole nature of the human, or to bring about
in the spiritual realm what the American Revolution had inaugurated in the sociopolitical world. Kings and nobles had lost their
relevance to Americans; that hierarchy had been abolished. Joseph
Smith, in his final phase, pragmatically abolished the more fear-
some hierarchy of official Christianity. Plural marriage was to be
the secret key that unlocked the gate between the divine and the
human.

I emphasize again the profound affinity between Smith and the
Kabbalah, since in each the function of sanctified human sexual
intercourse essentially is theurgical. Either there was a more direct
Kabbalistic influence upon Smith than we know, or, far more
likely, his genius reinvented Kabbalah in the effort necessary to
restore archaic Judaism. Consider the following passage, taken
from Moshe Idel, in which I have substituted "Mormonism" or
"Mormon" for "Kabbalistic" or "Kabbalist" but otherwise have
altered nothing:

> The focus of the Mormon theurge is God, not man; the latter is
> given unimaginable powers, to be used in order to repair the
> divine glory or the divine image; only his initiative can improve
> Divinity . . . The theurgical Mormonism articulates a basic fea-
> ture of Jewish religion in general: because he concentrates more
> upon action than upon thought, the Jew is responsible for every-
> thing, including God, since his activity is crucial for the welfare
> of the cosmos in general.

Joseph Smith's emphasis upon human power necessarily
achieved an apotheosis in his exaltation of plural marriage, which
became for him the new and everlasting convenant between God
and the Latter-day Saints. Historians both Mormon and Gentile
have made clear that Smith went so far as to practice a kind of

polyandry with the wives of several highly placed Mormons. Again there are archaic precedents, including the complex career of Sabbatai Zvi, the Kabbalistic Messiah. Joseph Smith, far more than any other religious innovator in his century, authentically brought about a fresh breaking of the vessels. We underestimate his genius when we fail to see that he desired an ontological change in his followers, a new mode of being, however high the cost. The Mormonism of the last hundred years and of today is not my subject here, but plainly it is only a compromise with gentile America, rather than being the authentic vision of Joseph Smith. The sacredness of human sexuality, for Smith, was inseparable from the sacred mystery of embodiment, without which godhood would not be possible. God and Jesus are men of flesh and bone, and those who would progress to join them must be in the body also. Smith's theurgy, like that of the Kabbalists, is essentially sexual, and demanded a full realization of the prophet's desires.

One scholar, Mark Leone, has remarked upon "the virtually unfathomable complexity of Joseph Smith's early ideas and trials at plural marriage." Certainly the complexity is immensely intricate, as much so as the sinuous windings in the doctrines and conduct of Sabbatai Zvi, as described by Gershom Scholem. But the Kabbalistic Messiah espoused the Gnostic way of the antithetical; his prophet, the brilliant Nathan of Gaza, argued that Sabbatai had to descend into the broken shells in order to liberate the sparks, a pattern that Scholem called "redemption through sin." Smith's ascent into plural marriage was not antithetical but life-affirming, and indeed God-affirming. In simplest terms, I can accept the notion that the Prophet Joseph sought to follow the Jewish pattern, in which a religion becomes a people. Marked by the glory and stigma of plural marriage, the Mormons of 1850 through 1890 indeed became a peculiar people, a nation apart. But this formulation is reductive and inadequate; Joseph Smith did not wish merely to set his Saints apart. He wished them to become gods, and he decided that polygamy was necessary for that apotheosis. The truest mystery of what I would want to call Smith's Kabbalah or secret tradition is why and how he linked divinity and plural marriage. What was the imaginative form of that linkage?

Anthropologists have no more regard for Freud's *Totem and Taboo* than they have for the Book of Mormon, and neither Freudians nor Mormons would wish to see the two works juxtaposed. But *Totem and Taboo* is as much an effort of the religion-unmaking imagination as the Book of Mormon is of the religion-making kind. Smith's early scripture rejects polygamy, while hinting that a subsequent revelation might yet impose it. Freud's identification of God with the slain and cannibalized leader of a tribal horde, murdered by his sons for having monopolized all the women, can be read as Smith's later polygamous revelation reflected in a dark mirror. What the Church Fathers made into the close of their Old Testament, the latecomer prophet Malachi's final admonition turning the hearts of the fathers and the sons towards one another, is one of the biblical texts that most haunted Joseph Smith. Smith's vision of plural marriage is many mythmakings at once. Those Latter-day Saints who have the authority to sustain polygamy will become gods, and the sons of those gods will be reconciled with their fathers, and then become gods themselves. It was, I think, the early Mormon leader Orson Hyde who once speculated that Jesus had married Mary, Martha, and the other Mary, which is only a step short of speculating about the plural marriages of God.

One suspects that Joseph Smith had thought about patriarchal polygamy long before 1831, because his imagination was of the unfolding rather than the developing kind. National circumstances and human nature alike combined to dim the full audacity of Smith's vision, when his church retreated from him during the century from 1890 through 1990. Mormonism, born of Puritanism, has gone back to Puritanism, and has had to forget that Smith intended a religious reform as total as the birth of Islam. Smith's most original doctrines have the same relation to Protestantism that the Kabbalah has to the Talmud. Yet what is the status of those doctrines in Mormonism today? Before he was martyred in 1844, Joseph Smith evidently had himself crowned as king of the Kingdom of God. The LDS Church evades that crucial moment in its history, even as it evades the tradition that Brigham Young emulated Smith by an ultimate repetition of this sublime audacity. Yet to evade such sublimities is to cancel out, at least for a time, the powerful imaginative assertion that Mormonism could make, to the effect that it indeed is the American Religion, the spiritual embodiment of the American Sublime.

"Did the Prophet Joseph want every man's wife he asked for?" was a rhetorical question asked in a sermon by Jedediah Grant in 1854. Grant replied in the negative, asserting that Smith was testing his people, but no one ought to consider it other than an open question now. Joseph Smith and Brigham Young shared a vision of authority very different from any now tolerable among their descendants. Scholars, whether Mormon or Gentile, only can offer their misinterpretations, strong misreadings or weak misreadings, of Smith's vision. The strongest misreading, and so the best interpretation, necessarily was provided by Brigham Young, who founded his kingdom upon the Prophet Joseph's aspirations for plural marriage. For thirty years, Young led in very nearly the full meaning of leading. Though his complete legacy was voided thirteen years after his death, Young lived to see part of what Smith dreamed. Celestial Marriage and baptism for the dead are now Mormon abstractions, as they are not differences that make a difference without a system of plural marriage. Visionary and pragmatist at once, the Prophet Joseph had the American concern with the earthly paradise, and so he taught Young, at least by example, that the mysteries of the Kingdom had to be enacted in the here and now, privately if possible when hemmed in by Gentiles, and publicly though by no means universally when a stable Zion at last could be founded.

Whether Brigham Young had twenty-seven or fifty-five wives is one of those questions akin to scholarly speculation as to whether Joseph Smith had managed eighty-four marriages within the three years before his murder. Good clean or unclean fun, this erudite arithmetic at least establishes the high seriousness of the quest shared in by both men. Each understood that Celestial Marriage and consequent progression towards godhood were the true essence of becoming a Latter-day Saint, the heart of Mormon religion making. Without plural marriage as the instrumental modality for Celestial Marriage, their quest would have seemed to both seers to have become the tragedy of *Hamlet* without the prince. The true epiphany of Mormonism did not take place in Smith's lifetime, but must be identified with the August 1852 public proclamation of plural marriage by the Church, certainly the most courageous act of spiritual defiance in all of American history. Orson Pratt's grand discourse on Celestial Marriage is of course not part of Mormon scripture, but perhaps someday it yet will be, for the spirit of Joseph Smith breathes through it.

Orson Pratt's truthful and realistic assumption is that the difference between a vigorous gentile male of talent, intellect, and power and his Latter-day Saint counterpart is that the Gentile is a hypocrite and an adulterer, while the Saint need not be and is not either. Male nature being polygamous, the restoration of all things demanded a sanctification of that polygamy, rather than an abolishment of a nature that could not be corrected. Joseph Smith had found in himself a polygamous nature, and evidently had come to understand that his prophetic gift would perish if that nature were to be balked or voided. When some Mormons say now that Smith instituted plural marriage against his own will, threatened by a divinely commissioned angel with a drawn sword, lest prophecy cease, they perhaps fail to see precisely what the metaphor intimates. Orson Pratt saw and said what was intimated. Either our bodies, like the body of the Prophet Joseph, were to be tabernacles towards the building of the Celestial Kingdom, or they were to be sepulchres for adultery. Gentile America refused to accept this as religion, and so as protected by the Constitution, but gentile America, then as now, had become a country in which prophecy had ceased. When William Blake declared that one law for the ox and the lion was oppression, then he prophesied the embattled stance of Brigham Young and the underground exile of John Taylor.

There have been many other religion-making imaginations in America before, contemporary with, and since Joseph Smith's, but not one of them came near his in courage, vitality, or comprehensiveness, or in so honest a realization of the consequences of a charismatic endowment. In retrospect, it is clear enough why Smith and Parley Pratt and so many other Mormons were murdered, and why the Saints were driven west from state to state, territory to territory, by a furious rabblement of endlessly violent persecutors. If Joseph Smith was a true prophet, and spoke with authority, then America was nothing but a vast Sodom, rushing onward to inevitable destruction, in exile from God and from Christ's own visit to the American continent. Mormonism today is one of the centers of the American establishment, one more exaltation of the way things are in this best of all possible societies. But Joseph Smith, for all his genial and loving nature, prophesied against the way things were in a fallen and unjust society. Biblical prophets practice a most dangerous profession and live in expectation of potential martyrdom. Joseph Smith, the most gifted and authentic of all American prophets, was too robust an American humorist not to be able to see the irony of his mixed legacy, if he returned now.

Prophecy is a difficult mode; religion making is so impossibly difficult an adventure that no one could hope to set standards for it. On the giant scale of Muhammad's imagination, Smith's might be dwarfed. After all, an angel's voice speaks the Book of Mormon, while the only voice we hear in the Koran is that of Allah himself. Smith's Saints have survived and prospered, but they constitute perhaps two percent of their own nation, and a fraction of a percent of the world. I speak out of a stance separate from Christianity or Islam when I observe that Islam indubitably is closer to Muhammad's teaching than Mormonism now is to the complete vision of Joseph Smith. History, in our country, stands neither at an origin nor at an end. The material continuity of Smith's imaginings is assured, and will endure at least as long as our nation endures. But the Prophet Joseph centered upon the law of consecration: the spirit and temporality were to dwell together. Mormonism is as much a separate revelation as ever Judaism, Christianity, and Islam were, and a total revelation is a kind of giant form, with dimensions somewhat beyond our faculties of discernment. Like the prior revelations, the religion of the Latter-day Saints moves on in ways both seen and unseen, and is certain only to confound all our expectations.

Except for such visionaries as the Christian mystics, Jewish Kabbalists, and Islamic Sufis, there is little enough precedent in Western religion for Joseph Smith's heroic enterprise in lessening the difference between God and man. But Smith wisely declined to live a life of continuous ecstasy. The March 1836 dedication of the Kirtland temple was unique in Joseph's and the Saints' history, and the prophet never sought to revive such raptures and visitations. It is as though he wished to rely more upon his own authority as revelator than upon peak experiences, whether communal or personal. Since Smith denied the dogma of original sin, he could regard himself as untainted by history, and fully capable of reigning over the Kingdom of God upon this earth.

I myself suspect that Joseph Smith was the source of Brigham Young's near identification of God, Adam, and Michael, which I earlier traced back to the same archaic Jewish traditions that gave Kabbalah the formula that Enoch was Metatron or Michael. In the imagination of Joseph Smith, five figures may have become a composite, comprising God or the Ancient of Days, Adam, Michael, Enoch, and Smith himself. Though many Mormons are now uncomfortable with their very human God, their prophet was emphatic in his insistence that God had begun as a man upon our common earth, and had earned godhood through his own efforts. A God who progresses through crises has much to do with the archaic Yahweh of the Yahwist or J Writer, but very little to do with the infinite and transcendent power of orthodoxy, whether Jewish, Christian, or Islamic. Monotheism in Israel certainly evolved from a cult in which Yahweh, though chief of gods, was surrounded by many gods, to a cult of Yahweh alone. Smith, studying the Bible, shrewdly surmised this development, and desired to restore the archaic polytheism, but only so that we too, as Americans, might become gods.

Latter-day Saints, however much their Church may have had to stray from his paths, have been almost alone in apprehending the greatness of Joseph Smith. An entire century after the Mormon repudiation of plural marriage, their prophet remains without honor among most of his countrymen. But insofar as there is an American Religion that is almost universal among us, whatever our professed beliefs, then Smith may be considered to be in many respects its unacknowledged forerunner. His imagination created a particular religion, but the contours of his imagination may mark the limits of every post-Christian spirituality in our America.

6

Baptism for the Dead, Spirits for the Unborn

MORMON theology is nowhere near so enigmatic as Southern Baptist theology, since the Mormons are not suspicious of everything in religion that is not experiential. And since the Gnostic components of Mormonism are overt, though called by other terms, one has less difficulty in expounding the American elements in this most ambitious and hard-driven version of the American Religion. But since, for a century now, the Church of Jesus Christ of Latter-day Saints has been edging away from Joseph Smith's extraordinary spiritual originality, what precisely is or is not Mormon doctrine is problematic. Whether, in their innermost circle, the current powers of the Church actually adhere to esoteric beliefs and rituals now out of public fashion is of course not known by me. I surmise, though, that the heirs of Smith and of Brigham Young have not altogether given up the aspiration to achieve the Mormon vision of the Kingdom of God in America. No one really knows what portion of the liquid wealth in America's portfolios is held by the Latter-day Saints Church. Yet it is clear that Mormon financial and political power is exerted in Washington to a degree far beyond what one would expect from one voter in fifty. The Republican regimes of Reagan and Bush have enjoyed fierce Mormon financial and moral support, and the Salt Lake City hierarchy in turn can make itself heard in the White House. The nation will not always be only two percent Mormon. The Saints outlive the rest of us, have more children than all but a few American groups, and convert on a grand scale, both here and abroad. I do not know what figures they project for their increase in the next generation, but my own guess is that by the year 2020 (when I will not be here), they could well form at least ten percent of our population, and probably rather more than that. Their future is immense: the Mormon people consistently are the hardest-working, most cohesive bloc in our society; only Asian-Americans rival them in zeal, ambition, and intensity. Salt Lake City may yet become the religious capital of the United States.

This chapter will seek to fulfill one of the functions of religious criticism (as I conceive it), which is to give a final overview of the inner shape of Mormon spirituality, even if part of what I say would not be approved by the current Church authorities. Still, the Mormons have in common with their enemies, the Southern Baptists, an aversion to absolutely formal creeds. If it is difficult to say exactly what Moderate (or authentic) Southern Baptists believe, because it is a formidable exercise to translate experiential religion into language, it is difficult in quite another way to say exactly what Mormons believe, because they are likely to believe very different, even contradictory doctrines. Mormon theology, rather deliberately, has been left incomplete, which encourages Mormons, like ancient Valentinian Gnostics, to invent for themselves, in some respects. There is also the peculiarity that the Mormons believe in continuous revelation, and do not let themselves forget the dry remark of Joseph Smith that he had learned only while laboring upon the Book of Abraham (1835, now in the Pearl of Great Price) that the father of Jesus, God himself, had a father, who in turn had a father, and so on. Smith had arrived at the Mormon doctrine termed "plurality of gods," since the Mormon Church still refuses to be called what it most certainly is, polytheistic. I see nothing wrong with polytheism, once we set aside the ancient Hebrew prejudice against it. The Yahwist clearly uses Elohim to refer to a variety of divine beings, and Joseph Smith, as I have observed before, had an impulse of genius in finding his own way back to the J Writer, whose Yahweh was one of the Elohim, surrounded by others. Joseph Smith's gods, it will be remembered, were not only plural, but of flesh and bone, like the Yahwist's quite substantial Yahweh and his attendant Elohim. Smith and Brigham Young, as I remarked earlier, also returned to Kabbalistic speculations by surmising that the gods once had been men upon earth, or as Young happily put it, that God, Adam, and the Archangel Michael were the same personage.

Sterling McMurrin with superb clarity develops the crucial argument that the Mormon God is *not* a creator. Pragmatically, neither is the resurrected Jesus of the Moderate Southern Baptists. But I come here to a central argument of this book. The God of the American Religion is not a creator-God, because the American never *was* created, and so the American has at least part of the God within herself. Freedom for an American, as I have intimated throughout, means two things: being free of the Creation, and being free of the presence of other humans. The Mormons rejoice in the first freedom, while fleeing the solitude of the second, which is to be alone with Jesus, as is granted to the Southern Baptist Moderates. Mormons have a Gnostic freedom from the world of nature, a necessary liberty for men who aspire to become gods, each with his own planet, a world altogether his own. I find that the difference between Mormons and Southern Baptists here is not pragmatically a true difference, since what is alone with Jesus in the Baptist is itself something in the spirit that never was created. As for the Mormon, he may never be alone with Jesus, but he aspires finally to govern without rivals in his own world, alone with his wife (or wives) and his varied progeny. The darkest and most authentic impulse of the American Religion is shared finally by what must seem at first the unlikeliest of trios: R. W. Emerson, Joseph Smith, Jr., E. Y. Mullins. Each stands in the Abyss *before* the Fall into Creation, and each experiences the Freedom that is Wildness, the perfect Solitude (itself creative) of the American visionary. My language here is Emerson's, but the metaphysics pertains equally to the Mormon prophet and the belated founder of Moderate Southern Baptism. Here Smith remains my center, and I return to his denial of the traditional Christian account of a creation out of nothing by an absolute God, the God of the Priestly Author who wrote what is now the first chapter of Genesis. Smith's God is shrewdly compared by Sterling McMurrin to the Platonic Demiurge, satirized both by the Gnostics and by Blake as being a false deity. Smith's Gnosticism inverts the ancient variety and celebrates what McMurrin pictures as a hard-working God, fit model for the Mormons, who from the start through now have been perhaps the most industrious people on the American continent:

As a constructor or artisan God, not entirely unlike Plato's demiurge of the *Timaeus*, the Mormon deity informs the continuing processes of reality and determines the world's configurations, but he is not the creator of the most ultimate constituents of the world, either the fundamental material entities or the space and time that locate them. God's environment is the physical universe, the minds and selves which exist but are not identified with him, the principles under which reality is structured, and perhaps even the value absolutes which govern the divine will. In any case, it is entirely evident that it is a basic article of Mormon theology that God is related to a world environment for the being of which he is not the ultimate ground and by which he therefore is in some sense conditioned. This means that God is a being among beings rather than *being* as such or the ground of being, and that he is therefore finite rather than absolute. (*The Theological Foundations of the Mormon Religion* [1965], p. 29)

The Mormon God is certainly American, and so is appropriately subject to space and to time. It is of course a scandal, in the contexts of Judaism, Christianity, and Islam, to posit so limited and contingent a God. The awesome sublimity departs, but so do many of the enigmas of theodicy, if God once was human and still has a body. McMurrin emphasizes the shock of the Mormon God's immersion in temporality, while I suspect that the spatial limitation is just as disconcerting. Joseph Smith's God, unlike Yahweh, cannot say that he will be wherever and whenever he chooses to be. There can be no Mormon Book of Job, and the followers of Joseph Smith never had to despair because God did not rescue their prophet from his martyrdom. Original sin and God's culpability have vanished together. The Mormon God can organize, but he cannot create. He has a human father's responsibilities, and his powers differ only in degree, not in kind, from those of any other father.

There are immense confusions in Mormon theology, partly because Smith changed his mind so often, the inevitable consequence of one man attempting to reimagine the whole of Western religion.

Smith's untimely murder is necessarily part of the problem also; the evolution from his earlier to his later theology had not been completed. A further complication stems from Brigham Young's revelations, some of which clearly departed from Smith's, and few of which are now accepted by the Mormons. There is also a bevy of Mormon theologians, who for more than a century have attempted to fill out the structure of their faith while reconciling what contradictions they could. The combined effect is startling; at first, it all seems contrived and arbitrary. But as one meditates upon it, two realizations grow. One is that Mormonism, a religion truly as different from Christianity as Islam is, exposes how contrived and arbitrary all theology is, indeed how strange and unexpected all religion evidently has to be. The other is that Tolstoy was accurate when he told Andrew Dickson White (the first president of Cornell University) that "the Mormon people teach the American Religion." Though so much of current Mormonism seems only a more exotic American Protestantism, nothing is left of Protestantism in it, but much that is singularly American abides. The Mormon Gods are a sequence of American fathers, each progressing from human to divine on the basis of hard work and obedience to the laws of the universe, which turn out to be the maxims of the Latter-day Saints Church. Organization, replacing creation, becomes a sacred idea, and every good Mormon indeed remains an organization man or woman. The visitor to Salt Lake City, after just four days, has learned to tell the difference between certain Mormons and most Gentiles at first sight. There is something *organized* about the expressions on many Mormon faces as they go by in the street. It is therefore all the more refreshing that everyone has so much difficulty in organizing Mormon theology, but surely that suggests why Joseph Smith, Jr., and Brigham Young, charismatic expressionists and passionate prophets, might not flourish in contemporary Utah.

Mormon theology now identifies Jesus with Jehovah as "God of the Old Testament" while naming Jehovah's own father as Elohim. This weirdness has the sanction neither of Smith nor of Young, and seems to me simply an arbitrary error on the part of the Church. Its history (though he declines to call it error) is told by Boyd Kirkland in a courageous essay on how the Mormon concept of God developed (see *Line by Line*, edited by G. J. Bergera, 1989). Kirkland traces the sequence of Mormon leaders—Cannon, Richards, Talmage, Penrose—who prevailed in having the LDS Church adopt the identity of Jesus and Jehovah, and the notion that Elohim fathered this being. Since there is nothing in the Bible, nothing in Smith's writings, and nothing in the oral teachings of Smith and Young to support these oddities, one must ask: why did they become doctrine? There seems no answer available, and Kirkland does not venture one, though he hints at a kind of fine desperation in Mormons when they are confronted by the baffling intricacies of their own doctrine. My own best guess is that the Church was in fierce retreat from Brigham Young, an even wilder speculator than Joseph Smith. Somehow Young had found his way back to ancient Gnostic or Kabbalistic identifications in which Yahweh, Michael (or Metatron, Enoch), and Adam were three names for one being. Moshe Idel has noted the affinities between Kabbalah and ancient rabbinical texts that hint at a Hermetic unity between God, angel, and man in the beginning. Young, autocratic and brutal though always resourceful for and ultimately benign towards his own people, was much more of a theomorphic biblical patriarch than the mercurial, frequently quixotic, endlessly charming Smith. Ambitious enough to crown himself as king of the Kingdom of God upon earth, Smith nevertheless was likelier to see himself as Muhammad than as God himself. Brigham Young may well have thought of himself as the American Adam, and so as an American Archangel Michael and even an American God. What better candidate could any of us find now, in the nineteenth century, for the role of American Adam, than Brigham Young? Historians like to refer to him as the American Moses, leading the Exodus of Mormons through the Wilderness into what is now the Utah of the Saints. But Young was hardly a reluctant, stammering prophet, like the self-torturing Moses of the J Writer. The Mormon God is the great Organizer, and that was Young. What creed would be more natural for Brigham than the Adam-God doctrine, for that had been his experience of life and of himself. I would venture that Brigham Young was Joseph Smith's finest work. Joseph labored to prophesy a new man, a truly American Adam, theomorphic and capable, made ontologically different through fresh rituals, plural marriages, and an ultimate progression to divinization. Young pragmatically was audacious enough to manifest some version of all that, far more than any other American of his century, or perhaps ever. Dying at seventy-six of a ruptured appendix, Young was reported by his daughter Zina to have cried out: "Joseph! Joseph! Joseph!" as his final words, an appropriate tribute to the seer who had organized, in the Mormon sense, an authentic genius at organization.

Modern Mormonism, for a century now, has manifested a very complex anxiety of influence towards its two great founders, whom it consciously reveres, yet who set goals and standards for it that had to be compromised, and indeed perhaps betrayed. Where there is devastating revisionism, there will be ambivalence, however concealed or unconscious, and much of contemporary Mormon doctrine seems to me a reaction-formation against both Joseph Smith and Brigham Young. This is hardly unique in the history of religion, and has many parallels in other realms. There is, to begin with, simply the question of the human diminishment in scale as one moves from Joseph Smith, whether he be considered as outrageous charlatan or as inspired prophet, through Brigham Young, however his power be regarded, on to Ezra Taft Benson, whose abilities and views alike seem to have been decently veiled by the Latter-day Saints Church. And there is the broad change in Mormon strategy, now ongoing for about sixty years, in which the Saints rival Fundamentalist Baptists and other American Evangelicals in having become socially, politically, and economically reactionary bastions of the American establishment. Mormons have extended their missionary work from the American public and foreign nations to our federal government, so that the FBI, CIA, and allied organizations have become very Mormon indeed.

When a faith's ambitions are this enormous, it seems just for religious criticism to center upon the precise nature of such ambitions, if the dominant contribution of such criticism is to be made at all. This chapter's title brings together the two largest assertions of its own spirituality by the Latter-day Saints Church: baptism for the dead and gaining entry to life for the spirits of the unborn. The first has become a vast, almost unbelievable effort in genealogy and in organization, while the second has taken the place of Joseph Smith's now unrealizable dream of a perfect polygamy. Both testify to the ferocious, indeed the fanatical, sincerity of the Mormon people, who have made their stance towards death and birth a kind of giant quest romance, a huge metaphor for the whole of their drive towards dominion.

Little as we know about the original Baptizer, John who baptized

Jesus, we can be certain that as an apparent Essene, or perhaps an independent akin to the Essenes, he would have been astonished, even horrified at the extraordinary notion of baptizing the dead. How do you therapeutically cleanse or purify the dead? Rebirth is the burden of baptism, whether administered to infants or to adults, which must be why the ancient Gnostics so bitterly observed that many "go down into the water and come up having received nothing." That is the Valentinian *Gospel of Philip*, deploring what the Gnostics condemned as the Church's easy universalism. Joseph Smith, despite his vast exfoliation of a personal Gnosis, was fiercely attached to a vision of adult baptism. In his "Inspired Version" of Genesis, he thoughtfully baptizes Adam by immersion, and he seems to have believed that everyone should be baptized at the mature age of eight. On January 19, 1841, during his final and most audacious phase, the vision of baptism for the dead came to him, taking him back to a curious moment in I Corinthians 15:29:

> Otherwise, what do people mean by being baptized on behalf of the dead? If the dead are not raised at all, why are people baptized on their behalf?

Saint Paul seems neither to approve nor disapprove of this odd practice, which was carried out later, from the second century on, by such Enthusiastic and Gnostic covens as Montanists, Marcionites, and Cerinthians. It was characteristic of Smith to revive a mode of ritual endemic among the Mormons' most authentic precursors. At Nauvoo, Illinois, the revelation came for the building of a new temple, where the ancient ceremony could be restored:

> For there is not a place found on earth that he may come to and restore again that which was lost unto you, or which he hath taken away, even the fulness of the priesthood.
> For a baptismal font there is not upon the earth, that they, my saints, may be baptized for those who are dead. (Doctrine and Covenants 124:28–29)

Smith returned to this matter in Doctrine and Covenants 127 and 128, where he specifies that "the baptismal font was instituted as a similitude of the grave," since the ceremony signifies resurrection. The true point emerges when the prophet insists that this ritual guarantees possession again of the ancient Holy Priesthood. At the very center of Smith's motivation is a text that always haunted him, the words of Malachi the prophet that the Christians chose to conclude their Old Testament:

> Behold, I will send you Elijah the prophet before the coming of the great and dreadful day of the Lord:
> And he shall turn the heart of the fathers to the children, and the heart of the children to their fathers, lest I come and smite the earth with a curse. (Malachi 4:4–5)

For Smith and the Mormons, the first part of Malachi's prophecy had been fulfilled on April 3, 1836, when Elijah appeared to the Mormon prophet and Oliver Cowdery during the ecstatic dedication of the temple in Kirtland. Four figures manifested themselves to Smith and Cowdery, Elijah being preceded by Jesus, Moses, and one "Elias" (Smith evidently was not aware that this was the Greek equivalent of Elijah's name). Doctrine and Covenants 110 contains Elijah's explanation that he had come to give Smith and Cowdery "the keys of this dispensation." Since Elijah then quoted Malachi's prophecy, Smith's clear implication was that baptism for the dead was the instrumentality for turning the hearts of the fathers and of the children to one another.

Audacious as all this was and is, it remains one of Joseph Smith's most remarkable innovations, with its own curious logic. As the prophet who restores the only true Church, Smith again confronts the dilemma of his own belatedness. How are all the millions who lived and died between Jesus and himself to be saved? This question, added to Smith's Judaic sense of family, provoked the urgent doctrine in which one's own salvation is linked to effort in the salvation of one's ancestors, however remote. The palpable sincerity and intensity of the religion of our Mormon contemporaries is nowhere, for Gentiles, demonstrated more overwhelmingly than in the immense effort that goes into baptism for the dead. A splendid essay, "The Mountain of Names," by Alex Shoumatoff, appeared in The New Yorker's "A Reporter at Large" series, on May 13, 1985 and was subsequently published in book form. Visiting Salt Lake City in November 1990, in order to lecture upon Joseph Smith at the University of Utah, I was driven out to the Mountain of Names by friends, and found myself gawking in disbelief at what is surely one of the wonders of the world. The Granite Mountain Records Vault of the Genealogical Society of Utah rises up some twenty-two miles south of Salt Lake City. It now contains (by some accounts) nearly two billion names of the dead, safely stored where no earthquake, no nuclear bomb-blast, nothing short of an asteroid impact could obliterate them. Shoumatoff emphasized that "no genealogical archive is remotely comparable. The Mormon collection is the closest there is, and the closest there will ever be, to a catalogue of catalogues for the human race."

At enormous expense in time and in money, the Mormons work constantly at baptizing the dead, their own ancestors *and others*, since Smith insisted that the dead were free to accept or refuse what is done for them in the temples. Many Gentiles (a category which, to Mormons, includes Jews) are at the least nervous, if not indignant, at this apparently forced conversion of their ancestors, and are not particularly pacified by Mormon assurances that there is perfect free will in the spirit world. But it is difficult for me not to be moved by the vast imagination at work in this enterprise, which is another exemplification both of Mormon industriousness and of the reverberating strength of Smith's spiritual originality. Shoumatoff quotes from the speech of Spencer Kimball, then the Prophet, Seer, and Revelator, while dedicating the Mormon temple in Washington, D.C., in 1974:

> The day is coming not too far ahead of us when all temples on this earth will be going day and night. There will be shifts and people will be coming in the morning hours and in the day hours . . . because of the great number of people who lie asleep in eternity and who are craving, needing, the blessings we can bring them. (p. 86)

By 1990, Kimball's prophecy had been fulfilled; some of the temples, at least, are open all night, as Mormons keep arriving to stand in as proxies for the dead. Perhaps the coming on of the year 2000 is spurring this process, even though there is not (so far as I know) an official stance by the Latter-day Saints Church on any likelihood of the millennium coming on at that date. There are a large number of Mormon Fundamentalists, many of them polygamy-practicing Brighamites, who fully believe that A.D. 2000 will mark the beginning of the end time, but they hardly represent the Mormon mainstream, except that the urgency for baptizing the dead does seem a general concern among the Mormons. It is so remarkable a doctrine and practice that it is worth considerable meditation for the religious criticism of this most original and ambitious version of the American Religion. As a revelation, baptism for the dead inaugurated Joseph Smith's major phase as a seer, in January 1841. Three and a half years later, the great visionary was murdered, but that phase introduced most of the faith's great innovations: plural marriage, the new, strangely Masonic temple "endowments," sealing for eternity in marriage, whether single or plural, and the ultimate audacity-of-audacities, the crowning of Joseph Smith as king of the Kingdom of God. It is fascinating to speculate what would have happened had Joseph lived, and eventually led the Mormons westward as Brigham Young did. Until the federal government intervened, Young ruled the Mormon desert state as a pragmatic theocracy, but he was not Joseph Smith, to whom Jehovah and Jesus had appeared and spoken face to face. Had Smith lived another thirty years or more, as he ought to have done, then American history might have been very different. The West might now be fully as different an American culture as the South is, because much if not most of the West could well have become Smith's Kingdom of God in America. No one ought to underestimate the Mormons; a people who grow at the steady pace of six percent a year may yet turn the West into such a kingdom, say by the year 2020 or so. The next Mormon Prophet, Seer, and Revelator probably will be the very capable Thomas S. Monson, potentially the strongest figure in the Church since Smith and Young. What dreams he dreams one cannot know, but a considerable part of our national future is incarnated in him.

When Joseph formulated baptism for the dead, he interpreted it inwardly as the authentic reception by him of the keys to the Kingdom. A religious critic, struggling to comprehend the really shocking spiritual ambition, indeed the aggressive drive, of Mormon baptism for the dead, is unlikely to find any true parallel to it in modern religious history. Jan Shipps, the most sympathetic gentile scholar of Mormonism, sums up her understanding of this "new religious tradition" by placing the emphasis upon what might be called a corporate Gnosis:

Although the "unit of salvation" in Mormonism remains the individual, salvation itself depends on knowing Christ, knowledge that can only be gained with the legitimation of the LDS priesthood and within the corporate structure of the LDS Church. In addition, although the gospel is available to all, the "unit of exaltation" is the family rather than the individual. Consequently, the ultimate goal of the Latter-day Saints is not eternity somehow spent in the presence of the Lord Jesus Christ in heaven. Mormonism holds up a different goal: "eternal progression" toward godhood. (*Mormonism*, pp. 148–49)

What kind of "knowing" Christ is this, though? Is the saving "knowledge" actually "of" Jesus? If one employs Moderate Southern Baptism's great metaphor of "walking and talking with Jesus," then we are vast distances remote from Mormonism. So extraordinarily intense is the mediation of the corporately structured LDS church that Jesus becomes pragmatically unnecessary in the work of salvation. Mormonism, as Shipps clearly conveys, is no more a kind of Christianity than Islam is. Instead, Mormonism is a purely American Gnosis, for which Joseph Smith was and is a far more crucial figure than Jesus could be. Smith is not just "a" prophet, another prophet, but he is the essential prophet of these latter days, leading into the end time, whenever it comes. We cannot say in Mormonism that "Jesus saves." No Fundamentalist Southern Baptist (not even one from Texas) would ever say that the Southern Baptist Convention itself mediates salvation through Jesus. How shall we understand the full position that the Prophet Joseph continues to occupy, even in a Mormonism that has been compelled to renounce polygamy? And who can believe that the Mormons ever would have turned away from the practice of Celestial Marriage, if it were not for federal pressure? No one, least of all in Salt Lake City, will be much inclined to accept a religious critic's foretellings, but I cheerfully do prophesy that some day, not too far on in the twenty-first century, the Mormons will have enough political and financial power to sanction polygamy again. Without it, in some form or other, the complete vision of Joseph Smith never can be fulfilled.

But at just this point, I need to move from baptism for the dead to an even more enigmatic assertion of Joseph Smith's genius,

which is a metaphysical vision of birth as the building of a redeemed tabernacle for spirit to inhabit, the great doctrine of providing spirits for the unborn. I ascribe that to Joseph Smith, but
only as an informed surmise, because this is a vexed matter, on
which Smith left us mostly an oral tradition. Yet the vexedness
itself is a deep entry into the strangeness and unfinished nature of
a religion whose prophet was murdered even as he underwent an
extraordinary self-revision. Mormons today are taught that all of
us emerge from an unborn state where a god and his wife (or one
of his wives) make love and so quite literally beget our spirits. After
we die and are resurrected elsewhere, we will perform the same
pleasant labor of begetting "spirit children" for later universes. The
peculiarity of this double vision is that no Mormon theologian can
cite the writings of Joseph Smith, canonical or other, to support
such now pervasive convictions. Indeed, Smith's passionate belief
(wholly Gnostic) that our spirit or intelligence is as old as God and
the gods, and so need never have been begotten, is rather clearly at
variance with the doctrine of spirits being engendered for the unborn. We have the anomaly of a doctrine of Spirit Birth that not
only has no sanction in the scriptures that Smith composed, but
that also seems to violate one of his most basic principles.

Van Hale, a contemporary Mormon publisher and essayist, has
a very useful discussion of this difficulty, "The Origin of the
Human Spirit in Early Mormon Thought" (in *Line upon Line*, ed.
G. J. Bergera, 1989). After noting that, for Smith, "spirit," "soul,"
"intelligence," and "mind" were synonyms, Hale compiles an impressive catalog of the prophet's pronouncements to the effect that
the human spirit is coeternal with God. This listing concludes with
the King Follett Discourse, the furthest frontier of Smith's prophecy before his martyrdom. As the prophet grandly says: "The
mind of man is as immortal as God himself." That mind or spirit
therefore need not be begotten by God upon a heavenly wife, yet
this contradictory doctrine was taught by Orson Pratt while Smith
yet was among the living. Parley Pratt reported an oral teaching of
Smith (in 1840) that eternal marriage would go on producing children after the Resurrection. Hale sensibly implies that Smith
would have cleared this matter up, could he have lived to preside
over the completion of the Nauvoo temple, which was accomplished under Brigham Young's supervision as a mystical gesture
to Joseph before the great exodus to the West.

What we seem to have then is an oral teaching, perhaps one left incomplete, with unresolved contradictions. This raises the wonderful question that ought to haunt all religious critics of Mormonism. Is it not likely that Smith left other secret teachings, that have been handed down only within the hierarchy? It seems to me a wholly likely premise, since the Church has never affirmed that everything most crucial to it ever has been made public to the Gentiles, or even to most Mormons. Whether I am deluded or not, there does seem to be some partly repressed teaching of Smith involved in the doctrine of spirits for the unborn. Here the authority is the remarkable B. H. Roberts, who interpreted the King Follett discourse as meaning that the human spirit was begotten in heaven, while its mind or intelligence was separate, and had always existed. Hale demonstrates that Roberts worked with a doctored text (put together back in 1855) of the 1844 King Follett discourse, and firmly rejects Roberts's conclusions:

> While this teaching is closer to Smith's belief and represents the interpretation which will probably endure in Mormonism, I do not believe that it represents the doctrine of Joseph Smith on the topic. (p. 123)

We are left with the likelihood again of a private or secret teaching by Smith, one that he himself had not fully worked through, since disputes between Orson Pratt and Brigham Young continued for decades in Utah on preexistence, and on the nature of God and man, and both Pratt and Young had been in Smith's confidence. Standing outside Mormonism, I am compelled to attribute this difficulty again to the extraordinary ontological quest that drove the Prophet Joseph so furiously onward in the final years of his short life. Far more than an ancient Gnostic seer like Valentinus or Basilides, Smith urgently hoped to produce an utterly new kind of man, starting presumably with himself. In the previous chapter, I cited Lawrence Foster's argument that polygamy was the pragmatic instrument through which Smith hoped to create a new people. Clearly, there are inevitable links between polygamy as the highest form of Celestial Marriage, and the two apparently bizarre doctrines of baptism for the dead and spirit bodies for the unborn. If you have denied original sin and any salvation by grace, and if you have materialized and limited God, then you have placed a particular burden upon the religious capabilities of the human spirit. Sterling McMurrin gently calls this "a liberal doctrine of man"; I would think it might be called something rather more breathtaking. McMurrin also categorizes Mormon theology as "a modern Pelagianism in a Puritan religion," which is another shrewd understatement. Joseph Smith's American Gnosticism had produced a new Kabbalah, in which the destiny of the divine became wholly dependent upon sexual theurgy and the extreme limits of the human capacity for family affection. Mormon polygamy, rather than breaking down the family unit, was intended to extend and strengthen it, a paradox evidently operative today among the illegal but numerous polygamists in the Mormon backcountry. Progression towards godhood, for Smith, was not to be distinguished from plural marriage, but one senses a larger form in all of this, for which Celestial Marriage itself is a kind of metaphor or myth. It is as though Smith wished to make all of his followers share in his own preternatural capacity for ecstasy.

I will return to the Mormons in the final chapter of this book, in order to compare them to the American belief that both opposes yet strangely complements theirs, that of the Moderate Southern Baptists. In these three chapters I have centered necessarily upon the religion-making genius of Joseph Smith. What is a valid estimate of him, from the stance of what I have been calling religious criticism? The largest problem is that of the clash of two perspectives, the rest of us and the Mormons. Smith demanded to be accepted as the true, the only prophet of this latter dispensation. To the Mormons, he was, is, always will be that. By his own doctrine, he was more even than a prophet, or rather he is now doubtless a god, having progressed in the almost one hundred and fifty years since his death. Some later nineteenth-century Mormons even speculated that the preexistent Joseph Smith had been among the beings who had helped God in the initial organization of this world. The Mormon perspective is available only to Mormons, or to those few who can imagine themselves into that people.

If one decides that Joseph Smith was no prophet, let alone king of the Kingdom of God, then one's dominant emotion towards him must be wonder. There is no other figure remotely like him in our entire national history, and it is unlikely that anyone like him ever can come again. Most Americans have never heard of him, and most of those who have remember him as a fascinating scamp or charlatan who invented the story of the Angel Moroni and the gold plates, and then forged the Book of Mormon as a follow-up. Since the Book of Mormon, more even than the King James Bible, exists in more unread copies than any other work, that is poor fame indeed for a charismatic unmatched in our history. I myself can think of not another American, except for Emerson and Whitman, who so moves and alters my own imagination. For someone who is not a Mormon, what matters most about Joseph Smith is how American both the man and his religion have proved to be. So self-created was he that he transcends Emerson and Whitman in my imaginative response, and takes his place with the great figures of our fiction, since at moments he appears far larger than life, in the mode of a Shakespearean character. So rich and varied a personality, so vital a spark of divinity, is almost beyond the limits of the human, as normally we construe those limits. To one who does not believe in him, but who has studied him intensely, Smith becomes almost a mythology in himself. In the midst of writing this, I paused to reread Morton Smith's remarkable *Jesus the Magician* (1978), and found myself rewriting the book as I went along, substituting Joseph Smith for Jesus, and Joseph Smith's circumstances and associates for those of Jesus. No Mormon (presumably) would sanction such impiety, but it is strikingly instructive. Joseph Smith the Magician is no more or less arbitrary a figure than Morton Smith's persuasive mythmaker.

I end as I began, with wonder. We do not know Joseph Smith, as he prophesied that even his own could never hope to know him. He requires strong poets, major novelists, accomplished dramatists to tell his history, and they have not yet come to him. He is as enigmatic as Abraham Lincoln, his contemporary, but even if we do not know Lincoln, we at least keep learning what it is that we cannot quite understand. But with Joseph Smith, we cannot be certain precisely what baffles us most. As an unbeliever, I marvel at his intuitive understanding of the permanent religious dilemmas of our country. Traditional Christianity suits the United States about as well as European culture does, which means scarcely at all. Our deep need for originality gave us Joseph Smith even as it gave us Emerson and Emily Dickinson, Whitman and Melville, Henry and William James, even as it gave us Lincoln, who founded our all-but-all-powerful Presidency. There is something of Joseph Smith's spirit in every manifestation of the American Religion.

Joseph *knew* that he was no part of the creation, *knew* that what was best and oldest in him already was God. And he knew also, more humanly, that despite his prophetic vocation and communal vision, he was essentially alone, and could experience his own spiritual freedom only in prophetic solitude.

III

RIVAL
AMERICAN
ORIGINALS

7
Christian Science: The Fortunate Fall in Lynn, Massachusetts

OF all American Dualists, Mrs. Eddy was the most confused, and so presented her science as a Monism. But then, she was a figure of heroic pathos, and willed herself into religious history without much intellect or knowledge to aid her. Her will sufficed, and though her religion now scarcely claims one American in a thou sand, it still maintains a tenacious life among us. Since, in this book, I have taken on the burden of religious criticism, I need to remind myself of William Blake's great apothegm: "Everything Possible to be Believed is an Image of Truth." Christian Science, however it wearies the patience of an empiricist, retains an irreducibly spiritual element. It is the religion of those who refuse to accept reality testing, who refuse the enlightened wisdom that culminates in Sigmund Freud's reality-principle, which is our necessity for coming to terms with our own inevitable death. That is the pathos of Christian Science, considerably less heroic than Mrs. Eddy's stubborn pathos.

The prose style of Mary Baker Eddy, long ago ironically celebrated by Mark Twain, is one of the great ordeals of the American Religion. As an incessant, indeed an obsessed, reader, I have made my way through most of the current text of *Science and Health with Key to the Scriptures*, but am not prepared to commend it to anyone else. Still, one *can* get through, whereas I am defeated every time I attempt a New Age volume. Here I am concerned only with Eddy's notion of God, "notion" being a rather deliberate word on my part. I cannot speak either of Eddy's "vision" of God, or her "concept" or "idea" of God, because her God is the ultimate product of that long process in which the original Yahweh of the J Writer, a God who was an exuberant personality, has been vaporized into a gaseous entity. Philo of Alexandria, father of Western theology, is not one of my personal favorites, but he would be justly punished if, in some Dantesque realm, he has had to encounter the Founder of Christian Science. Popular Platonism, endlessly seething, has given us nothing else quite as idealized (inadequate word!) as the God of Mary Baker Eddy. No figure in the entire span of Western religious life has been as horrified by an anthropomorphic God as Eddy was. Sin, illness, and death itself, she insisted, had come into the world because of "the belief that Spirit materialized into a body, infinity became finity, or man, and the eternal entered the temporal."

That assertion is contained in an essay that Eddy called "The People's Idea of God: Its Effect on Health and Christianity," where the priority of "Health" is made quite palpable, though in fairness to Eddy one must admit that, to her, health and Christianity were all but identical. After the Fortunate Fall upon the ice in Lynn, Massachusetts, in early February 1866, Eddy achieved not a revelation but a scientific understanding of God. The science involved was ancient enough, since its founding principle was that God had not created the natural world. Eddy surpassed the Gnostics, however, by refusing empiricism: not only was matter altogether unreal, but seeing, hearing, touching, tasting, smelling were unreal also, since they too partook of death. With confidence, Eddy affirmed her new creed: "Christian Science rejects the validity of the testimony of the senses, which take evidence of their own—sickness, disease, and death." If Christian Science today is so dwindling a sect among us, that may be the reason: the superb strain of equating all evidence—everything we see and hear, everything we touch, taste, smell—with death.

And yet, though Christian Science ebbs among us, it was for more than a century a crucial strand in the American Religion. Its origins, frequently denied by Christian Scientists, are not in its antiempiricist Founder, but in the marvelously named Phineas

Parkhurst Quimby (1802–1866), who healed Mary Morse Baker
Eddy (1821–1910) in 1862. Quimby, an ex-mesmerist, professed
to follow Jesus as a healer, and seems to have invented the term
"Christian Science." He did not invent Mary Baker Eddy; that was
her life's work. But she is inconceivable without Quimby, though
she and her followers denied her indebtedness. A Maine clock-
repairman, self-educated and humane, the kindly Quimby cured
his own neuroses by self-hypnotism and amiably turned to healing
others. Hypnotism soon was set aside by Quimby in favor of mental suggestion. "Mind Cure," as the mode came to be known, was
part of Quimby's "science of health," essentially a spiritual rather
than a psychological doctrine. Though always careful to distinguish himself from Jesus, Quimby associated his cures with those
of Jesus, and seems to have postulated a kind of universal human
mind, itself a manifestation of the mind of God.

Mary Baker, when she came to Quimby, was an extraordinary
wreck, a monumental hysteric of classical dimensions, indeed a
kind of anthology of nineteenth-century nervous ailments. After
being cured by Quimby, she went through a phase of being his
disciple, an attachment that lasted until the master's death. The
loss of Quimby undid the cure; one month after his death, she
slipped on the ice in Lynn, Massachusetts, and became again the
invalid she had been before Quimby. Known still to Christian
Scientists as "the Fall in Lynn," this singular event of February 1,
1866, might be considered the American version of the Fortunate
Fall. The apple, for this new Savior, was associated however not
with Adam, but with Newton:

> My immediate recovery from the effects of an injury caused by
> an accident, an injury that neither medicine nor surgery could
> reach, was the falling apple that led me to the discovery how to
> be well myself, and how to make others so.

Mark Twain, in his book on Christian Science, has made lesser
humorists unnecessary. The figure of Mrs. Eddy lacks the charm
and insouciance of Joseph Smith, but as a religion-maker she is
second only to him among American heresiarchs. An outline of
Christian Science is not my purpose here, as they are plentifully
available. Religious criticism, applied to the Southern Baptists or
to the Mormons, confronts enigmatic creeds, but their irreducible

spirituality is not to be denied. Christian Science purports to be a pure spirituality, and indeed seems to be nothing else. But its denial of empirical reality sometimes makes it akin to Scientology, in the mode of science fiction crossing over into the religious sphere.

Mary Baker Eddy's God is the Gnostic Godhead, despite all denials by believers and scholars, since again we encounter the alien or stranger God, who dwells outside our unreal cosmos, and beyond any realm of mere matter. Instead, Christian Science gives us what it terms "the seven deific synonyms," summarized by Mrs. Eddy with her customary positive emphasis: "God is incorporeal, divine, infinite Mind, Spirit, Soul, Principle, Life, Truth, Love." The interesting word there has to be "Life," which certainly cannot be life as we all of us naturally enjoy and endure it. As for Mrs. Eddy's "Love," it must be something of a mystery, since her God is not a person, or even a personality. And whatever it is that God loves in us, it is certainly not our bodies, since they are far too flawed for him to have made. Though my numbed readings back and forth in *Science and Health with Key to the Scriptures* have not uncovered any references to God as Scientist, the Jesus Christ of Mrs. Eddy notoriously is described as a Scientist, rather than as a prophet or magician. Indeed, as Scientist, Jesus is granted the dignity of being the First Coming to Mrs. Eddy's Second, rather as though the Crucifixion were the initial "Fall in Lynn." Since there is no reality to evil or to suffering, to pain or to disease or to death, the Crucifixion necessarily was rather less of an ordeal than that productive slip upon the February ice. Death, according to Mrs. Eddy, cannot destroy life in any of us, so Christ is hardly unique. If there is no death, then there is no Resurrection, no raising either of Lazarus or of Jesus from the tomb. There is only a waking up from deep sleep, which alas has not yet been accomplished by Mrs. Eddy or by any other Christian Scientist, but which remains the crucial hope that this doctrine continues to promise us. Doubtless this is the rock, not of Christian Science's foundation, but of its perpetual self-destruction. How can the dead learn not to believe in death, when even Jesus and Mrs. Eddy have failed (so far) to learn not to believe in it?

The sophisticated Christian Science reply adumbrates Mrs. Eddy's somewhat desperate adage: "Resurrection from the dead (that is, from the belief in death) must come to all sooner or later."

"Sooner or later" allows a vast temporal latitude for what Mrs. Eddy called "progression and probation," particularly upon the other side of passing away. Yet the Apocalypse of Mary Baker Eddy had come already:

> . . . we can become conscious, here and now, of a cessation of death, sorrow, and pain. This is indeed a foretaste of absolute Christian Science. Take heart, dear sufferer, for this reality of being will surely appear sometime and in some way.

"Absolute Christian Science" was, however, what even Mrs. Eddy could not attain, since she did sicken and (apparently) die. The *spiritual* body was, for her, "the incorporeal idea," but she came too early, according to her believers, to know the Absolute. Yet it is always already there to be known, and I suppose that each Christian Scientist is free to believe that she or he yet will surpass Mrs. Eddy, and come to inhabit the Absolute. The dream of not dying has extraordinary capacity for pathos, in a great poet or in a religious genius. Mrs. Eddy was a lifelong verse writer, whose published work reminds me throughout of Oscar Wilde's sadly truthful reflection, "All bad poetry is sincere." Was Mrs. Eddy a religious genius? The question is wholly sincere on my part, and is a legitimate concern of the religious criticism that I seek to develop. What after all was it, is it, that gave and gives Christian Science the dignity of its evident permanence as a sect?

Though it rejects nature, and human nature, Christian Science paradoxically is a religion of the will. Mrs. Eddy's most crucial (yet most confused) distinction is between "mortal mind" and "divine Mind," the principle of healing. Mortal mind, an agency of evil, is the source of the dreaded M.A.M., "Malicious Animal Magnetism." Here Mrs. Eddy dwelled in a kind of perpetual borderline condition, as the first edition of *Science and Health* (p. 123) manifested:

> In coming years the person or mind that hates his neighbor will have no need to traverse his fields to destroy his flocks and herds and spoil his vines; or to enter his house to demoralize his household; for the evil mind will do this enough through mesmerism; and not *in propria persona* to be seen admitting the deed. Unless this terrible hour be met and restrained by *Science*, mesmerism,

the scourge of man, will leave nothing sacred when mind begins
to act under the direction of conscious power.

Paranoia, according to the sage William Burroughs, is just knowing all the facts, an insight modified by Thomas Pynchon into the
accurate observation that even paranoids have enemies. Stephen
Gottschalk, in the highly restrained *The Emergence of Christian Science in American Religious Life*, is compelled to admit just enough of
his Founder's obsessions to make us stare at his pages with some
incredulity. We are told of her close student Richard Kennedy,
who consciously tried to cause her personal suffering through his
exercise of malign animal magnetism. Then comes the death of her
husband, Asa Gilbert Eddy, "mentally assassinated" by Edward J.
Arens, another alienated former student. But Gottschalk evades
the magnitude of all this malign magnetism. For that one must turn
to Edwin Franden Dakin's *Mrs. Eddy* (1929), a biography that the
Christian Scientists did everything they could to suppress. Much
of Dakin's book, justly and inevitably, is devoted to Mrs. Eddy's
obsessive fear of Malicious Animal Magnetism. M.A.M. became
the composite evil against which Christian Science struggled, but
what was M.A.M.? Simply ill will, or any will except Mrs. Eddy's
own, or that of her loyal followers:

> The students were delegated to sit in a certain pew and defend
> Mrs. Eddy, while she spoke, against Malicious Animal Magne-
> tism . . . When Mrs. Eddy arose in the morning she could ascer-
> tain, from the sort of depression that she experienced, or from
> the color of her mood and thoughts, just which kind of M.A.M.
> was being directed toward her, and which one of her enemies—
> Kennedy, Spofford, or Arens—was seeking to take control of her
> for the day. Sometimes all three set on her at once, and then the
> day was lost. The administrations of every student available
> would be required in these terrible emergencies. (p. 159)

Animal magnetism, whether malicious or benevolent, was the
invention of Friedrich Mesmer, German physician and perfor-
mance artist, who dazzled Paris towards the end of the eighteenth
century. Mesmer, the Jacques Lacan (rather than the Freud) of his
day, saw animal magnetism as the medium linking body and mind.
A hypnotist of undoubted genius, Mesmer largely discredited the

therapeutic uses of hypnotism. It was not until the later nineteenth century that the precursors of Freud—Charcot, Janet, Breuer—restored "mesmerism" to its proper status in medicine. Quimby, Mrs. Eddy's only begetter, was courageous in working his "mind-cures" during an era when the shadow of the charlatan Mesmer still darkened the uses of suggestion in psychiatry. Mrs. Eddy, by dualistically dividing animal magnetism into the ill will of others and her own Jesus-like divine mind, contributed little to Quimby's enterprise. But then, it was not as a healer that Mrs. Eddy made her contribution. Her own heroism lay in the enterprise of her own will, despite all her denials. As such she performed her own remarkable crossing from an imported Protestantism to another new version of the American Religion.

Mark Twain enjoyed the Christian Science quasi-identification of Mary Baker Eddy with the Virgin Mary, a parallel still regarded as "clear" by current Christian Science exegetes, such as Gottschalk (p. 167). Mrs. Eddy herself, in the tradition of Mother Ann Lee of the Shakers, sometimes played with the fancy of seeing herself as the woman "clothed with the sun" in Revelation 12:1–5. In this last decade of the twentieth century, we can expect some Christian Scientists to revert to such an apocalyptic vision of their sublime Founder. Though not herself a prophet, seer, and revelator in the mode of Joseph Smith, Mrs. Eddy nevertheless was given to statements of divine authority: "*God* does speak through me to this age." Since her own will-to-healing was thus necessarily the Will of God, Mrs. Eddy was able to accomplish a triumph of the will without parallel in nineteenth-century religious speculation, if we except Thomas Carlyle, who seems to me her hidden source. True, she never read Carlyle, or any other Victorian sage, at all extensively, but she took what she needed from him (and from John Ruskin) by gleanings from a single popular anthology, *Philosophic Nuggets* (1899), edited by one Joanne G. Pennington. Dakin, in an appendix, charts her plagiarisms from Carlyle and Ruskin, but they seem to me less interesting than her palpable debt to Carlyle's heroic exaltation of the will.

An obsessive believer in M.A.M. and plagiarist of Thomas Carlyle would not seem a likely heroine of the American Religion, but I do not hesitate in judging Mrs. Eddy to have been of that eminence. Without her teachings, we would hardly know certain boundless aspects of the American will. Though the faith-healing element in Christian Science is anything but unique in the American Religion—it is shared by many Baptist Fundamentalists, by Pentecostals, by Seventh-day Adventists (with a difference), and even by some Mormons—still Christian Science healing remains very much a revelation of what we should call the American will. As always, Emerson and William James are the appropriate theorists here. Emerson's Will to Vital Power and James's Will to Believe are very different indeed from Mrs. Eddy's Divine Mind, yet on a lower register she too votes for possibility, a fairer house than prose. Her crucial proof-text, which restored her after the Fortunate Fall in Lynn, is Matthew 9:1–5:

And he entered into a ship, and passed over, and came into his own city.

And, behold, they brought to him a man sick of the palsy, lying on a bed: and Jesus seeing their faith said unto the sick of the palsy; Son, be of good cheer; thy sins be forgiven thee.

And, behold, certain of the scribes said within themselves, This man blasphemeth.

And Jesus knowing their thoughts said, Wherefore think ye evil in your hearts?

For whether is easier, to say, Thy sins be forgiven thee; or to say, Arise and walk?

Mrs. Eddy arose and walked, and about one quarter of one percent of her fellow countrywomen and men these days attempt to arise and walk with her, to arise and walk in the will, which she has taught them to believe is the mind of God. Since Christian Science denies all empirical evidence, it is technically the most Idealist religious formulation that the West ever has known. Joseph Smith had a powerful religion-making imagination, whereas Mary Baker Eddy had close to no imagination at all. It is true that Smith was what W. B. Yeats wrongly thought William Blake to have been, a literalist of his own imagination, but since Mrs. Eddy denied the natural completely, then the natural imagination died in her also. Her doctrine is neither literal nor figurative; it is pure will. Her will does the work of Joseph Smith's imagination, and places us in a world without color, light, and sound.

Stephen Gottschalk weirdly concludes his apologia for Christian Science with a chapter that attempts to fit Mrs. Eddy's doctrine into what Gottschalk calls "the American Pragmatic Orientation." Invoking the spirit of William James, Gottschalk insists that "Christian Science stands, therefore, for the idea of an experience-able absolute" (p. 282). This remarkable insistence leads to a more startling statement: "her assertion of the nothingness of evil amounts pragmatically to the claim that the conditions of experience make it possible to actually reduce evil to nothingness in specific situations." With evil thus eradicated, at least pragmatically, Gottschalk is emboldened to proclaim that Christian Science has transcended Protestantism:

. . . Mrs. Eddy asserted that man and creation understood in Science are the expression of God, hence that the belief in a God-created material universe and man are the products of a radical misconception of true being. Salvation in Christian Science, therefore, means the full demonstration of the spiritual fact and is predicated upon the understanding of the truth of being in Science as differentiated from the mortal picture of being as presented to the physical senses. Protestantism, however, accepts as true that very picture of man and the universe which Mrs. Eddy declares is a misconception of being, understands man's material-ity as natural to him in his creaturely estate, and conceives of salvation as the moral transformation of a fallen man rather than the demonstration of man's inherent perfection as the son of God (pp. 286–87).

Presumably without knowing it, Gottschalk propounds an ancient Gnostic alternative to Christianity. To find pragmatic and experiential a religion that denies the natural world and the natural man and woman is to have redefined the pragmatic and the experiential, and to have abandoned William James of Harvard for Basilides of Alexandria. Yet Gottschalk is accurate enough in seeing that Mrs. Eddy's contentions cannot be Protestant. We hear again the great formulae of the American Religion: what is best and oldest in Mrs. Eddy is no part of the Creation, and Mrs. Eddy's freedom, her escape from Malicious Animal Magnetism, flowered only in perfect solitude, or in the solipsism where her quasi-sacred person could be protected by disciples actively exercising their minds as overt defenses against her assassins or heretical disciples.

Against Gnosticism, Mrs. Eddy's followers tend to affirm her

Idealist Monism, her passionate faith in the only real principle, the Mind of God. There are Gnosticisms and Gnosticisms, and Mrs. Eddy's may be granted its own flavor, a kind of tutti-frutti of the spirit. Too narrow a definition of Gnosticism underlies Mary Farrell Bednarowski's account of Christian Science's affinity with or distance from the ancient heresy, in her *New Religions and the Theological Imagination in America* (1989):

> Whereas gnosticism and Scientology are dualistic systems, positing the reality, if not the equality, of spirit and matter, the theology of Christian Science is monistic in nature. A study of Christian Science yields no concept of a demiurge who has created the material world as a trap for humankind. If there is anything villainous in Christian Science, it is mortal mind; but mortal mind refers to a false mode of thinking rather than to a cosmic antagonist of God. Further, the god of Christian Science is not a radically transcendent, "unknowable" god as is the god of gnosticism. Nor is this god immanent. (p. 34)

This neglects the demiurgical entity Malicious Animal Magnetism, aside from misrepresenting the bewildering variety of Gnostic formulations. Mrs. Eddy's God is of course no more transcendent or immanent than Mrs. Eddy herself; if the demiurge of her system was M.A.M., then the God of her science might be called B.A.M., or Benign Animal Magnetism. For we approach at last the essence of Mrs. Eddy's authentic originality as a prophetess of the American Religion. Healing is an act of the will, and proceeds when the will is utterly divorced from nature. The art of healing, Christian Science, is a Gnosticism that teaches again the ancient discipline of how to separate one's mind from nature. Mrs. Eddy's God, and not nature, is our authentic narcissistic mirror. God is perfect and good, and so Mrs. Eddy, as his truest reflection, is also perfect and good. When we perceive ourselves as Mrs. Eddy, then we too will be perfect and good, and absolutely healed. We will not be mortal, and all aches—whether of head or belly—will vanish from us. And being free of illness, we will be free to prosper, and so become both very wealthy and immortal to boot.

Irony ensues only because mortality and materiality afflict our sense of language. Mrs. Eddy, master of Christian Science, had considerable trouble with language, which is too much infected by empirical woes. Confronted by perfection, whether in her God or in Mrs. Eddy, the reader of *Science and Health* is likely to feel somewhat unfinished. What most marks Mrs. Eddy's God is his perfect finish; he-she or Father-Mother has nothing incomplete in or about him-her. Incompleteness ensues in sin, error, pain, sickness, suffering, death, and also in sexual love, humor, and the arts. The author of *Science and Health*, who was beyond irony, teaches us these truths with a steady fervor almost unmatched in the chronicle of Western spirituality. Sexuality, humor, and the arts hardly were her concern, nor should they have been. *Science and Health* is the antithesis of humor or good writing, as it is the antithesis also of the erotic drive. More than any version of the American Religion since the Shakers, it achieves perfection by evading or negating the realities and values of the human body.

All human sexual travail is judged by Christian Science to stem from our failure to see that we are spiritual beings rather than sexual individuals. In her chapter on marriage in *Science and Health*, Mrs. Eddy looked forward to a future in which children could be produced without that roiling about in mere matter that is sexual intercourse. One gets the impression frequently in reading Mrs. Eddy, or in reading about her life, that there was for her a peculiarly sexual menace in Malicious Animal Magnetism. Perhaps M.A.M. is the Christian Science equivalent of the dread Freudian Return of the Repressed, or perhaps the physical and the sexual had become synonyms for Mrs. Eddy. Since, to her, we were reflections of God, and God's own splendor precluded sexuality, our sexuality could be no part of the truth. Like cancer, like war, like death, sex is only another illusion. There is very little in life, let alone in love, that was not illusion for Mary Baker Eddy. Only another step or two would have taken Mrs. Eddy over into the religious vision of Mother Ann Lee, in which case the Christian Scientists, like the Shakers, would now be extinct.

This may seem like an unsympathetic account, whether of Mrs. Eddy or of her creed, but that is certainly not my intention. I turn to a closer look at Mrs. Eddy in action, as it were, in order to analyze more closely the authentic triumph of her will, or of what Blake called the Female Will in her organization and doctrine. Moving in closer will not render the material less bizarre, but then it is the particular strength of the American Religion that its modes must seem excessive and eccentric in relation to older spiritual establishments. Certainly Mrs. Eddy herself could be singularly fearless in her pronouncements:

> Even the Scriptures gave no direct interpretation of the scientific basis for demonstrating the Spiritual Principle of healing, until our heavenly Father saw fit, through the Key to the Scriptures in Science and Health, to unlock this "mystery of godliness."

Sometimes the courage became something else, not easy to name, as in this apparently modest disavowal:

> No person can take the individual place of the Virgin Mary. No person can compass or fulfill the individual mission of Jesus of Nazareth. No person can take the place of the author of *Science and Health*, the Discoverer and Founder of Christian Science. Each individual must fill his own niche in time and eternity.

Heresiarchs generally foster their own rivals; schism begets schism, and cults proliferate into sub-cults. Mrs. Eddy had reason to fear those who would take her place, not so much the M.A.M. triad of Daniel Harrison Spofford, Richard Kennedy, and Edward J. Arens, former students cast out by her, as two extraordinary women disciples, Mrs. Augusta Stetson and Mrs. Josephine Curtis Woodbury. Mrs. Woodbury, the more flamboyant though less consequential figure, dared to challenge Mrs. Eddy in Boston, home of the Mother Church. Notorious for her charm and sexual dynamism, Mrs. Woodbury went too far in 1890, when she experienced a virginal conception and bore a son to no one, she announced, except herself. Though Mrs. Woodbury proclaimed that this miracle had come about under the influence of Mrs. Eddy's spiritual prophecies, Mrs. Eddy herself was not at all pleased. A further Woodburian venture in floating an "air engine" stock scheme led to Mrs. Eddy's final expulsion of the troublesome beauty. Mrs. Woodbury, in the Founder's anxieties, joined the dangerous company of those who, night and day, exuded Malicious Animal Magnetism towards her home and person.

Mrs. Woodbury is comic relief in the somber chronicles of Christian Science; the center of the story is Mrs. Augusta Stetson, who went from being Mrs. Eddy's most valued disciple to being the most feared and rejected by the Founder. Edwin Dakin, in his persuasive biography of Mrs. Eddy, attributes both the rise and fall of the talented Mrs. Stetson to her intense love for Mrs. Eddy. Indeed, Mrs. Stetson first to last believed in the divinity of Mrs. Eddy, for Mrs. Stetson, a confirmed mystic, was the true Enthusiast of the movement. Dakin quotes from a letter of Mrs. Stetson's sent to Mrs. Eddy (November 1, 1906) a passage almost unique in the varied ecstasies of the American Religion:

My students, assembled to-day at the annual meeting of their Association, unite with me in conveying to you our loyal love. We re-affirm our instant, constant allegiance. We are individually watching and working with you, realizing that we also rise with you in proportion to our understanding and demonstration of your teaching, by precept and example, of the eternal law which governs and controls all created things. Because, in this sacred hour, from your cloistered communion in the secret place of the Most High, *you* are demonstrating the immortality of Life manifest in individual man, *we* look for the appearing of the ideal man, made in God's image and likeness, never to disappear, reflecting forever the presence, power, and peace of the eternal Mind. (Dakin, p. 336)

The *you* and *we* are Mrs. Stetson's own italics, helping acutely to emphasize the authentic accent of the enthusiast. Alas, Mrs. Stetson was not saved from the inevitable rejection endured by any figure who might intrude upon the aura of Mrs. Eddy. As healer, teacher, organizer, fund raiser, Mrs. Stetson outperformed her godlike original. What Mrs. Stetson understood, better even than Mrs. Eddy, was one of the central truths of the American Religion, the equation of poverty with error, and the belief that such error brought forth illness, sin, and death. Strong in will, Mrs. Stetson surpassed all other leaders of Christian Science in her exercise of Malicious Animal Magnetism. She went at last too far by leading her practitioners in "treating" Mrs. Eddy's Board of Directors of the Mother Church, such treatment to M.A.M. being intended to remove them from this world. Her credentials withdrawn by Mrs. Eddy, Mrs. Stetson suicidally accepted her eventual excommunication and continued to worship the divinity of Mrs. Eddy.

Even so rapid an exposition is compelled to touch upon what must seem zaniness, but again I disavow any intention of ridicule.

Mrs. Eddy, a lifelong semi-invalid before being rescued by Quimby, does seem to have become paranoid after Quimby's death. But many (perhaps most) religious geniuses are psychically unbalanced, from a secular perspective. Mrs. Eddy's one gift was a strong religious will, ultimately the will to deny the reality principle or the necessity of dying. Her healing powers, like Quimby's, were based upon what may as well be named animal magnetism, whether malicious or benign. The Christian Science passion, from Mrs. Eddy to the present day, for denouncing and denying mesmerism is a revealing indication that Christian Science essentially is a belated American spiritualization of the grand charlatan Mesmer. J. H. van den Berg, in his marvelous "Introduction to a Historical Psychology," *The Changing Nature of Man* (1961), gives us a subtle disquisition on "the changing character of the miracle":

> The miracles of our time are subtle miracles. Apparently God is not allowed to show Himself in any way except the way that things appear to us; not in the things themselves. And it is quite clear why. The things have suffered so much from the treatment of many ages, that the damage cannot be undone, not even by God. Especially not by God, because the damage is His absence. The only thing God can still do is to put Himself "against" the substratum of things; He can pretend, and pretending, He can bring back to our minds a past that was more glorious, more real. A past of a fair reality, which tolerated God, and in which He walked in and out. (p. 207)

Mrs. Eddy, perhaps unwisely, refused to believe "that the damage cannot be undone, not even by God." But then, Christian Science declines to distinguish between women and men, and God, the ultimate mother-father, even while it rejects an anthropomorphic God, who could walk in and out. But that is because Mrs. Eddy rejected our walking in and out. To her, we were Divine Mind, or we were nothing. Whatever one thinks of the consequences, human and medical, of her insistences, her audacity remains both impressive and American. Divine Mind in praxis reduced to animal magnetism, benevolently working to heal the unreality of illness and pain. To extend such power to suggestion, or animal magnetism, was to open the way to those malicious influxes that so terrified Mrs. Eddy.

The religious dream of America, like its secular reveries, centers on freedom and on victory, not the Great Defeat (as Emerson called it) of Golgotha, but a triumph to the senses as well as to the soul (Emerson again). Mrs. Eddy's stance is an inevitable parody of our religious dream. Her narcissism is absolute: "Whatever is possible to God, is possible to man *as God's reflection*." And though the possibility may not have been actualized by Jesus, it was by Mrs. Eddy, according to Mrs. Eddy. Her contrasts between Jesus and herself tend to give her the advantage, since her rejection of the body far surpasses any dismissal that she could ascribe to him.

Of the major American cults, Christian Science does not export as universally as Mormonism, Jehovah's Witnesses, the Pentecostals, and Seventh-day Adventism. They convert many races, many languages, but Christian Science abroad remains mostly an English-speaking affair, with some favor among Germans. Why should it be an Anglo-Saxon phenomenon, unlike our other lasting indigenous faiths? This surely has little to do with any untranslatability of Mrs. Eddy's *Science and Health*, which Mark Twain wanted translated into English. Nor can it be that Christian Science is somehow more American even than Mormonism, or than the Southern Baptists. It seems rather to be a class phenomenon; urban and rural masses do not become Christian Scientists. To deny the reality of matter and of the body you must be very clean, well fed and housed and clothed, and easily able to afford medical care when benign animal magnetism falls short.

Christian Science takes August 23, 1879, as its origin, as on that day The Church of Christ (Scientist) was incorporated in Boston. The function of the Church, according to the *Church Manual*, was "to commemorate the word and works of our Master, which should reinstate primitive Christianity and its lost element of healing." The American quest for the Primitive Church is doubtless unending, going back as it does to Puritan biblical Primitivism and proceeding on through similar strands in American Methodism and among American Baptists until its complex triumphs in the Restorationism of the Mormons, the early Pentecostals, and in the three groups that stem from the Campbells and Barton Stone: Churches of Christ, Disciples of Christ, Independent Christian Churches. Yet Mrs. Eddy hardly can be considered a Restorationist, and her vision of primitive Christianity did not extend beyond faith healing. She was not searching for "True Antiquity" or for "Soul Liberty," or for any of the other goals of American Protestantism. A true American, Mrs. Eddy searched for and found herself, and had no other truth or wisdom to give than what she herself incarnated. Indeed, she had not even that, as she rejected all incarnation or embodiment whatsoever. She had her will to power, over her health or anyone's health who would turn to her. But the shadow side of her will stayed with her also. Living by the will to heal through benevolent animal magnetism, she feared dying through the Malicious Animal Magnetism of her own rebel or cast-off disciples. Her life, and her now-waning Church, teach us that even in America the will alone cannot suffice to create a faith. The American Religion, fierce and fecund, continues to burgeon, but increasingly Christian Science seems to have become one of its epiphenomena.

8

Seventh-day Adventism: Health, Prophecy, and Ellen Harmon White

RAISED as a Maine Methodist, Ellen Harmon White (1827–1915) may have been overdetermined in her prophetic vocation by a catastrophe suffered at the age of nine. Walking home from school, the child was knocked unconscious by a stone thrown into her face by an older girl. Her nose broken, her entire face disfigured, Ellen Harmon survived a long subsequent trauma, and emerged as an exemplification of Nietzsche's great maxim: "That which does not destroy me strengthens me." A self-proclaimed prophetess, although barely readable she remains the indubitable founder of a highly original and permanent American faith that scarcely is a trust in America. Though the Seventh-day Adventists do not join Jehovah's Witnesses in a refusal of patriotism, they began just as much in opposition to the American vision as Jehovah's Witnesses did. What initially allied the two sects was their mutual origin in the Millerite Great Disappointment, but there is now very little in common between them. The greatest oddity of Seventh-day Adventism is its evolution from a stance set against the American Religion to a position of being all but absorbed by our national shamanism.

Today, the Adventists vie with the Witnesses and the Mormons in conversions abroad, while at home a formerly racist church increasingly is constituted of African-Americans and Hispanics. It is a nice irony that the most prominent Seventh-day Adventists are no longer the prophetess Ellen White and her quondam disciple, Dr. John Harvey Kellogg, inventor of Kellogg's Corn Flakes, but rather two eminent vocalists, Little Richard and Prince, just as our leading Jehovah's Witness now most certainly is the moondancer, Michael Jackson. Adventism, unlike Jehovah's Witnesses, has not become part of American popular mythology, nor has it given us such imaginative constructs as the Jonadabs or Mrs. Eddy's Malicious Animal Magnetism. The public associates the Adventists with a Saturday, or Jewish, Sabbath and with a vast and benign medical establishment. Sometimes, indeed, the Adventists, like the Mormons, seem in danger of becoming just another Protestant denomination, or just another shade or variety of Fundamentalism. And yet the Adventists have a theology peculiar to them, one that is revelatory of an American spirituality quite different from any other.

The most informed study of Adventism, Malcolm Bull and Keith Lockhart's *Seeking a Sanctuary* (1989), warns against any simplistic understanding of the paradoxes of the faith:

> Adventism had defined itself as a negation of the American dream of unlimited material and spiritual progress. The millennium would not take place on American soil, for the nation was in league with the devil, and its achievements were doomed to destruction. The way to salvation and the experience of a heavenly millennium was to sink a sanctuary among the band of Sabbath keepers who were moving toward perfection. From the first, Adventism presented itself as a more effective means of realizing the spiritual objectives for which the rest of society was striving. Interestingly enough, Adventism has also proved to be an effective means of gaining the material and social benefits for which most Americans yearn. But the accelerated upward mobility that Adventists achieve depends on their deviation from the mainstream. It is precisely because Adventism has developed an alternative network of schools and institutions that it is possible to rise so rapidly within it. Adventism's deviant ideology has provided a justification for the replication of state institutions. This, in turn, has provided a way to realize more rapidly the goal of material prosperity. Through negating the American dream, Adventism has made it into a reality. (p. 268)

The Oneida Community, we can recall, came apart primarily because Noyes aged and could not continue to lead, but a contributing factor was the group's economic prowess (in making and selling animal traps!), a perpetual undoing element in American sects. What Bull and Lockhart see as uniquely Adventist is rather an American repetition, embracing also Quakers, Shakers, and the makers of modern Mormonism. Perhaps the new influxes of African-Americans and Hispanics will return the Adventists to their apocalyptic critique of the American dream, but more likely the Adventist genius for discipline, health, and organization will elevate their converts into the American middle class. Bull and Lockhart may err in their estimate of Adventist uniqueness, but their study firmly demonstrates how little of the earlier Adventism survives today. But again, this is eminently true of the Mormons, proud pillars of the Republican Party in the mountain states and in Southern California. Does anything remain in the Adventists that is not mainstream Protestant Fundamentalism? There abides enough wildness in the Mormons so as to continue their American shamanism, but what of the ostensible followers of the entranced prophetess Ellen White?

Preparing for this book I have attempted to read Ellen White in some depth, with mixed success. I have gotten through *The Great Controversy* (1888), but bogged down in the multivolume *Spiritual Gifts* (1858–64) and *Spirit of Prophecy* (1870–84). She is more readable than Mrs. Eddy or the New Age authors, but that is all one can give her. Bull and Lockhart describe her earlier narrative style as "simple but compelling"; "simplistic and compulsive" would be more accurate. As with Mrs. Eddy, there is evidence of multiple authorship and of generous plagiarism, yet these do not much alleviate Ellen White's murky drabness. This founder of a persistent American sect badly needed education in religious writing. Should this seem harsh, here is a climactic passage from *The Great Controversy*, representing Ellen White at her most inspired moment, one absolutely central to her followers:

There must be an examination of the books of record to determine who, through repentance of sin and faith in Christ, are entitled to the benefits of His atonement. The cleansing of the sanctuary therefore involves a work of investigation,—a work of judgment. This work must be performed prior to the coming of

Christ to redeem His people; for when He comes, His reward is with Him to give to every man according to his works. (p. 422)

"Examination of the books," "entitled to the benefits," "a work of investigation": though Ellen White was given to composing in frequent trances and in ecstasy, her diction remained faithful to a Maine lawyer's office. Jesus appears here as the Great Accountant, accomplishing the cleansing of the Temple so that God can get the accurate figures on repentance and faith (sales and profits). The Great Controversy between Christ and Satan begins to resemble not a great debate but a dispute concerning double-entry bookkeeping. "Who cooks the books?" will be heard upon earth, even as it was heard in heaven.

No American faith, not even Jehovah's Witnesses, has a theology so convoluted as that of Seventh-day Adventism. I observe this in admiration, not in disrespect. Though limited in her expressiveness, Ellen White possessed a remarkably labyrinthine religious imagination, inspired as it was by the Millerite Great Disappointment of October 22, 1844. She was then seventeen, and met her own share of regret that the world went on by commencing her visions just two months later. The visions continued for a third of a century, at the average rate of about half a dozen per year. Unlike Saint Paul and Joseph Smith, Ellen White may be said to have domesticated, even routinized, her visions. They answered a crying need of the Adventists, who accorded them the status of Testimonies. Acceptance of the Testimonies as being inspired by the Spirit of Prophecy remains the validating entry into Seventh-day Adventism, even as Mormonism assigns the same function to accepting the authenticity of the early visions of Joseph Smith, more even than to the truth of the Book of Mormon.

Smith was a charismatic personality; Ellen White decidedly was not. The best biography, *Prophetess of Health* by Ronald L. Numbers, is very useful, yet cannot unriddle the enigma of her authority for her followers down to the present time. The best hint is by Bull and Lockhart, which I cite gratefully, but only in order to twist it inside out:

Unlike the Mormon prophet Joseph Smith, Ellen White did not proclaim her revelation and gather a following; rather, she had a particular kind of religious experience that came to be accepted as authoritative in an existing group. The prophetic ministry of Ellen White was an aspect of Adventist social experience, not just the psychological experience of a single individual. (p. 25)

One must respond by observing that the Adventists did not enjoy group visions; Ellen White had a highly individual psychological experience, and then repeated it two hundred times or so. It remained *her* experience, and became communal because the disappointed had to have their faith in the spiritual world constantly renewed. Bull and Lockhart's true point is that authority had to be bestowed upon Ellen White, because she was initially too shy to assert it for herself. Her husband, and then their son after James White's death, made many of the assertions for her. But any reader who has gotten through *The Great Controversy* ceases to think of Ellen White as being in any way diffident. She is an endlessly firm dogmatist, even though the dogma is very curious and idiosyncratic. Her leading characteristic is persistence. She may not wear you down, but she has the air of always going on until she is stopped, and she never is stopped. Though the dogma began as a group inheritance and always seems to be presented as impersonal, it is shaped throughout by a sensibility not much at home in nature or in the United States of America of mid-century and after in the great age of the American Religion, our nineteenth century.

Since Seventh-day Adventism in the 1990s is very much a this-worldly religion, intent upon health, it remains startling that the movement's theology is so centered upon a heavenly sanctuary. This world did not end on October 22, 1844, but on that very day Jesus Christ entered the Holy of Holies up in heaven and started to scrub away our sins. Alas, after a hundred and fifty years he continues to clean up after us, so many are our sins. If the Adventists were to employ this vision as a prophetic witness against our contemporary America, then it would be to some purpose, but they have ceased to see it as a criticism of American life in terms of real injustices and amoralities. AIDS, crack, and homelessness are not cleansed by Christ, despite the Adventists' abiding concern for their own health, and to some degree, for the health of the nation.

Health, an inevitable obsession for Ellen White, has become the pragmatic theology of the Adventists. From an initial program that included a strong preference for Kellogg's Corn Flakes over masturbation, the Adventist drive for health has become a worldwide medical crusade that has benefitted millions of Africans and Asians, and that has exalted doctors beyond ministers in the Adventist hierarchy. It could be argued that the advantage of Ellen Harmon White over Mary Baker Eddy is the paradox that the Adventist prophetess has improved the world's health while longing only for heaven, while the Christian Science magus has jeopardized the health of many while driving hard towards material prosperity even as she denied the existence of material reality. One need not hesitate in awarding the palm to Mrs. White over Mrs. Eddy, but then Mrs. Eddy is hardly a standard for the Religious Sublime. Seventh-day Adventism, despite its original crusade against last century's America, remains part of the American Religion, our extraordinary blend of Christianity, Orphism, Gnosticism, and our ongoing shamanism. The standard to set Adventism against is provided by Mormonism and Southern Baptism, our most original and vital contributions to the world's religious imagination. But first I return to the extraordinary features that mark Mrs. White's spiritual Testimonies, all of them following upon the vision of Christ's labor at cleansing the Sanctuary.

That vision was not in fact originally Ellen White's, but came to Hiram Edson, who kept vigil, with other devoted Millerites, all through the non-fateful night of the Great Disappointment, on October 22, 1844, not too far from Rochester, in burned-over New York State. On the morning of October 23, after consuming a rather sad postapocalyptic breakfast, Edson wandered into a cornfield and looked up to behold heaven opening before him. Quite plainly, Edson saw precisely *how* William Miller had gotten it wrong. Christ had not descended to cleanse the earthly sanctuary, but rather had only just entered "the second apartment" of the heavenly Holy of Holies. Though Miller himself found this unpersuasive and remained Disappointed, Ellen White helped guide other Adventists to the Edson vision. These included Joseph Bates, a retired ship captain of Massachusetts, who had pioneered among Adventists in the cause of adopting Saturday as the Sabbath, after the model of the Seventh-day Baptists. Ellen White, at first cold to this innovation, later adopted it herself as the seal of God upon her movement.

Numbers, in his *Prophetess of Health*, remarks that while one particular angel always accompanied Ellen White in her trances, the prophetess herself never named her heavenly guide. Tradition from the Apocrypha through the Kabbalists to Joseph Smith always has been very specific about the naming of angels, but Ellen White kept the secret to herself. This anonymity helps give a particular tone to her Testimonies, enhancing their odd impersonality. Her wanderings in eternal places were precisely opposite to those of Swedenborg, whose weird greatness of personality informs everything he saw. Here is her vision of Satan (reprinted by Numbers, p. 20) as a kind of mid-century American scamp, fallen from middle-class respectability:

> That brow which was once so noble, I particularly noticed. His forehead commenced from his eyes to recede backward. I saw that he had demeaned himself so long, that every good quality was debased, and every evil trait was developed. His eyes were cunning, sly, and showed great penetration. His frame was large, but the flesh hung loosely about his hands and face. As I beheld him, his chin was resting upon his left hand. He appeared to be in deep thought. A smile was upon his countenance, which made me tremble, it was so full of evil, and Satanic slyness.

"What kind of slyness, Mrs. White?" one asks, and "Satanic slyness," one is told. Nothing else in American spirituality is quite as baffling as Ellen White's Testimonies. Their appeal, initial or protracted, is irrecoverable, even by many Adventist believers. The Disappointment demanded some supernatural evidences of consolation, and there were only her visions to provide it. But she lacked the religion-making imagination of Joseph Smith; audacity and humor were no part of her. Something else, stubborn and complex, took their place and endures still, though more in the outward armature of Seventh-day Adventist theology than as a manifestation of what might merit being called the spirit of prophecy. Call it Ellen White's desperate will-to-health, a quest for survival amidst every kind of disappointment, secular and spiritual. It is the exercise of that will, still flickering on among Adventists around the world, that keeps her church a cult rather than another Evangelical Protestant denomination, which in so many ways it has become.

Anthony A. Hoekema, in *The Four Major Cults* (1963), pp. 388–403, catalogs the elements in Adventist theology that are unacceptable to traditional Protestantism. They include: the extra-Scriptural source of authority in Ellen White's writings; a wavering on justification by grace alone, since later deeds can cancel out earlier sanctification; the Investigative Judgment, in which Christ counts up the good and ill deeds; giving the Mark of the Beast to those who do not keep the Seventh-day Sabbath; various limitations in Christ; an identification of the Adventist Church as playing a unique role in the Apocalypse, and as representing the remnant that can be saved. That is an imposing list, and I am hardly convinced when Bull and Lockhart, apologists for the Adventist Church, dismiss Hoekema for having the narrow stance of "evangelicals in the Reformed tradition" and thus giving "a view of one American minority from the perspective of another." Their other defense is to insist that Adventists enjoy a "plurality of opinion" and have no single doctrine, particularly since they have so peculiar an origin:

> Seventh-day Adventism is thus not the estranged child of any mainstream American Protestant body, but the orphaned offspring of a brief liaison among several Protestant groups. There is, accordingly, no single doctrine or historical event that separates Adventists from the mainstream. There is no one mainstream group with which Adventists can forget their differences and reunite . . . Adventist identity does not hinge on a few doctrines that deviate from those of the mainstream . . . but on a unique and isolated history. (p. 86)

Except for the first sentence, that applies far more precisely to the Mormons than to the Adventists. Like the Jews, the Mormons are a religion that has become a people, but the Adventists were a particular people, the Millerite Disappointed, who became a religion. Since very few American Adventists now are descended from Millerite ancestors, only the religion is left, and Hoekema seems to me merely accurate in his perception that Seventh-day Adventism remains in some respects scarcely Christian, in any Protestant, let alone Catholic, sense. It is an American Religion of Health, crossed by the postapocalyptic dream of an end time never to be. To trace the theology of the Adventists is to chart the passage of Ellen White's prophecies from Heaven's investigative judgment to the investigative judgments of stethoscopes and blood-transfusions, of surgeons and of nurses. Adventists now vie with Mormons in out-living all other Americans, a curious fate for believers whose pre-cursors did not expect to outlive October 22, 1844. New converts to the Adventists now learn a somewhat modified version of the original doctrines, but rather more centrally they learn the Seven Principles that will help them to live at least six extra years: good air, good water, nutrition, scheduling, rest, exercise, and moderate eating.

All this began with a vision that came to Ellen White in 1863, in the midst of our Civil War. Health Reform had been an American crusade throughout the nineteenth century, but Ellen White, de-spite her invariable bad health, came surprisingly late to her most characteristic emphasis. Perhaps war brought her to a higher awareness of the religious significance of health, or more likely her persistent distaste for human sexuality gave her the visionary in-sight that sex, being for her an unhealthy and irreligious phenom-enon, might best be transcended by a mingled concern for bodily and spiritual welfare. Her chance references to the body as God's temple (following Saint Paul, at a considerable distance) have meant more to modern Seventh-day Adventism than ever they did to her, and yet have greatly affected Adventist abstention from alcohol, tobacco, drugs, coffee, tea, most meat, and even from strong condiments. Mrs. White herself rarely could avoid such backslidings as fried chicken, though eventually she is believed to have rarefied herself into vegetarianism. One returns always, in considering Ellen White, to the central mystery of her appeal to her followers. Distinctly not a charismatic leader and hardly an inspiring writer, most certainly not an organizer or an originator, she nevertheless remains today a worldwide presence. Numbers, though her best biographer, cannot do much with the paradoxes of her career. A kind, good person, she was remarkable only for her tendency to experience visions, drab as they tended to be in them-selves. I turn at last to a meditation upon her theology, since only there can her curious strength be fathomed.

The most interesting aspects of Adventist theology doubtless are its American heresies, when considered from the perspectives of normative Protestantism. I therefore set aside here everything that they share in common with contemporary American Fundamental-ism, which is very substantial, and begin instead with their flat denial that we are born with immortal souls. Though they endorse

Ellen White's cosmological dualism, or the Great Controversy between Christ and Satan, they follow her also in refusing to see
individual persons as being other than unitary. Doubtless, Ellen
White's passion for Health Reform is the operative principle here:
body and soul constitute a monistic entity, so that the body thus is
guarded from devaluation of any kind whatsoever. This refreshing
repudiation of Christian dualism is mitigated unfortunately by the
key Adventist doctrine of the Investigative Judgment. Since 1844,
Jesus Christ has been at work blotting out sin, which turns out to
mean something very different from forgiving sin. Adventists part
from Southern Baptist Fundamentalists, for one instance, in that
repentance and forgiveness are hardly even provisional. You can
die utterly repentant, and apparently forgiven, and yet your bad
influence ongoing long after your death still can be held against
you. Salvation will come only when all sins are blotted out by
being placed by Christ upon poor Satan, the universal scapegoat,
after which Christ will descend again to earth, as it was hoped
initially he would have done on October 22, 1844.

I cannot think of another American doctrine, even among the
Jehovah's Witnesses, that assigns so crucial a role to Satan. Were
that malign spirit to be blotted out prematurely, then there could
be no salvation for Seventh-day Adventists. Ellen White's Jesus is
more a defense attorney for mankind than he is the bearer of the
Atonement. In a mad literalization of the rituals of Leviticus, the
necessity of the Christian Atonement vanishes. Satan, unwillingly
of course, takes upon himself the sins of the world, and so we are
given what in effect has to be called a Satanic Atonement. Perhaps
that is the final vengeance of those who suffered the Millerite Great
Disappointment of 1844. Ellen White's sturdy frustrations are at
last set aside at the expense of the ultimate scapegoat. Amiable as
Ellen White was, there is something dangerously unamiable about
this doctrine, and one need not be a Christian theologian to observe
that it is scarcely Christian. Pragmatically, the vicarious nature of
the Atonement has passed from Christ to Satan, with some rather
dark psychological consequences in Adventist believers. One can
cite the African-American novelist Richard Wright, who in his
eloquent autobiography, *Black Boy*, recalls his youthful dread of

a gospel clogged with images of vast lakes of eternal fire, of seas
vanishing, of valleys of dry bones, of the sun burning to ashes, of

the moon turning to blood . . . a salvation that teemed with fantastic beasts having multiple heads and horns and eyes and feet.

A Satanic scapegoating leads to horrid figurations of the end time, surpassed only by the ugly speculations of Jehovah's Witnesses. If you teach children that failure to keep the Seventh-day Sabbath will bring upon them the Mark of the Beast, then you are in danger of scapegoating children. Official Adventism now avoids this by asserting that only those who fail to keep the true Sabbath just before Christ's return will be lost, but this fine distinction frequently vanishes among Adventists. As a "remnant church," Adventism is subject to an outcast pride that not even its alliance with Fundamentalism has greatly altered, and which they share with Jehovah's Witnesses. Alas, the vision of the Last Things in Adventism is strikingly akin to that among the Witnesses, perhaps because of their common origins in Millerism. Like the ferocious Anabaptists of the sixteenth century, both Adventists and Witnesses hold that there is a "soul-sleep" after body and soul die together. Between death and resurrection, we are unconscious, and if we are not saved, then we will rise up only to be forever annihilated. There is considerably less lust for slaughter and sadistic delight in Adventist apocalypses than in Witnesses accounts, but the Health Reform aspect of Adventism seems rather difficult to reconcile with the still quite inhumane visions of the End by Ellen White and by her followers down to the present moment.

Bull and Lockhart dryly deprecate any such conclusions:

In the postwar world, the Second Coming has become more distant, and doctrinal modification has become necessary for believers whose expectation of translation is less vital than that of their forebears. (p. 90)

"Less vital" is indeed the crucial phrase in that sentence. Like the Mormons, though on a less grand scale, the Adventists of the older stock have achieved upper-middle-class respectability, but the faith described by Bull and Lockhart will dwindle away into a purely medical sect if such "doctrinal modification" goes much further. The essential paradox of the prophetic Ellen White cannot be resolved by any absorption into the Fundamentalist desert of middle-class morality. Either Adventism will return to her version of shamanism as a branch of the American Religion, or it will vanish from among us except as a vast medical legacy. It is the final irony of the Millerite remnant that it can survive, whether at home or abroad, only through the apocalyptic yearnings of Africans and Asians, whose zest and zeal are the last echo of Ellen White's patient and stubborn voice.

9

Jehovah's Witnesses: Against the American Religion

EVERY national faith is bound to call forth its antitype, and ours has produced its antithesis in the peculiarly stark phenomenon of the Jehovah's Witnesses. As a sect, they could have begun only in the United States, and indeed they represent the likely final upsurge of nineteenth-century American Adventism. The Millerite fiasco of 1843–44, when the world did not end, led to the Seventh-day Adventism of Ellen Harmon White, which we have seen as a positive version of the American Religion, despite its origins. But Jehovah's Witnesses, moving out of much the same source, was and remains an altogether different movement, violently dissenting from everything that is distinctively American, whether in government, religion, or economic matters. All these are assigned to Satan and are set aside, even as the Witnesses await the end of all things.

Jehovah's Witnesses take their start from Charles Taze Russell (1852–1916), who had gone through Presbyterianism and Congregationalism but found himself only when he encountered Adventist preaching. Convinced that the Second Coming would be spiritual rather than fleshly, Russell abandoned the Adventists and prophesied that a forty-year harvest period would go from 1874 through 1914, after which the gentile times would end. The world did not end in 1914, but World War I began, which saved the movement.

Russell, a fairly brazen impostor, nevertheless did not seek to tyrannize over his fellow Bible Students (as then they were called). At his death in 1916, the movement passed to its legal advisor, Joseph F. Rutherford, a sort of millenarian Tamerlane, who ruled it from 1917 through 1938. Today there are about three million Witnesses here and throughout the world, at the least, not counting almost as many peripheral adherents. Unlike the Mormons, the Seventh-day Adventists, and many Pentecostals and Fundamentalists, the Witnesses remain fiercely expectant of the imminent end time. With the year 2000 coming so soon, they are unlikely to lose their zest, despite their perpetual self-mystifications as to dating the Apocalypse.

The Jehovah of the Witnesses is a solitary majesty, rather than the first person of a Trinity; in contrast to him, Jesus is a god, but not God. And though Jehovah is the universal father, to us as to Jesus, he is not a particularly loving father. Power, not love, is his true attribute always. What this Jehovah seeks is supremacy, and a universal acknowledgment of his sway. The Jehovah of the Witnesses is remarkably like the Jehovah that the ancient Gnostics satirized and opposed, but where the Gnostics dissented, the Witnesses worship. What this Jehovah most wishes is his ultimate victory at Armageddon, in order to establish his name forever. The mission of Christ is not so much to redeem mankind as it is to help celebrate and vindicate the power of Jehovah. The power of Jehovah is the obsessive concern of the Witnesses. So intense is this exaltation of power in the Witnesses' writings that I must categorize it as pathological. By the criterion I have proposed for religious criticism, Jehovah's Witnesses is certainly the most dubious movement among our country's indigenous faiths. To find its irreducible spirituality is an agonizing quest. Mrs. Eddy's writings require translation to achieve coherence, but they offend only one's sense of reality. The writings of Russell and of Rutherford offend anyone's sense of human dignity, provided such a sense exists. They propose a theocratic Fascism that is not mitigated by assigning the dictatorship to a tyrant they call Jehovah.

Why then did Jehovah's Witnesses spring up in the United States? And why does it retain a distinctively American aura? This most extreme of all millenarian cults had to emerge from the most apocalyptic of nations, and our country continues to see itself as the world's redeemer. Fiercely unpatriotic, the Witnesses subtracted from American millenarianism only America. Ahlstrom gives the Witnesses as his prime example of what he calls "Radical Adventism." For the Witnesses the end time already has come, in 1975, when the six thousand years of human existence were completed, but so radical is their Adventism that they continue to abide in hope, though what they regard as hope most among us would call by another name. This is not to deprecate the belief in "the Rapture" of many American Fundamentalists, but rather to suggest that rapture for Jehovah's Witnesses is not necessarily going to be rapture for everyone else.

The intricacies of apocalyptic arithmetic are too ponderous for the wings of wit; one's mind sinks under them. Even if one were to expound this aspect of Jehovah's Witnesses, there would be inevitable misrepresentation, because the movement has not told one story and one story only about these matters. It is appropriate that the best book on the subject, by M. James Penton (1985), should be entitled *Apocalypse Delayed*. Most of us doubtless feel that a delayed Apocalypse is the best kind, but in the pure good of theory the Witnesses would not agree. The disappointments of the movement began with 1878, and have been regularly repeated up to the extraordinary disappointment of 1975. The coming change keeps coming, and the Witnesses are not exactly of the temperament of the proverbial rabbi who is at work planting a flower when told by an excited disciple that the Messiah has come. Being a sage, the rabbi finished planting the flower before going off to check the report. Jehovah's Witnesses are at the opposite extreme from the most Jewish of all writers, Franz Kafka:

The Messiah will come only when he is no longer necessary; he will come only on the day after his arrival; he will come, not on the last day, but on the very last.

Kafka goes on planting the flower; the Jehovah's Witnesses now believe that human existence ended in 1975. Once again, nothing in this book is meant to discredit even the most extravagant of American religious beliefs. The night before writing these pages (March 13, 1991), I walked into my kitchen in New Haven, idly switched on the television, and was bemused at breaking into a clerical discussion of the precise relation between the aftermath of the Persian Gulf War and the texts of Daniel and Revelation. The

Reverend Pat Robertson and guest clergymen were calibrating the fall of Babylon (Saddam Hussein) in terms of the sacred arithmetic. Many millions of Americans, of varied denominations, have been expecting Armageddon, and still are, in the shape of a Russian-Arab assault upon the state of Israel. A trust in Biblical inerrancy must have its consequences, and Jehovah's Witnesses remain only the most extreme wing of a mental habit that is prevalent among an enormous percentage of us. What makes the Jehovah's Witnesses different is not their expectation of destruction, but their violent hatred of what will be destroyed, which is to say: our country, our world, our common planet. The passion for destruction may be a creative passion, as the anarchist Bakunin insisted, but in the Witnesses it is not creative of anything. There are no positive elements in existence that the Witnesses seek to salvage; they wish to see all of us vanish, and as quickly as possible.

To consider Jehovah's Witnesses in the here-and-now necessarily has to be a somewhat painful intellectual experience. Anti-intellectualism among millenarians and Bible literalists is a recurrent phenomenon, but no other religious movement in America ever has been as programatically set against its intellect as are Jehovah's Witnesses. The Fundamentalist majority wing of the Southern Baptist Convention are devotees of pure reason compared to Jehovah's Witnesses. Disdain for the intellect or for knowledge from the perspective of Bible inerrancy is very different from a hatred of mind, a hatred that surpasses even the Witnesses' loathing for government, all other religion, and business. It may be that the most theocratic movement in America is bound to fear and hate intelligence. One could also surmise that the chagrin of perpetually delayed apocalyse turns the Witnesses against any rational apprehension of self-contradiction. But I suspect that the true origin of the aggressiveness and hostility of Jehovah's Witnesses is to be found in their preferred text, the Revelation of Saint John the Divine. The influence of Revelation always has been out of all proportion to its literary strength or spiritual value. Though it has affected the strongest poets, from Dante and Spenser through Milton on to Blake and Shelley, it also has enthralled the quacks and cranks of all ages down to the present moment in America. A lurid and inhumane work, very poorly composed in the original, the Apocalypse of St. John was rightly called one of the "nightmares of anxiety and triumph" by the late Northrop Frye. It *is* a nightmare of a book: without wisdom, goodness, kindness, or affection of any kind. D. H. Lawrence judged it pungently: "The Apocalypse does not worship power. It wants to murder the powerful, to seize power itself, the weakling." There, in my own judgment, is the heart of the aspiration of Jehovah's Witnesses. Like the book they study incessantly, they too wish to murder the powerful: in the churches, in government, in commerce. Their psychic need is what Lawrence associates with John of Patmos, archetype of all the pale priests of resentment. Intellectually weak, spiritually empty, Jehovah's Witnesses dreams of seizing power itself, so as to share in the majesty of the great Theocrat, Jehovah.

The principal doctrines of this most apocalyptic of religious movements are few and rudimentary, and cannot be said to constitute a theology, which after all demands thought and some effort to resolve self-contradictions. The central dogma, according to Penton in *Apocalypse Delayed* is that of the "faithful and discreet slave," who is always the reigning theocrat, the more-than-Pope of Jehovah's Witnesses. The President of the Watchtower Society, to give him his formal title, is the authorized interpreter of the Bible, which the individual Witness most certainly is not free to read for himself. Nor is the Witness free to inquire why the Rapture is continually postponed. Russell prophesied it first for 1878, then for 1881, then 1914. Rutherford named 1925 as the year, and from 1965 on the Society pointed toward 1975. No sublime year has since replaced 1975, and perhaps none will be ventured until we touch the year 2000. It is one of the functions of the faithful and discreet slave of Jehovah to hush these speculations, presumably until the powerful slave progresses further in revelation. A related crux, also not to be pondered except by authority, is the very identity of the faithful. Witness dogma brings together Matthew 24:45, where Jesus speaks of "the faithful and discreet slave whom his master appointed over his domestics to give them food at the proper time," and Revelation 7:4–8 and 14:1–3, where the redeemed Israel is counted as precisely 144,000 souls, or 12,000 from each of the twelve tribes. That might seem to allow for only 144,000 Jehovah's Witnesses, and so to exclude several million of the devout. Russell had identified his early followers as the nucleus of the 144,000 king-priests who would serve Jesus Christ throughout the millennium, while insisting that the great bulk of mankind would be resurrected into a restored earthly paradise. Later *Watch-*

tower seers had pointed to a third rabblement, the "great multi-tude" of Revelation 7:9, who would hold on also in a less glorious manner. These would be the "sheep" of Matthew 25:31–46, who would be separated out from the hopeless fourth rabblement or "goats." President Rutherford, in his most picturesque insight, found the foretype of the "sheep" in Jonadab the Rechabite, who assisted Jehu of Israel in his purge of Jezebel's Baalite priests (2 Kings 10:15). In 1935, Rutherford set in motion the still-ongoing missionary enterprise of the Witnesses by arguing that all the "great multitude," all the class of "sheep," were "Jonadabs" who will live forever in this world in return for obedience to the Watch-tower Society. Since Rutherford also proclaimed in 1935 that all of the sacred 144,000 had already been chosen, so that only a few "replacements" would be allowed for those who had fallen away, it would seem that most Jonadabs were relegated forever to a kind of secondary status. In *praxis*, however, the Witnesses have been very shrewd, and on a day-to-day basis it has become far better to be a Jonadab than one of the Elect. Until 1973, the movement's leaders were confident that the "remnant" of the Elect would shrink as Armageddon hovered closer. But from 1973 to 1975, so many new converts announced themselves as called to the Lord's Supper of the "anointed" Elect that manifestly there were more than the mys-tic 144,000 claiming that status! The society's pragmatic response has been plain nastiness exerted against any Witness, not yet in old age, who asserted election. A convert to the movement thus is welcomed graciously if she or he is a Jonadab, and well nigh ostra-cized if one of the Elect, however intense the mystical conviction may be.

It is Watchtower teaching that the selection of the Elect began at Pentecost, so most of the congregation have been selected, died, and from 1918 onward have been roused to heavenly life. Thus, only a remnant of "kingdom heirs," now just over 9,000 in number, are left among us today. The great crowd of Jonadabs are not actually part of Christ's New Covenant, and so have no mediator. Therefore they are not sanctified, thus justified by faith, and will be only after the advent of Armageddon has brought about the millennium of Christ's reign on earth. During that thousand years the faithful and fortunate Jonadabs will endure two major tests by Satan and his legions. If they pass, then they will be saved, thus justifying finally what might now be termed the pragmatic motto of Jehovah's Witnesses: "Don't pride yourself upon being one of the 144,000; be glad you are a Jonadab!" Since human existence ended anyway in 1975, we all are posthumous and to be a Jonadab is certainly a step up from being a kind of ghost.

Jonadabs, I venture, are to Jehovah's Witnesses what Malicious Animal Magnetism is to Christian Science: a superb contribution to American mythology, each quite as inventive as anything to be found in Herman Melville or in Thomas Pynchon. A brief chart of the Watchtower Society's current chronology is another substantial augmentation of the mythical imagination:

607 B.C.	Fall of Jerusalem and start of the "Times of the Gentiles"
455 B.C.	Decree to rebuild Jerusalem's walls and start of the 70 weeks of Daniel 9:24
A.D. 29	Baptism of Christ
A.D. 33	The death of Christ
A.D. 36	The end of the 70 weeks of Daniel
A.D. 1914	End of Times of the Gentiles and start of Time of the End
A.D. 1918	Christ's coming to his temple for judgment
A.D. 1919	Fall of Babylon the Great and birth of the New Nation of Jehovah's Witnesses
A.D. 1975	End of the 6,000 years of human existence

Daniel 9:24 is a proclamation by the Angel Gabriel, to the effect that seventy weeks will suffice to restore Jerusalem. In Witness lore, the seventy weeks extend from 455 B.C. through A.D. 36, which is four hundred and eighty-one years, a number not easily divisible by seven. But no one, including the major theocrats of the Watchtower Society, ever fully understands the Witnesses' chronology. Chronology has followed chronology, and will be followed by more. It is not the dates or even the patterns of chronology that seem to matter, but rather the idea of a chronology itself. Definite numbers are an amazing comfort to millenarians; they convey the illusions of power and of knowledge, and seem to provide a shield against reality. No other sect has so abounded in the mystical mathematics of the city of heaven, or has so gratified the American appetite for supposed fact. That there are no immutable dates, or even unchanging doctrines, does not seem to bother the majority

of Witnesses. There is something not unimaginative, even if a touch zany, about the movement's capacity for absorbing changes in doctrine. One might think that the resurrection of the dead would be a crucial enough event so that some clear expectation could be fostered, but no one would ever pass an examination question that said: "Give a historical account of Jehovah's Witnesses in regard to the resurrection of the dead." Russell held that the 144,000 Elect would be resurrected in heaven to immortality from 1878 on, a date now shifted to 1918. As for the great crowd of Jonadabs, Russell added that they would also be resurrected, but at a secondary time. Then, at last, everyone else would come back to life during the millennium, particularly the "ancient worthies" of the Old and New Testaments. But in the boisterous years of the American twenties, Rutherford had second thoughts, and began to resurrect the worthies even ahead of the saintly 144,000. In the mid-thirties, a darker time, Rutherford denied that even ancient men of faith, let alone dying sinners, would ever return. Only Saints and Jonadabs could live again. In 1950 a subsequent theocrat, Frederick Franz, in his broodings upon Armageddon decided that the pious of old could be resurrected once the great battle had been fought. When the 1960s brought on the counterculture, the movement reacted by giving preference to ancient sinners over contemporary ones. Those who died in Sodom would be resurrected, but all American clergymen were consigned forever to Gehenna.

The manifest permanence of Jehovah's Witnesses as a movement opens again one of this book's incessant concerns: what truths about America and Americans give rise to such extraordinary sects, and what is it that sustains, here and abroad, so inhumane a vision as that of Russell, Rutherford, and their heirs? The supreme fact about Jehovah's Witnesses is that it sets itself against the American Religion by laboring to widen immensely the distance between the heaven-dwelling Theocrat-of-theocrats Jehovah and his American subjects. The God of Joseph Smith and Brigham Young was an exalted man self-elevated into heaven, while Mrs. Eddy shared so deeply in the Divine Mind that she had but to read her own will in order to read God's. Southern Baptists experience a mystical solitude, alone in the garden with Jesus, while Pentecostals can be wholly seized by the descending Paraclete. Seventh-day Adventists, like Shakers before them, share in the ecstasies of women who bordered upon being female Christs, and nearly all American Fundamentalists have intimations of divinity through their experience of the Second Birth. Only the Witnesses dissent, and continue in the dreadfully modest hope that they may yet be regarded as faithful and discreet slaves of a Jehovah altogether intoxicated with his own majesty.

As a public, we think of the Witnesses with some embarrassment, since they seem to offend many of the justified norms of American society. Their refusal of patriotism offends primarily in wartime; in peace it seems not much more bothersome than their reputed denial of birthday celebrations, even to little children. Far more serious is their fierce stand against blood transfusions, since in the name of sanctifying life they so often pragmatically welcome death. Their primary rancor sets them against the State, the Church, the Marketplace, the University, and every other institution of our lives. If they did this in the name of some humanizing hope, some mitigation of the unkindness of our hearts, then we could see them as addled prophets, innocents of a literal reductionism. Alas, their critique of America is the weakest ever offered us. They would make us a nation of Jonadabs, of sanctified assassins cutting down the priests of Baal, for whom read Catholic priests, Protestant ministers, Jewish rabbis, and all sectarian teachers of spirituality. They are the good haters whom D. H. Lawrence feared, the lovers of Apocalypse for its own sake.

Yet what a superb imaginative achievement they would be if they were American fiction rather than American fact. Even our most apocalyptic writers could not have conceived Russell, Rutherford, and their followers. If the entire movement had been created in the writings of Herman Melville or Nathanael West or Thomas Pynchon, we would find no grander invention in those dark visionaries of our culture. Mark Twain was sincerely outraged by Mrs. Eddy's willed denial of the reality of death, yet on a repressed level she also may have outraged his inability to have created her, despite all his satiric gifts. What is humanly offensive about the doctrines of Jehovah's Witnesses in mere reality would be transformed utterly if they were edifying fictions. I will try out this formula by giving a plain paraphrase, as accurate as I can make it, of the Witnesses' accounts of their favorite event, the Battle of Armageddon. What the wretched Saddam Hussein failed to give us, the Mother of All Battles, is promised to us by the Witnesses.

Nathan Knorr, the reigning theocrat at the 1953 Assembly of Witnesses at Yankee Stadium, said that Armageddon would be the worst event ever in the history of man. The relish of that assertion is palpable, and I would venture that the most characteristic quality of Jehovah's Witnesses in general is their group relish in contemplating the Last Things. Let us begin to explicate this relish by first examining its prime textual source, Revelation 16:14–16, which tells us as little as possible about Armageddon:

> For they are the spirits of devils, working miracles, which go forth unto the kings of the earth and of the whole world, to gather them to the battle of that great day of God Almighty.
> Behold, I come as a thief. Blessed is he that watcheth, and keepeth his garments, lest he walk naked, and they see his shame.
> And he gathered them together into a place called in the Hebrew tongue Armageddon.

This slight foundation is the site for the Witnesses' elaborate mythology of Armageddon, which they see as Jehovah's crucial battle against everything, supernatural and natural, that opposes him. The most distinguished literary account of a roughly parallel combat is John Milton's vision of war in heaven in *Paradise Lost*. All that Milton and the fiercely anti-intellectual, anti-literary sectarians have in common is the role of Jesus Christ as commander of Jehovah's legions against Satan's. Armageddon, for the Witnesses, still has its curious link to World War I, since they see the first fighting between Christ and Satan as having taken place from 1914 through 1918. The second and decisive battle will be Armageddon (though even it will not be the last battle), and those slain in it will not be raised up again in the millennium. But the Witnesses—both Elect and Jonadabs—are promised they will not die at Armageddon. As for Armageddon itself, the conflict will not be between America and Russia, or America and Iraq, nor will it be a general, worldwide nuclear confrontation. Rather, *all* nations (since all are Satan's) will fight against the Witnesses everywhere, sometime soon but charmingly unspecified. In 1952, the Witnesses stated that it would be within a generation, and in 1958 they insisted that many alive in 1914 would still be alive at Armageddon. Since that was seventy-seven years ago (as I write) Armageddon cannot be much longer delayed.

Whenever, we will stand at Armageddon, which will be where you are, wherever you are. What will we see? If we are the Witnesses, or New Israel, we will be greatly outnumbered: a few thousand still here of the mystical 144,000 and a couple of million sheepish Jonadabs standing up to the United Nations, all the false religions of the world, and billions of goats, mostly human ones. But it does not matter that we are so few, because we will not fight anyway. Christ and invisible armies will fight for us, assisted by Jehovah's full arsenal: forest fires, floods, avalanches, earthquakes, hailstorms, great winds, and terrible plagues. Against this, Satan and the United Nations (including the American armed forces) will have only a poor if rather sublimely anachronistic blend of spears and hydrogen bombs, poison gas, and bows and arrows. But whether the goats are skewered or burned alive, well over two billion will be slain, including all intellectuals whatsoever.

Still, the survivors—saints and Jonadabs alike—will be given a grisly task in the aftermath of the slaughter. They must gather up the bones of all the dead, and then beat a few swords into ploughshares, for use in the millennium. As for Satan and his principal devils, they will survive the carnage, but they will be thrown by Christ into a convenient abyss, a place of nonbeing where they will abide passively until they are needed again to torment and test Jonadabs. In the restored earth of the millennium, no one will die anymore, and the Last Judgment will be based not upon anything good or bad done in this life, the here and now, but only upon what one does in the millennium. Satan's last battle will be his temptation of everyone at the end of the millennium. Those who follow him will be consigned by Jehovah to a great lake of burning sulfur, where they will be annihilated forever with Satan. But Jehovah's obedient ones will remain forever upon a perpetually paradisal earth. And so the story as told by the disciples of Russell and Rutherford comes to its close.

I have omitted a mass of details, but they do little to alter this pattern. What can most of us do with such a narrative? Lurid and cruel, it contrasts poorly with the apocalyptic elements in early Mormonism or even with the eschatological longings of Seventh-day Adventism. Though there are a number of rather savage apocalyptic scenarios current among American Fundamentalists, I am aware of none quite so inhumane as the Jehovah's Witnesses' accounts of the End of our Time. There is something peculiarly childish in these Watchtower yearnings: they remind me of why very small children cannot be left alone with wounded and suffering household pets.

10
Pentecostalism: Swaggart Slain in the Spirit

TONGUES on fire with strange words and stranger nonwords: this phenomenon is as old as Christianity, and, one suspects, even older. For nearly a century it has been an indigenous American sect, and now vies with the Southern Baptists and the Mormons as one of the three most vital ongoing movements in what I have chosen to call the American Religion. The spiritual power that moves the Assemblies of God, our largest grouping of Pentecostals, is hardly to be denied, whatever we take its origins to be. To attend a Pentecostal service, when the Spirit descends upon and among the congregation, is to hear and see the unloosing of authentic forces that seem to emerge from the recesses of being. An unbeliever sits and stands amidst a storm of ecstasy, and may be reminded of the great metaphor by which John Bunyan characterized the unbeliever: "He sleeps on the top of a mast." One sits, eyes half closed, like the protagonist of Elizabeth Bishop's "The Unbeliever," a grand variation on Bunyan, murmuring: "I must not fall." My one experience of a Hispanic Pentecostal service was a humbling and informative occasion.

The prophet Joel can be considered the precursor of Pentecost, in his extraordinary vision of "the latter rain":

Be glad then, ye children of Zion, and rejoice in the Lord your God: for he hath given you the former rain moderately, and he will cause to come down for you the rain, the former rain, and the latter rain in the first month.

. . . .

And it shall come to pass afterward, that I will pour out my spirit upon all flesh; and your sons and your daughters shall prophesy, your old men shall dream dreams, your young men shall see visions. (Joel 2:23, 28)

The apostle Peter, in the second chapter of Acts, quotes Joel's prophecy as the foretelling of the Descent of the Holy Ghost:

And when the day of Pentecost was fully come, they were all with one accord in one place.

And suddenly there came a sound from heaven as of a rushing mighty wind, and it filled all the house where they were sitting.

And there appeared unto them cloven tongues like as of fire, and it sat upon each of them.

And they were all filled with the Holy Ghost, and began to speak with other tongues, as the Spirit gave them utterance. (Acts 2:1–4)

Saint Paul remained true to his Pharisaic education by eloquently deprecating speaking with tongues in 1 Corinthians 14. One hears the pupil of the great rabbi Gamaliel when Paul reminds the Corinthians that "the spirits of the prophets are subject to the prophets." Unlike the descent of the Spirit at Pentecost in Acts 2, where the babbling seems both glossolalia (meaningless vocalizing) and xenoglossy (words and phrases of a real language one doesn't speak), what Paul describes is exclusively glossolalia. So far as I know, there are no verified reports, ancient or modern, of xenoglossy, and so Acts 2 would be unique in Christian tradition, unless indeed we misunderstand it. Paul was arguing against Corinthian Enthusiasts or Gnostics, and yet I wonder why his strictures have not discouraged American Pentecostals more than they seem to have done. The issue is scarcely theology; it is largely one of authority. Charismatic experience is privileged over every other aspect of Christianity by the Pentecostals. Though the Assemblies of God are not about to honor as founders the Montanist Enthusiasts of second-century Phrygia, they actually have far more in common with Montanus, Maximilla, and Prisca than they do with the apostolic author of Corinthians.

Though Pentecostals insist upon being the heirs of a continuous tradition, from the initial Pentecost until now, they are an almost purely American phenomenon, whose true ancestry begins at Cane Ridge. Mother Ann Lee's Shakers and the early Mormons spoke in tongues, but otherwise had nothing in common with our Pentecostalism. It seems odd to us now, but the Assemblies of God ultimately stems from the Methodists and from the Holiness movement that followed the celebration of the centennial of American Methodism in 1866. By the later 1870s, Holiness began to break away from the Methodist Church, both South and North, and by 1890 the movement essentially was a separate religion. The center of Holiness, and of Pentecostalism after it, remained a Wesleyan legacy transformed almost beyond recognition, the doctrine of Christian Perfection. John Wesley proclaimed that a perfect sanctification could come to all who were justified, and not just to an elect. A more Calvinist view, emanating from the British Keswick movement of the 1870s, severely modified this Wesleyan generosity, and resulted in the crucial Pentecostal notion of a third blessing or act of God's grace, a Baptism in the Holy Spirit, made evident by a speaking with tongues.

The twentieth century was ushered in on January 1, 1901, at Topeka, Kansas, where Charles Fox Parham led his Bible School of Holiness followers in an ecstatic celebration of Baptism in the Holy Ghost. Agnes Ozman, previously ignorant of Chinese, asserted that for three days following she spoke Chinese and wrote Chinese characters. This encouraged the rest of the group to emulate Miss Ozman in many other languages, to the background of white fire. Parham himself praised God in what he took to be Swedish, but the episode passed away, and little seemed to have come of it. But in Houston, in 1906, Parham recruited William Seymour, an African-American preacher, who carried the new vision out to Los Angeles. The San Francisco earthquake (April 18, 1906) stimulated religious sentiments throughout the nation, but particularly in Orphic California. At the Azusa mission in Los Angeles, William Seymour led his followers into a perpetual storm of Pentecost. By the autumn of 1906, the Azusa speaking with tongues had begun to spread around the nation, and thence around all the world. After a meeting in Hot Springs, Arkansas, in April 1914, the Pentecostals soon founded the Assemblies of God, the dominant white group in the rapidly segregating movement. African-American Pentecostalism has never ceased, and it remains an irony of the American Religion that the authentic founder of our Pentecostalism was William Seymour, who did what his teacher Parham could not do. The Assemblies of God, to the best of my knowledge, does not honor Seymour, but without him they would not exist.

Pentecostalism is the fifth of the American sects that clearly will survive as long as the nation does, but it has very little in common with Mormonism, Christian Science, Seventh-day Adventism, and Jehovah's Witnesses. In a sense, it has more in common with certain aspects of the Fundamentalist majority in the Southern Baptist Convention than it does with the indigenous sects. Like the Southern Baptists, the Pentecostals manifest an almost wholly experiential faith, but the Pentecostal mode of experience is far more restricted—one might even term it "specialized." Ecstasy has been routinized by the Pentecostals, who after all tend to be the insulted and injured, of whatever race or origin. Southern Baptists are the Established or Catholic Church of the American South and Southwest, but the Assemblies of God and the African-American and Hispanic Pentecostals hardly constitute any part of an establishment, in a national sense. The Southern Baptists are now best known to the rest of us because of their internal battles between Moderates and Fundamentalists, while the Assemblies of God are most notorious for Jimmy Swaggart and Jim and Tammy Bakker. Respectability in any case is hardly likely to descend upon Pentecostals. In a legitimate way, they do continue the ancient tradition of Enthusiasm, more in its Evangelical than in its Mystical mode, to resort again to Ronald Knox's distinction. Evangelical Enthusiasm, however routinized, is a wild phenomenon, aptly symbolized by the flames of Pentecost.

The best study of American Pentecostalism down to the Depression years is by Robert Mapes Anderson, who tellingly called it *Vision of the Disinherited* (1979). Anderson interprets Pentecostalism as socially serving the interests of the American establishment: "the Pentecostals have been ideal workers and citizens in every respect except for their cultivation of ecstasy" (p. 239). Doubtless, Anderson is right, but his observation would be as valid for nearly every organized faith in the United States. Pentecostal ecstasy dismisses social concerns by so acute a devaluation that no real parallel can be found among the adherents of other groupings, and yet Pentecostals are not necessarily the most right-wing among all American religionists. They are however perhaps the most spiritually extreme citizens of every nation where they are organized, an extremity that is the source of their peculiar power of attraction to the socially disinherited, to use Anderson's word. If you share in the force of the Holy Ghost, with your tongue on fire and miraculous healing breaking out upon every side of you, then you may well scorn every lesser manifestation of power. Pentecostals participate in miracle; nature, reason, and society are dwarfed by the apparent realities of Pentecostal worship. The charismatic, for the Assemblies of God, is not merely a function of the leadership. Every man and every woman is also his or her own charismatic. The ecstacy emerges from your own lips, and where there is Baptism in the Holy Spirit, then prophecy, healing, and miracle must be present as well.

What is American about Pentecostalism? The question may seem absurd, since ecstasy (of whatever sort) clearly must be a universal endowment. Again, if one rejects sociological and anthropological reductions of religion, as I do, any quest for national characteristics in spiritual matters is likely to be thwarted. But why should Pentecostalism have waited to spring up until the start of the twentieth century, and then locate itself in Topeka and Los Angeles? Mormonism and Southern Baptism are perhaps the most American of religions, as this book attempts to demonstrate, but I do not think that Pentecostalism comes far behind. There is something stubborn as well as violent in Pentecostal ecstasy, and something profoundly withdrawn, gone out and away from neighbors and the sun. The phenomena involved are overdetermined instances of possession, or of the will-to-be-possessed. By what? The Holy Spirit is one name for what shamans evoke by their very varied techniques of ecstasy. Pentecostalism is American shamanism, even though Jimmy Swaggart does not journey in trance to the underworld or to a northern paradise, and even though Jim Bakker cannot escape incarceration by transforming himself into a bird or practicing bilocation. The Pentecostal charismatics may or may not be sorcerers, but they share with shamans archaic and modern such stigmata as trances, spirit voices, healings through exorcism, manifestations of light or fire, and above all, visionary transport, or "prophecy" as the Assemblies of God phrase it. There are also clearly shamanistic elements in such Pentecostal activities as Jericho marching (while shouting out prayers and singing hymns), dancing in the Spirit (where the Spirit presumably takes over the body), and being "slain in the Spirit" (where one falls, generally backwards, while the congregation prays over one). Rather than adumbrate American qualities in all these ecstasies, I prefer to seek them at the true center of Pentecostalism: speaking with tongues and its relation to Baptism in the Spirit. At this center, the matter under discussion is *the experience of power*, and not really any particular degree of sanctification. As in Emerson, theologian of the American Religion (here again I follow Sydney Ahlstrom), ecstasy and power are intimately related. The experience of the Holy Spirit is one of influx, and the shock of the flowing-in is manifested by the glossolalia.

Let us return momentarily to Miss Agnes Ozman, who helped begin the twentieth century by speaking in tongues at Charles Fox Parham's Bible School in Kansas. Parham, and his Azusa Street disciple William Seymour, regarded glossolalia as evidence that Baptism in the Holy Spirit had taken place. The chanting in Chinese reported by Miss Ozman was therefore an authentic witness of the descent of the dove, the fiery advent of the Comforter. What the Assemblies of God term "the enduement of power for life and service" transfused itself into Agnes Ozman, even if she may have mistaken the identity of the foreign language upon her lips. Margaret M. Poloma, in her very thorough *The Assemblies of God at the Crossroads* (1989), reflects upon some of the vagaries of glossolalia. Though one in five Americans asserts she or he is a Pentecostal, only one in twenty-five dares to affirm that she or he has spoken in tongues. Perhaps a certain shyness is involved, or a kind of wistfulness, but the implication surely is that most people at a Pentecostal service content themselves with hearing the evidence of others, usually of their pastors. The Holy Spirit presumably has a particular preference for the Jimmy Swaggarts, the charismatics who are unashamed in their intensities.

Ecstasy, from Cane Ridge to the present, always has been the essence of the American Religion. How could it be otherwise? To know that one's own spirit is part of the Holy Spirit, existent before the foundation of the world, is an exhilarating experience.

To know also that one is completely free—the Emersonian Wild-ness—because one's solitude is shared with the Holy Spirit, carries the rapture to a Sublime elevation. And though Assemblies of God theology is officially Trinitarian, in *praxis* the Pentecostal knows only Oneness, and calls the Holy Spirit by the name of Jesus, not the Jesus of the Gospels or even the Christ of Paul, but the American Jesus, a Pentecostal like oneself. As the speaking with tongues proceeds, whether you overhear yourself or listen to your pastor, direct evidence of the Spirit's influx is vouchsafed to you. Mortality falls away, as when you are slain in the Spirit, for where the Spirit is, there can be nothing else. And what is the Holy Spirit to an American Pentecostal, if it is not the power to negate everything that is not the occult self, and the survival of that self. Here, in the belatedness of the Evening Land, surely the Holy Spirit has found its new home. Pentecostalism flourishes much more abroad than in the United States, because shamanism is more universally accepted in Asia, Africa, and Latin America than it is here. Yet Pentecostal-ism had to begin here, because its extreme supernaturalism had to be a reaction against a triumphant naturalism, against a society where power was enshrined in an abundant materialism. Scholars rightly emphasize that the inaugural wave of American Pentecos-talism was a reaction against the Gilded Age, while the second wave was part of the general charismatic upheaval of the 1960s. Without the blatant power of American material achievement, there would have been no stimulus for the antithetical intensity of Pentecostalism.

As the Assemblies of God has progressed into middle-class pros-perity, this earlier edge has vanished, and we have passed into the Age of Reagan and Bush, when the prominent Assemblies of God layman James Watt could serve as Reagan's apocalyptic Secretary of the Interior. The ineffable Watt opposed conservation because, as he explained to the nation, this world would pass away within a generation or two. Watt was a mere ripple compared to the public exposures of the two most celebrated Assemblies of God pastors, the marvelous Jimmy Swaggart (of whose televangelism I remain a sincere and ardent fan) and the less interesting Jim Bakker. Swag-gart, a superb performer, is the archetype of a Pentecostal preacher old-style, apparently possessed, and famously convinced of his di-rect relationship to the Holy Spirit. His articles in *The Evangelist* (published in Baton Rouge by The Voice of Jimmy Swaggart Min-

istries) lack the urgency of his effectively frenzied oral performances, but they possess obsessive force as they cry out against
"abortion, atheism, evolution, communism, liberalism, infanticide,
euthanasia, ERA, homosexuality, lesbianism, and perversion." Evidently Swaggart does not know the differences between these
eleven "sins," though presumably it was not "liberalism" he sought
in some of his wanderings. A passionate opponent of "psychology,
psychiatry, psychoanalysis" (not so much, for him, a triple-headed
beast, but evidently three words for the same evil), Swaggart suffered the fictive, indeed comic-book catastrophe of the biter bit.
His compulsive concern with the pornographic victimized the Pentecostal prophet, and culminated in the most extraordinary and
masterful of his television appearances, as he cried: "I have sinned!"
to enthralled onlookers, myself included. Swaggart, the first cousin
of Jerry Lee Lewis, is his kinsman's rival as a charismatic performer, despite the evangelist's disapproval of the rock star. One
could suggest that Swaggart's genius resides in his adversary
stance, an aggressivity so intense that it led him to destroy his
Assemblies of God colleagues, Jim Bakker and Marvin Gorman.
Though repudiated (for a time) by the Assemblies of God, Swaggart goes on more strongly than ever, and I try never to miss one
of his telecasts. Without irony, it should be observed that Swaggart, whatever his greeds and failings, is the pure product of the
Pentecostal tradition. Bakker, with his new style gospel of domestic
love, was banal in comparison. As Americans, we are compelled to
judge Pentecostalism and the Assemblies of God as being incarnated in Jimmy Swaggart. He is as authentic a national image as
Billy Graham, and reflects something in all of us, even as Graham
does. Swaggart's doom-eagerness catches up the essence of Pentecostalism as American popular religion; his extreme and open emotions are an equivalent to the rattlesnake handling and "salvation
cocktail" (strychnine) drinking of Holy Ghost cultists in Appala-
chia. I cite a vivid passage from *Popular Religion in America* by Peter
W. Williams (1980):

On one level, these practices can be seen simply as an extremely
literal interpretation of Mark 16:17–18, which promises that the
followers of Jesus shall cast out demons, speak in new tongues,
and not be harmed by taking up serpents or drinking deadly

things. This does not resolve the question as to why this, as opposed to numerous other passages in Scripture which raise rather serious problems when taken at face value, should have been chosen for literal adherence. One suggestion is offered by Wayne Elzey, who argues that such practices involve a symbolism of inversion. Where such practices as drinking, gambling, and non-marital sexuality fall under a taboo in daily life, structurally similar practices become positively sacred when performed in a sacred context. Thus intoxication and sexual ecstasy, though forbidden in secular life, are signs of possession by the Spirit when they seize the participant at a Pentecostal worship service. Similarly, gambling—in this case with one's life, by playing with rattlesnakes, poison, or fire—takes on a similar "positive charge" when performed in a sacred manner. (p. 145)

Elzey and Williams both were writing long before the public ordeal of Jimmy Swaggart, but they state the dialectic of his descent and his recovery. Visiting a prostitute was Swaggart's equivalent of the Holy Ghost cultist passing a lighted blowtorch over hands or face. We are in the pattern that Gershom Scholem, meditating upon such Kabbalistic figures as Nathan of Gaza and Jacob Frank, named "Redemption through Sin." Swaggart's genius was to convert his falling forward on his face, as it were, into being slain in the Spirit, thus falling back into the arms of the congregation, his television viewers. Pentecostalism, as Williams rightly indicates, moves onto shamanistic ground when many in the congregation dance and sing in the Spirit, in an ecstasy scarcely distinguishable from sexual transport.

Of all versions of the American Religion, Pentecostalism is experientially the most daring, in trespassing upon so many taboos. It is said that certain Pentecostals even attempt to raise the dead, which is only a kind of ultimate faith healing. The pure version of an American shamanism, Pentecostalism breaks through every snare devised by the supposedly rational structure of our society. Jimmy Swaggart, whatever his limitations, moves across the television screen with the charismatic energy of the ultimate American shaman, protesting our bindings and unbindings. I recall the marvelous acting of Burt Lancaster as Elmer Gantry in the film version of Sinclair Lewis's novel. As Gantry, Lancaster moved with the restless, displaced sexual energy of the holy Swaggart, furious to manifest his doom-eagerness, his playing with serpents and with the audience's repressions and hungerings.

There are no interpretive fictions that will encompass American Pentecostalism, even as it is a movement too large and urgent to be adequately held in any American narrative fiction to date. Americans never will stop questing for the Primitive Church, in itself a remarkable American interpretive fiction. We will have Pentecostals among us until the end of time, or until the end of the republic. On a much higher register, our American poetry is a kind of Pentecostalism, a speaking with tongues, from Walt Whitman to the present day. The same impulse that drove Parham, and that holds together the Assemblies of God, has governed much of American spirituality, from Cane Ridge through Woodstock. It is a very long span from the disciplined Hermeticism of our father Walt Whitman (as James Wright called him) to the croonings, fierce whisperings, clamorous shouts, and mystical weeping of Jimmy Swaggart, but the two extremes share a curious affirmation of self that aspires only to dissolve into a communal ecstasy. Freedom is solitude for the American Religionist, alone with the Spirit, but alone in a way that points to our shamanistic tendency to merge into one another. Pentecostalism affirms the American sense of the primal abyss, the fullness that preceded creation. In resisting the apparent Dionysiac qualities of a Pentecostal service, the American actually resists being reminded of her and his own two deepest and most Orphic convictions: that she and he ultimately are older and higher than the Creation, and that they also know freedom only when they are sublimely solitary, alone with the Holy Spirit.

11

The New Age:
California Orphism

CALIFORNIA, for most of this century, has been our new Burned-over District, replacing the western reserve of New York State, which was the religious hothouse of the nineteenth century. Though the New Age cults have no more than about thirty thousand members, their fellow travelers are an untold multitude. Virtually all our bookstores feature a New Age section, ranging from Shirley MacLaine recalling her previous incarnations to the memoirs of prehistoric warriors, Schwarzkopfs of 35,000 years ago. Networking in our America, these days, takes place either among the politically correct academics of the high camp of Resentment, or among the dank cranks of the belated Aquarian Conspiracy, trying to float our planet off into cosmic consciousness.

Religious criticism cannot be applied to Scientology, or to the Moonie Unification Church, any more than literary criticism can find its texts-for-discussion in Alice Walker or in Danielle Steel. The New Age is a borderline case, like Allen Ginsberg or John Updike. The warlocks and the mediums of California Orphism aren't exactly Emanuel Swedenborg or even Madame Helena Petrovna Blavatsky, of whom W. B. Yeats sublimely remarked: "Of course she gets up spurious miracles, but what *is* a woman of genius to do in the nineteenth century!" The spurious miracles of the New

Age are the comic outreaches of the American Religion, and might yield a few amiable insights to a properly disinterested religious criticism. The way not to criticize the New Age is simply to denounce it, which is the practice of Christian apologists such as Kerry D. McRoberts in his *New Age or Old Lie* (1989), an Evangelical ferocity of a treatise:

> Concerns by some Christian writers that an ominous system, like the New Age, could usher in the reign of Antichrist are valid, yet they are easily sensationalized. The biblical record clearly illustrates that we live in a theistic universe, not one left to the conscious, random reordering on a world-wide scale by diabolical co-conspirators independent of God's foreordained "plan."

Easily sensationalized? Hardly, since New Age fantasies are beyond further sensationalizing. Their ultimate American ancestor is Emerson, who would have had grand entertainment from them, and yet Emerson hardly would have rejoiced in his varied progeny. To have given us Walt Whitman and Wallace Stevens is one kind of achievement; to have helped foster Norman Vincent Peale and the wild apostles of Harmonial religion is quite another. Sydney Ahlstrom's definition of Harmonial religion is now classic:

> Harmonial religion encompasses those forms of piety and belief in which spiritual composure, physical health, and even economic well-being are understood to flow from a person's rapport with the cosmos. Human beatitude and immortality are believed to depend to a great degree on one's being "in tune with the infinite."

That last phrase is the title of Ralph Waldo Trine's book of 1897, which preached a universal religion in which God and man were seen as differing only in degree, not in essence. Hailing his namesake Emerson as prophet of the new Harmonial era, Trine set the pattern for a long procession of similar diffusers of the sage of Concord. The late President Bart Giamatti of Yale (later baseball commissioner) accurately remarked to me once that the actual Emerson was "as sweet as barbed wire," a truth lost upon the Harmonials.

Health and Harmony worthies, after Trine, memorably included Emmet Fox, Norman Vincent Peale, Anne Morrow Lindbergh, Thomas Merton, and all of our current New Age prophets, seers, and shamans. These are legion, yet are surprisingly homogenous, despite their descent from such varied ancestors as Swedenborg, Madame Blavatsky, and the Jesuit scientist Pierre Teilhard de Chardin. The American 1960s doubtless originated the ferment out of which the New Age emanated, but the movement essentially was revived in the California of the later 1970s and may have achieved its greatest prominence throughout the 1980s. Its most enthusiastic (and uncritical) chronicler remains Marilyn Ferguson, who celebrated its promise in *The Aquarian Conspiracy* (1980). Her catalog of gurus began with Teilhard de Chardin, Jung, Aldous Huxley, and J. Krishnamurti, and then went on to include a remarkable mingling (among others) of Tillich, Buber, Gregory Bateson, assorted Swamis, Marshall McLuhan, Buckminster Fuller, and even Werner Erhard. California, she declared, was the "Laboratory for Transformation," and the inevitable location for sparking a return to "the God within." We are well within the belated repetition of what I have called American Orphism when we contemplate California Orphism.

Having read his way through Mrs. Eddy, Mrs. White, and the Book of Mormon, the religious critic encounters his inevitable defeat in the pages of Matthew Fox, David Spangler, David Toolan, Chogyam Trungpa, and the other major New Age authors. One reads the same passages over again, worried that one has missed the point, only to discover that points belong to the wrong mindset. Here, absolutely at random, is Trungpa:

> Sometimes if your clothes fit you well, you feel that they are too tight. If you dress up, you may feel constricted by wearing a necktie or a suit or a tight fitting skirt or dress. The idea of invoking internal drala is not to give in to the allure of casualness. The occasional irritation coming from your neck, the crotch of your pants, or your waist is usually a good sign. It means that your clothes fit you well, but your neurosis doesn't fit your clothes. (*Shambhala, the Sacred Path of the Warrior* [1984], p. 85)

We are told (p. 79) that drala is "the living magic of reality," but the definition does not aid me in the difficult act of interpreting whether or not looser garments will bring me nearer to such living magic. New Age prose is its own genre, and the wonder of the New Age, at its advent, will be how the newagers will manage to read their own edifying discourses. Rather than pursue the pith of their doctrine in particular authorities, I will summarize the burden of what my doughty efforts have contrived to dredge up, so far. Somewhere in the background of the New Age is the lucid and beautiful anthology edited by Aldous Huxley, *The Perennial Philosophy* (1945). Huxley's spiritual authorities were the great seers and mystics of the ages, among them William Law, Thomas Traherne, the Bhagavad Gita, Meister Eckhart, and Saint Augustine. In the contemplative brilliance of Huxley's own prose as frame, the profundities of Law and Eckhart acquired fresh reverberation. By recourse to Huxley, you can sometimes construe a New Age passage and hazard some guess as to more or less what some California sage hoped she or he might mean. Otherwise, the student of the New Age must be resigned to that proverbial picnic, to which the authors bring the words (or some of them, anyway) and the readers bring the meanings.

Elevated consciousness would appear to be the common goal of all New Age Enthusiasts, including Ms. Shirley MacLaine, certainly the handsomest of the movement's public figures. Monistic ecologists of the spirit, they proclaim that now is the acceptable time for a great leap forward in paradigms, despite one's gloomy sense that the era belongs to Reagan, Bush, and similar anchors of the Old Age. If one must have apocalyptics, far better that they should be of the California Orphic variety than our multitude of Fundamentalist literalizers of the Revelation of St. John the Divine and the Book of Daniel. Californian apocalypses are by no means all benign: any reader of Nathanael West's *The Day of the Locust* can recall the fury that descends there on Los Angeles, and can wonder how ominous a prophecy it may prove to be. But New Age apocalypse is humane, indeed even sentimental. Our planet is not about to float off into a cosmic greenpeace, but at least it is heartening that the New Age Orphics dream of so amiable a conclusion.

God, for the New Age, is rather too purged of the anthropomorphic for my taste, and I assume that the Theosophical legacy is responsible for so otherwise uncharacteristic a Californian dehumanization of God. A God immanent both in outward nature and in consciousness evades the intervening space of incarnation. Christianity therefore is mostly irrelevant to the New Age, except inso-

far as Christianity already has been modified into the American
Religion, of which the New Age is sometimes a charming parody.
One might say that the New Age is to the American Religion what
Oscar Wilde's *The Importance of Being Earnest* is to Shakespearean
drama: a great shadow's last embellishment. The Mormon aspiration of mounting to godhood, or the Southern Baptist experience
of an uncreated self within one, is replaced by the entertainment
of the notion that one's own consciousness is God. And the Mormon ambition of populating a planet only with one's own family,
or the Southern Baptist passion for being alone with Jesus, is taken
to the lunatic apotheosis that one's very own spirit guide is built
into the ecology of one's own mind. American Gnosticism and
American Enthusiasm are splendidly parodied by California Orphism, by a metamorphic glamour that dissolves the last empiric
constraints which the universe of death exercises against our drive
for spirituality.

Aldous Huxley, in his introduction to *The Perennial Philosophy*,
gave a warning that New Age Enthusiasts, like everyone else, will
receive nothing for nothing:

> The Perennial Philosophy is primarily concerned with the one,
> divine Reality substantial to the manifold world of things and
> lives and minds. But the nature of this one Reality is such that it
> cannot be directly and immediately apprehended except by those
> who have chosen to fulfill certain conditions, making themselves
> loving, pure in heart, and poor in spirit.

California Orphism, skipping over Huxley's monitory remark,
apprehends Reality directly and immediately, at no inner expense
whatsoever. Marilyn Ferguson, in the accents of a benign con-
sumerism, excitedly assured her Aquarian conspirators that even
death had surrendered to their aspirations:

> A number of those filling out the Aquarian Conspiracy question-
> naire commented that their experiences had forced them to give
> up their previous assumption that bodily death ends conscious-
> ness. Despite their disaffiliation with formal religion, 53 percent
> expressed strong belief in such survival and another 23 percent
> said they were "moderately sure," a total of 75 percent. Only 5
> percent were skeptical and 3 percent disbelieving. (pp. 383–84)

What the God of California shares with the God of the American Religion, and indeed of Christianity, is that he is the Reality you set against the Freudian reality principle, the necessity of dying, of really dying, once and for all. The Californian God differs in that he is a kind of public orange grove, where you can pick as and when you want, particularly since he is an orange grove within. His perpetual and universal immanence makes it difficult for a newager to distinguish between God and any experience whatsoever, but then why should such a distinction occur to a California Orphic? Matthew Fox, ostensibly a Catholic priest, has formulated a curious doctrine of "panentheism" to avoid this collapse into pantheism, but Fox is one of my defeats. Several attempts on my part to read through *The Coming of the Cosmic Christ* (1988) have failed, as no prose I have ever encountered can match Fox's in a blissful vacuity, where all things flow to all, as rivers to the sea.

The absolute immanence of the New Age God is, I suppose, the inescapable poem of California's climate, the cosmos as one grand orange, consciousness as its juice. "The sacramental consciousness of panentheism develops into a transparent and diaphanous consciousness wherein we can see events and beings as divine." If one substituted "oranges" for "divine" as the final word in that Foxian sentence, after substituting "juice" for the two appearances of "consciousness," then mere understanding might be advanced:

> The sacramental juice of panentheism develops into a transparent and diaphanous juice wherein we can see events and beings as oranges.

To render justice unto Fox and most followers of the New Age, he and they hedge the obsessive immanence of God with a touch of transcendence. There is thus a heavenly or archetypal orange somewhere, as well as the enveloping cosmic orange. But this difference makes so little difference, on a daily basis, as not to survive the pragmatic test. Fox has a nostalgia for the Church's sacraments but he, like all newagers, doesn't really need them.

The perfect concentrate of consciousness is the Grail for which the New Age quests, a Grail it rather surprisingly identifies with near-death experiences, which now constitute a considerable American growth industry. Here again I must mutter my defeat, since I cannot understand how any near-death experience whatsoever can give evidence of the survival of consciousness *after* death. Carol Zaleski's very useful *Otherworld Journeys: Accounts of Near-Death Experience in Medieval and Modern Times* (1987) notes the rise of IANDS (International Association of Near-Death Studies). IANDS has become a marvelous amalgam of near-death research with New Age ideology, complete with "maroon T-shirts, and a logo that combines the tunnel image with the Taoist yin-yang symbol," as well as a quarterly newsletter hopefully entitled *Vital Signs*. As Zaleski shows, this is nothing new, but was inaugurated as early as 1903 by the British psychic researcher F. W. H. Myers, himself a crucial influence upon my favorite modern literary critic, the late G. Wilson Knight. Still, the modern phase of near-death jamboree begins only with Raymond Moody's relatively careful *Life after Life* (1975), a threshold work that does not cross over into New Age exuberance. That achievement belongs to Kenneth Ring, a Moody disciple who made the great leap and oranged himself:

Near-death experiences collectively represent an evolutionary thrust toward higher consciousness for humanity as a whole. . . . People who have had near-death experiences, as well as many other people whose lives have been transformed by one or more deep spiritual experiences, all these people as a totality represent in effect a more highly advanced human being. . . . To my thinking, the emergence of this new strain of human being . . . on the planet now, signals a possibility that the dawning of the New Age is indeed upon us. (quoted in Zaleski, pp. 107–8)

Zaleski's own restrained conclusions are altogether different:

At this stage I see no justification for treating contemporary near-death testimony as the foundation for a new eschatology or religious movement. Near-death literature is at its best when it is modest and anecdotal; pressed into service as philosophy or prophecy, it sounds insipid. (p. 204)

But apostles of the New Age ignore such a warning, and rely not only upon Moody and Ring but also upon Elisabeth Kübler-Ross, author of *On Death and Dying* (1969, 1975) and its companion works. Kübler-Ross, by whatever means, has comforted both the dying and their survivors, while assuring all of us that there is no such thing as death, and also that dying is in itself rather a good thing. It is hardly a limitation of the New Age that so much of its appeal is founded upon thanatology. Christianity, after all, stakes everything upon the Resurrection; if Jesus Christ did not rise from the dead, in defiance of nature, then all of Christianity is simply an imposture. The American Religion, as I have argued throughout, is ultrasupernaturalistic, and its varieties demand even more violent miracles than are afforded by institutional and historical Christianity. Extravagant as the New Age is, it is only the most garish of all the American originals that have expressed our national spiritual exuberance.

IV

THE
SOUTHERN BAPTIST
CONVENTION

12

Baptists: From Roger Williams to E. Y. Mullins

A nation as religiously fragmented as the United States will not yield very readily to any predictions (however informed) as to its denominational future. Our vastly increasing Hispanic population, now divided between a waning Roman Catholicism and a ferociously vigorous Pentecostalism, doubtless will become more diverse in spiritual orientation as it gains in economic and political power. Our crucial Asian-American communities, who will provide much if not most of the next generation of advanced intellectuals and leaders in the professions, are all but impossible to foretell, in the area of religious concern. What seems certain, to me, is that my two principal paradigms of the American Religion —the Southern Baptists and the Mormons—will be at the center of what is to come, since more than any other groups they are imbued with the ambivalent vitalism of our national faith.

As I write these pages (in late September 1990), the Southern Baptists clearly are moving towards a vast fragmentation, perhaps indeed a decisive split, between their Fundamentalist majority and their strong Moderate minority. With two very much opposed varieties of Southern Baptists added to two Northern and Canadian Baptist groups, and to the numerous African-American Baptists, we will have five separate kinds of Baptists. Taken all together, the

Baptists are the largest of all our Protestant faiths, and the most experiential in their religious approach. It is difficult for them to know precisely what it is that they believe, and immensely difficult for outsiders to comprehend. But if the argument of this book has any validity, then the Baptists can be illuminated, in their strength and in their decisive dilemmas, by an understanding that theirs indeed is what I call the American Religion, and not European Protestantism or historical Christianity.

The Southern Baptist Convention was born in 1845; a century and a half later, it might almost be called the Southern American Religion, even as Mormonism may yet be named as the Western American Religion. Far more than the Methodists or the Presbyterians, the Southern Baptists have become very nearly the Established Church of the old Confederacy. This gives their spiritual stance a curious aura, one of cultural survival in the face of military and political defeat. But that aspect of the Southern Baptist Convention cannot be part of my subject here. Without some sense of Baptist history however, I also cannot take this analysis of the peculiar religious dilemmas of Southern Baptists very far, and so I need to give a very rough sketch of American Baptist history, tracing the apparently arbitrary rise of what has been called the Catholic Church of the Confederate states.

This history begins in self-contradiction, since its point of origin is the extraordinary figure of Roger Williams, who most certainly is *not* accepted by Southern Baptists as a founding father, or even as a forerunner. One of the many peculiarities of the Baptists (Southern ones in particular) is that they had no Luther or Calvin, no George Fox or John Wesley, no great original at their beginnings. And yet, though they do not honor Roger Williams, he illuminates much that is strongest in their ethos. Presumably any Southern Baptist, whether Fundamentalist or Moderate, would feel the sensation of recognition when encountering the historian Edmund S. Morgan's summation of Williams's stance on the business of government:

But if government could do nothing with its whips and scourges and prisons to make men Christian, Williams did not deny it all opportunity to advance Christ's kingdom. There was one thing government could do, though few governments had ever done it: government could protect the free exercise of conscience in religion.

As early as 1638, Williams had rejected the validity of his baptism, yet he remained always a Puritan, and like John Milton he ended as a sect of one. There is a famous letter to George Fox from Richard Scott, who had been a member of Williams's church in Providence, sometimes described as our very first Baptist church. Scott, himself to become a Quaker, evokes a figure who would not be a member of any group that would have him as a member:

I walked with him in the Baptists' way about three or four months, in which time he brake from the society, and declared at large the ground and reasons of it; that their baptism could not be right because it was not administered by an apostle. After that he set upon a way of seeking (with two or three of them that had dissented with him) by way of preaching and praying; and there he continued a year or two, till two of the three left him.

If there is any trace at all of this formidable individual left in the Southern Baptists, it has to be his genius for schism. The Baptist tradition in America, for all its fiery intensities, has as little to do with Roger Williams as with the German Anabaptists of the sixteenth century, whose lurid chronicle frightens contemporary Southern Baptists. American Baptists descend from two rival sects of Inner Light English Puritans of the early seventeenth century: General Baptists, who believed that everyone in general could be redeemed, and Particular Baptists, who held on to the Calvinist convictions that only those elected in particular would be saved. What the two groups had in common amounted to little more than the rejection of infant baptism. But in 1801, the year of the Cane Ridge Revival, which was decisive for Baptist history in America, the two sects combined on the basis of a creedal declaration that blurred the issue of general or particular salvation. This uncertain fusion helped in the enormous expansion of the Baptists, who offered the frontier what was already an experiential religion, stressing the peculiar importance of an individual's turning to Jesus. Sydney Ahlstrom adroitly stated the Baptist advantage over rival

Methodists and Presbyterians, who disputed the frontier with them:

> Baptists did not exceed Presbyterians in zeal, but they were un-
> hindered by the bottlenecks to evangelistic work created by strict
> educational requirements and a rigid presbyterial polity. The ge-
> nius of Baptist evangelism was also at the opposite pole from the
> Methodist insistence on order and authority. Its frontier hero was
> not the circuit rider but the farmer-preacher, who moved with
> the people into new areas. (p. 323)

Ahlstrom's judgment was based upon, and supported by, W. W. Sweet's remarkable compendium of source materials, *Religion on the American Frontier: The Baptists*, *1783–1830* (1932). Sweet's collection of documents shows how difficult it was for Baptists to institutionalize their essentially experiential faith, even just before Cane Ridge. The minutes of their meetings regularly speak of accepting new members on the evidence of "a relation of their experience," with their auditors judging the authenticity of the accounts, presumably by comparing these to memories of their own conversionary experiences. The followers of the Campbells and of Barton Stone merely confessed Jesus as their savior, without needing to personalize the confessions. In the same way, Baptist sinners would be readmitted to membership on their own testimony in regard to repenting of fighting, gambling, sexual misconduct, swearing, "immoral dancing," and Masonic activities.

Working forward in time, it is almost impossible to tell just when Baptists had evolved into what they became in the days of E. Y. Mullins. Looking backward in Sweet's documents, you can trace a cumulative process towards the creedless faith of Baptists. This is highlighted by the opposition to missions on the part of so many early nineteenth-century American Baptists. Though an aversion to Indians had an effect upon these frontier people, the dominant element in their dislike of missions was their distrust of preachers specifically trained for such evangelism. The Baptists of Kentucky would not believe that a missionary ought to be anyone but a man called from within. Only Jesus called you to call others to him, and charisma is not to be hired, or taught. There was and is something profound in Baptist sensibility that doubts whether the experience of conversion can be communicated at all. If it could pass by contagion, then one person could have the experience for another, and so would cease to be alone with Jesus. Mystical Baptists, illuminated by the inner light of the Lord's candle, tended to be skeptical of evangelicism. I find in this the seeds, however remote, of what the Southern Baptist Convention now calls the Controversy, the struggle between Moderates and Fundamentalists. But these seeds grew crookedly in the furrow, and the anti-intellectualism inherent in that crusade against missions eventually became the almost lunatic resentment of mind in the currently dominant Fundamentalists of the Southern Baptist Convention. The mystical inwardness went one way, the fear of learning the other, but that will be a later story.

It is a leap forward from the antimission agitation of the early decades of nineteenth-century Baptist religion in the South, to the actual rise of Southern Baptism as the Established Church of the Old South, and then of the Confederacy and Reconstruction and on into our own day. I am pretty well convinced, as I have intimated earlier, that Mormonism will become the dominant religion of the entire American West, a process that is already well under way. The Southern Baptist Convention is already the prevailing faith of the South and Southwest. These experiential beliefs are antithetical to one another; they are rival American Gnosticisms, and may well dispute the spiritual future of our nation. There is a shadow upon both religions, which each has attempted to eliminate. African-Americans are not numerous among the Mormons, but technically they are now welcome. So long and vexed is the Southern Baptist relation, first to slavery and then to the immense struggle for African-American rights, that I must evade any true sketch of it here. It is a dismal record, though not of course unique among the Christian churches of the United States. But there are unique elements in it, and those must be at least noted here, since out of the myth of the Lost Cause come some of the most enigmatic qualities of Southern Baptist beliefs, Fundamentalist and Moderate alike. The Fundamentalist desperation to reject nearly all of Western intellectual history in favor of an inerrant icon, the limp leather Bible as object, hardly even as Scripture to be read and understood, has in it a deep resentment against a great betrayal by history, the death of an independent Southern nation in 1865. Much more subtly, the inward turn of the Moderates, a Gnostic knowing of Jesus through direct acquaintance, is also a culminating reaction to

God's failure to have performed a saving act in history, the rescue of God's people from catastrophic defeat. Of the three authentic American chosen peoples—Mormons, Southern Baptists, African-Americans of several denominations—it is the Southern Baptists who sustained total defeat. More even than Southern Presbyterians and Southern Methodists, the Baptists provided the great mass of Confederate enlisted men. Their great defeat reverberates still, and helped unite them for more than a hundred years in the highly uneasy conglomerate of the Southern Baptist Convention, now at last coming apart. A coalition formed in 1845 is nearly shattered in 1991, and will be two separate organizations soon enough.

Southern Baptists have their own peculiar myths, and one is that the formation of their Convention in 1845 was only secondarily a defense of slavery. This, to a non-Southerner, seems a baffling untruth, palpably in contradiction of realities, and yet Moderates and Fundamentalists alike insist that they were formed as a missionary denomination. Yet the first president of the Convention, explaining the group's rejection of their Northern former co-religionists, bluntly stated that "these brethren, thus acted upon a sentiment they have failed to prove—that slavery is, in all circumstances, sinful." Slavery, in their own circumstances, did not seem sinful, even though the original Baptists of the South were rarely the large-scale slaveowners. The wealthy, landed, slaveowning class was composed mostly of Episcopalians at first, but by 1845 the upwardly mobile, industrious Baptists increasingly possessed slaves. Compounding their defense of the institution was an augmented sense of being the only true Christians, a conviction that stemmed from the very odd Landmark movement, or controversy, as it is sometimes called. This took its name from Proverbs 22:28, rather extravagantly interpreted as being an unbroken tradition stretching from John the Baptist and the primitive Christian Church, supposedly of Jerusalem, and then going on through various Gnostics and Enthusiasts to culminate in the continental Anabaptists. This is a considerable fiction for one amiable proverb to have sustained: "Remove not the ancient landmark, which thy fathers have set." J. R. Graves, who became editor of the *Tennessee Baptist* in 1848, at the age of twenty-eight, proclaimed that Baptists were at once wholly autonomous in their individual churches, but also the only authentic dwellers in the Kingdom of God, and the legitimate descendants of the ancient Christian tradition. Pragmatically, Graves was the precursor of the rightist Texans who now exercise Fundamentalist control of the Southern Baptist Convention, because he inverted the Inner Light doctrine of the spirit's autonomy. Each local church, in Graves's view, had the authority to dictate belief to its own members. Landmarkism, which was still strong after the Civil War, left a legacy of dogmatism and triumphalism highly inimical to Baptist soul liberty, a legacy taken up by today's Fundamentalists.

The crushing of the Confederacy by superior force led to a trauma in the Southern Baptist spirit, evidently a more severe aftershock than the other Southern denominations experienced. Precisely why this should have been so is rather a mystery, and I have found no persuasive explanation for it. But I would hazard again the suggestion that Baptists were unique in having no founder, no overwhelming visionary and leader in their past. The Southern Presbyterians had Calvin, the Southern Methodists had Wesley, but the Southern Baptists had found their heroic figures in the great generals of the Confederacy, in Stonewall Jackson and Robert E. Lee, neither of whom were Baptists but both of whom assumed a kind of angelic status. A vehement nostalgia was combined with a rejection of subsequent history, so that nearly every new idea of the last third of the nineteenth century came to be rejected by Southern Baptists, with the unhappy consequence that no other American denomination entered the twentieth century with so pervasive an investment in anti-intellectualism. That investment has overdetermined the nature of the Fundamentalists in the Southern Baptist Convention, and has led to the current, more-than-justified despair of the Moderates. The crusade of the Texas-led Fundamentalists has turned into a drive against thought itself, in a final revenge upon history for the refusal of God to give victory to the South. The Moderates, an instance of Lincoln's "almost chosen people," have been unable to counter the fanaticism of a chosen people, zealous and ever-angry.

Such worship of the Lost Cause does seem rather more High Romantic Faulknerian than Christian, but this is not at all my literary imagining. Here is Bill J. Leonard, our major contemporary authority on Southern Baptist church history:

What then was The Great Southern Baptist Myth? The denomination of the defeated, itself born of schism and racism, had become God's "last" and "only hope" for evangelizing the world according to New Testament principles. Its numerical, financial, and spiritual growth, as well as its evangelistic zeal, was evidence of God's blessing on its ministry, its mission, and its method. Schism would mean the death of the myth, so schism must be avoided at all cost. Nothing could be allowed to deter the South's most southern denomination from its calling to redeem itself and win the ultimate battle against evil. This passion for triumph, for spiritual and numerical success among Southern Baptists, cannot be understood apart from the surrender at Appomattox. (*God's Last and Only Hope* [1990], p. 13)

But that avoidance of schism, as with the Landmarkers, was an error, and helped contribute to the hopeless situation today of Moderates (like Leonard) in the Southern Baptist Convention. There has been a long process of development in Baptist thought that culminated in the work of E. Y. Mullins. The Baptists, who were the Puritan Radicals of New England in the seventeenth-century, agreed with the Congregationalists on emphasizing God's sovereignty, but rejected the Chosen People ideology of their neighbors. These early American Baptists were "willing to respect —indeed, to accept—any Christian Church founded on true Gospel piety" (Philip F. Gura, *A Glimpse of Sion's Glory* [1984], p. 125). Precisely this acceptance began to vanish with Landmarkism, and has been obliterated by the current Fundamentalism. But there had been many negative instances of Baptist triumphalism in between. The antimissionism of the earlier nineteenth century had produced the rather dreadful Hard-Shell Baptists, headed by a peculiar Gnostic, Daniel Parker, who brought many of the Hard-Shellers together under the dominion of his "Two-Seed-in-the-Spirit" ideology. This doctrine, an extraordinary throwback to second-century Sethian Gnosticism (about which Parker knew absolutely nothing), amounted to a savage predestinarianism. God had implanted one seed in Eve, and Satan another in the unfortunate mother of mankind. The good seed, the ancient Gnostics would have said, resulted in Seth, who replaced poor Abel, while the bad gave us Cain. Since everyone is the product of one or the other seed, effort or missionary work is irrelevant; one is seeded either elect or damned. For the rest of the nineteenth century, Parker's Primitive Baptists kept their vehemence. Mixed in with later Landmarkism, a kind of permanent agitation became endemic in the Southern Baptist Convention. This unrest surged on until the publication in 1896 of William H. Whitsitt's *A Question in Baptist History*. Whitsitt discarded the Landmarkers' fiction of a continuous Southern Baptist tradition since that grandest of Southern Baptists, the one who baptized Jesus, and the Landmarkers responded by forcing Whitsitt to resign as president of the denomination's major seminary. Mullins accepted the post, and a new phase of Southern Baptist history began.

Edgar Young Mullins I would nominate as the Calvin or Luther or Wesley of the Southern Baptists, but only in the belated American sense, because Mullins was not the founder of the Southern Baptists but their re-founder, the definer of their creedless faith. An endlessly subtle and original religious thinker, Mullins is the most neglected of major American theologians. Pragmatically he is more important than Jonathan Edwards, Horace Bushnell, and the Niebuhrs, because Mullins reformulated (perhaps even first formulated) the faith of a major American denomination. Leonard says of Mullins that he personified the Great Compromise only now breaking down in the Southern Baptist Convention. Mullins died in 1928, and his ideas prevailed for half a century more, only to be overwhelmed, not by other ideas, but by the contempt for all ideas that animated the Fundamentalist takeover of the Southern Baptists in 1979. As Leonard notes, Mullins was not a theological liberal, but a defender of Evangelical Baptism who nevertheless found no threat in science or philosophy to the religious. A thorough pragmatist, deeply influenced by William James, Mullins grounded his faith upon "experience" in James's sense. A deep and powerful subjectivity was the basis of Mullins's intellectual and spiritual strength, linked also to a profound understanding that Baptist belief depended upon a highly personal relation of each individual to God. I don't find it accidental that Mullins had memorized much of Milton's *Paradise Lost*, for Milton had made himself into a sect of one, and his theological position is scarcely distinguishable from that of Mullins. Milton's devotion to the Inner Light is at the heart of Mullins's doctrine, to which I turn now, in order to explore the enigma of just what it is that Moderate Southern Baptists believe.

13

The Enigma: What Do Southern Baptists Believe?

T H E best presentation of the authentic beliefs of the Southern Baptist Convention is to be found in *The Axioms of Religion* (1908) by Mullins. His emphasis upon the historical significance of the Baptists centered itself upon one doctrine, the "competency" of the soul in religion:

> Observe then that the idea of the competency of the soul in religion excludes at once all human interference, such as episcopacy, and infant baptism, and every form of religion by proxy. Religion is a personal matter between the soul and God. The principle is at the same time inclusive of all the particulars . . . It must include the doctrine of separation of Church and State because State churches stand on the assumption that civil government is necessary as a factor in man's life in order to a fulfillment of his religious destiny; that man without the aid of the State is incompetent in religion. Justification by faith is also included because this doctrine is simply one detail in the soul's general religious heritage, from Christ.
> Justification asserts man's competency to deal directly with God in the initial act of the Christian life. Regeneration is also implied in the principle of the soul's competency because it is the blessing which follows close upon the heels of justification or occurs at the

same time with it, as a result of the soul's direct dealing with God.

The soul's competency is at one with the soul's experience of the authority of Jesus Christ. Mullins illustrates such competency by contrasting the Baptists with the Roman Catholics. The sacraments of the Roman Church, in the Baptist view, insist upon mediation and so upon the soul's incompetency in matters of religion. Most crucially for Mullins, the Catholic is not free to interpret the Bible for herself or himself:

The doctrine of papal infallibility combined with that of an authoritative tradition forbids all private or divergent interpretations of Scripture.

With this as preamble, Mullins proceeded boldly to state the six Baptist "Axioms of Religion":

1. The theological axiom: The holy and loving God has a right to be sovereign.
2. The religious axiom: All souls have an equal right to direct access to God.
3. The ecclesiastical axiom: All believers have a right to equal privileges in the church.
4. The moral axiom: To be responsible man must be free.
5. The religio-civic axiom: A free Church in a free State.
6. The social axiom: Love your neighbor as yourself.

Even in association with soul competency, these axioms are so broadly Protestant that they scarcely seem Baptist to any particular degree. Mullins, the clearest voice ever among Southern Baptists, cannot give an adequate account of what differentiates Baptists from other Protestants. Like all Baptists, Mullins affirms that Jesus alone is the truth, a declaration that works to make all specific doctrine irrelevant. One sees why Baptists pride themselves upon not being a creedal religion. The Reverend John Doe, my guide in seeking to understand Southern Baptists as experiential believers, remarks that soul competency only can be defined negatively, in terms of what it is not. That Southern Baptism is an American experiential mode of negative theology seems to me crucial for the understanding of our largest Protestant denomination. Gnosticism, the most negative of all ancient negative theologies, emerges again in the Southern Baptists, but with the American pragmatic difference. Bentley Layton translates *gnosis* as "acquaintance" rather than as "knowledge," which is a very William Jamesian turn, and fits well the Southern Baptist way of encountering Jesus. Each Southern Baptist is at last alone in the garden with Jesus, to cite one of the principal Baptist hymns.

Herschel H. Hobbs, very much of the moderate school of E. Y. Mullins, gallantly attempted a positive outline of Southern Baptist belief in *The Baptist Faith and Message* (1971), a work that still enjoys official status. Starting with the principle of soul competency and with Mullins's six axioms of religion, Hobbs quickly centers upon the anxious assertion that Southern Baptists will not end in schism, because "they have a living faith, rather than a creedal one." But how does one describe a living faith, even in one hundred and fifty pages? Like so many American denominations (the Mormons included) the Southern Baptists affirm the priesthood of all believers, leaving to the preachers only the prime function of exhortation. Soul competency is remarkably like erotic competency (if I may be allowed that splendidly outrageous term), since there is no room for a third when the Baptist is alone with Jesus. Even as each of us must define eros for himself, so the Baptist must define his own soul competency. As John Doe subtly remarks: "Everyone is competent to understand soul competency as she or he sees fit." His further ruminations constitute the most brilliant and revelatory exegesis of Southern Baptist soul competency that I have been able to find:

I only know to think of soul competency in practical terms. To me it means that the individual Christian is unassailable in her interpretation of Scripture and in her own understanding of God's will for her life. It means that when someone says, "This is what the Bible means to me," I cannot tell her she is wrong. I can merely say that her understanding is meaningless for me. Only the preacher's understanding of Scripture is expected to be generally meaningful for the whole community, and it is up to each individual to decide whether the preacher's words are useful or not. Soul competency means to me that anything I understand to bring me closer to God is true and cannot be taken away from

me, because my life is unique and there is a way of understanding
Scripture which is unique to me. Soul competency means to me
that I find truth when I am furthest removed from the distrac-
tions and contingencies of people and things and authorities—
again, when truth takes forms which are unique to me and my
understanding of the Bible.

Soul competency, in this vivid and moving account, has in it an
element of isolation and of intense individuation. It is a very rough
version of Emersonian self-reliance, in that there is a necessary
element of origination in it. And, as in Emerson, there is a touch
of negative theology involved in it, as Doe has said. Doe shrewdly
notes that soul competency is held to be inherent in Scripture even
though there are no proof-texts to be found for it. About all that
Baptists can adduce as textual evidences are the supposed agon of
Jesus with the Pharisees, and the palpable struggle of Saint Paul
with the Judaizers, led by James the brother of Jesus. As Doe says,
Baptists would identify Judaizers and Pharisees with Roman Catholics and other proponents of creedal religion.

In another deft gesture, Doe insists on a rigorous distinction
between soul competency and the priesthood of the believer. Soul
competency pertains to Hindus, Moslems, and all other followers
of religion, as well as to Christians, but only Christians receive the
guidance of the Holy Spirit in interpreting Scripture, a guidance
that in itself constitutes the priesthood of the believer. Therefore,
Doe rightly concludes, in another gesture that might have chilled
even Mullins and Hobbs, that soul competency, which is the essence of Southern Baptist faith, nevertheless does *not* refer to an
unmediated relationship with Jesus:

An unmediated relationship may be its true end, the purpose for
which God granted us soul competency, but soul competency is
fully operative in the atheist and the Mormon, as well as the
Episcopalian or Baptist. Nevertheless, the fact remains that Baptists conceive of the Christian life as an unmediated fellowship
with God, and the Bible is indispensable for that fellowship; it is
just that the Bible does not count as a true mediator. Instead, it
is the immediacy of the Spirit which makes the Bible meaningful
in the first place, though only to those with open hearts. You get
the idea that the Bible is yours, personally, and not external to

you as with Luther's sacraments. The Bible is internal to you with the Holy Spirit.

Doe is a Moderate Southern Baptist intellectual, or what Ronald Knox called a Mystical Enthusiast, as compared to what Knox called an Evangelical Enthusiast, or Fundamentalist Southern Baptist. All Southern Baptists—whether Fundamentalist or Moderate —certainly are belated Enthusiasts, who rely upon an inner light, even if only the Moderates seek to read Scripture by it. The inner light or Holy Spirit internal to you, much deplored by the Anglo-Catholic T. S. Eliot, is the true center of Southern Baptist faith, and the enigma of enigmas of the entire American Religion. The element in the Southern Baptist creedless creed that is most vital is wholly personal, subjective, experiential and finally quite nameless, or to be named only by everything it is not. Conversion, or "getting saved" or "being born again," is the frantic center of the spiritual life, and is wholly inward. It is this frightening inwardness that compels the Southern Baptist to hold on so hard to the Bible. Jesus and miracles alike are in the past; the Bible surges on in the present, and promises some control of the future. Without the Real Presence of the body of Christ in a communion service, the Baptist is alone with his Bible. To be more precise, since the Bible will not read or interpret itself (the astonishing Fundamentalist assumption), the Baptist is alone with an interpretation of the Bible, his own if he is a Moderate, or a lowest-common-denominator reduction if he is a Fundamentalist. Either way, only an interpretation substitutes itself for what Catholics hold to be a symbolic yet real presence of Christ.

Mullins, shrewdest of Southern Baptist theoreticians, met this difficulty by a characteristic emphasis upon the *personality* of the Divine. In his *The Christian Religion*, he fell back upon a formulation far more acceptable to Gnostics, ancient and modern, than to Christian traditionalists: "That which we know most indubitably are the facts of inner experience" (p. 73). Doe, though very much of Mullins's school, points out that this is at least partly contradicted later in *The Christian Religion:*

Even our faith, which is the vital principle of all our Christian living, is a variable factor . . . It is not our subjective experience in any of its varying forms, in which we trust. It is God's great and gracious act addressed to our variable experience to sustain it amid all its changes and struggles. (p. 396)

The act of God in history is a Protestant rather than a Gnostic conception, and yet even the Divine act is here addressed to "our variable experience," and not to a fixed soul or will. I suspect that this is because the varieties of religious experience, for Mullins, culminate in the experience of encountering the resurrected Jesus. Ahlstrom, in an overview of Mullins's theology, stresses the use of "Christian experience" as central, and notes also the relative lack of concern for social ethics. The definitive answer of Mullins to the question: "What do Baptists believe?" would be simply that "Jesus is the Resurrection and the Life." Hans Frei, discussing the identity of Jesus Christ, subtly indicated that while it must be God who raises Jesus, the Gospels are strangely silent on so crucial a matter, and so could not be used to refute the contention that Jesus raises himself, much as earlier he had raised Lazarus. The second-century Gnostics believed that the general Resurrection had taken place spiritually when Jesus raised himself, a belief inevitable for those who identified their "spark," *pneuma*, or true self with the risen Jesus, who had in fact in their view never been crucified, since only a substitute or phantom had suffered upon the cross. If what was best and oldest in you, a divine spark, went back to before the Creation, then it could not die, any more than Jesus could die. In that sense, the Resurrection always already had taken place, in your oneness with Jesus.

The Baptist experience of knowing Jesus, in a solitary and re newable encounter, takes priority over public worship, doctrine, or acts of charity. And since what can know Jesus, in some way already is akin to Jesus, then the saved Baptist participates *now* in the Resurrection and the Life. Mystical Enthusiasm (in Knox's sense) is the heart of the American Religion, and the post-Mullins Moderate Southern Baptist joins the nineteenth-century Mormon in knowing this ecstasy as Resurrection. Surely this is related to what Mullins named as "soul competency," the power and right of the individual Baptist to an utterly singular relationship with Jesus. If one's undying spirit accepts the love of Jesus, walks with the resurrected Jesus, *knows* what it is to love Jesus in return, alone with Jesus in the only permanent and perfect communion that ever will be, then there can be no churchly authority over one. As for the authority of Scripture, even it must yield to the direct encounter with the resurrected Jesus. That encounter, in its full intensity, may come only once or twice in a lifetime, and perhaps never more than nine or ten times in a long life, but when it comes, it comes without rival. What we have among the authentic Southern Baptists is one of the few manifestations of the American Religion that involves mystical experience among a fairly large group of people. And though democratic (being open to all), its continued ecstasy necessarily is available only to an elite. The mystical enthusiasm still current among contemporary "moderate" Southern Baptists finds an American companion only in the brief ecstasy that came to Joseph Smith and his elite in the dedication of the Kirtland temple.

But all Southern Baptist spiritual experience, as represented by Mullins, finds its center in one doctrine alone, to which now I return full-scale: the competency of the solitary soul confronting the resurrected Jesus. What is unique in Southern Baptist spirituality always turns upon soul competency. I have tried, with the skilled assistance of the Reverend John Doe, to find some instance of the phrase "soul competency" before Mullins, but neither of us has uncovered it in Southern Baptist writing or anywhere else. Mullins invented it, and slyly made no fuss about this, but employed it as though it were traditional and as old as the Baptists themselves, or indeed as old as Christianity. It is what John Milton called Christian Liberty, and is so nuanced by Mullins that it seems a curious fusion of nature and grace, or birth in the image of God and rebirth through God's gift of regeneration. Certainly the absolute competency of the soul in all religious matters gives one a vision of the individual without limitations, and free of every overdetermination. No one can tell the free soul how to interpret the Bible, or how not to interpret it. The doctrine destroys Fundamentalism by sanctioning endless interpretive possibilities, so that the weird metaphor of a "literal" or "inerrant" reading totally vaporizes. Mullins shrewdly cites no specific biblical texts as authority for soul competency, since his point is that the doctrine is the whole meaning of Jesus's total stance: in all his attitudes, everything he says, every act he performs. This stance is interpreted by Mullins as being set against all creedal religion, and he identifies it with the Southern Baptists' fierce denunciation of the creedal structure of Roman Catholicism. Of all the American quests for that mythical entity, the Primitive Church, the Baptists' hunt seems to me to have yielded the most persuasive fiction. It is a dangerous fiction, as all American versions of a Protestant Primitivism have been dangerous, both because fictions that think themselves facts are dangerous, but also because they make living human beings into the carriers of essentially dead beliefs. Yet the Baptists, by shying away from every creed, could avert those dangers, according to Mullins, despite the dogmatisms of Landmarkism and Fundamentalism.

As a religious critic (self-appointed, but what else is possible?), I am moved to put certain questions to the faith that Mullins worked out for Southern Baptists. Even Mullins tended to define soul competency by negation, usually by comparing it to its opposite in the Roman Catholic hierarchy of authority in spiritual matters. If soul competency is simply a description of an absolutely unmediated and intimate relationship with Jesus, then what precisely is the function of reading and interpreting Scripture? In Baptist terms, cannot there be an unmediated dialogue with Jesus, who after all seemed to replace the Bible with himself? If you reject the Catholic idea that the Church is the mystical body of Christ, then why cannot you be free of congregation, preacher, and text, and so be wholly alone with Jesus, walking and talking, spirit with spirit, spirit to spirit? If your soul is ultimately competent, then the nakedness of the soul should suffice.

Mullins powerfully insisted that Baptists are *not* dualists, in the precise sense that those who baptize infants necessarily declare themselves to be. But how can you have a religion of experience, that is *not sacramental*, without a dualism, or division between knower and known, whether Jesus is known in direct encounter or through Scripture? The Baptist soul and Jesus, in their mutual act of acquaintance, renew an ancient Gnosis, with all the problems such a renewal brings about. In such a Gnosis, how can the justification of the redeemed soul not become a perpetual condition? Recall Kierkegaard's harrowing insistence that *becoming a Christian* was a lifelong struggle. If you are saved once and for all, experientially, what will keep you from becoming an antinomian, beyond good and evil? All of these queries fuse into one: How does the

Southern Baptist maintain the boundary between herself and
Jesus, so that she does not become him, with rather unfortunate
societal and psychical consequences?

Ronald Knox, writing on Wesley, but in the total context of his
splendid *Enthusiasm*, made the classic Catholic indictment of experiential religion:

> Let us note, from the first, that traditional Christianity is a bal-
> ance of doctrines, and not merely of doctrines but of emphases.
> You must not exaggerate in either direction, or the balance is
> disturbed. An excellent thing to abandon yourself, without
> reserve, into God's hands; if your own rhetoric leads you in-
> to fantastic expressions of the idea, there is no great harm
> done. But, teach on principle that it is an infidelity to wonder
> whether you are saved or lost, and you have overweighted your
> whole devotional structure; you have ruled out a whole type of
> religious self-expression. Conversely, it is a holy thing to trust
> in the redeeming merits of Christ. But, put it about that such
> confidence is the indispensable sign of being in God's favour,
> that, unless and until he is experimentally aware of it, a man
> is lost, and the balance has been disturbed at the opposite end;
> you have condemned one type of religious mind to despair.
> (pp. 580–81)

Southern Baptists, like all Enthusiasts, whether Mystical or
Evangelical, have their own balance of doctrines, and such balance
is antithetical to the Catholic mode. Knox condemns what he
would call Mystical Perfectionism and Evangelical Regeneration,
each a characteristic of different strains in the American Religion.
Knox's harshest condemnation is voiced against all those who fail
to see that the ship of authority is going down:

> Religion became identified in the popular mind with a series of
> moods, in which the worshipper, disposed thereto by all the arts
> of the revivalist, relished the flavors of spiritual peace. You
> needed neither a theology nor a liturgy; you did not take the
> strain of intellectual inquiry, nor associate yourself whole-heart-
> edly with any historic tradition of worship. You floated, safely
> enough, on the little raft of your own faith, eagerly throwing out
> the lifeline to such drowning neighbours as were ready to catch
> it; meanwhile the ship was foundering. (p. 589)

One reads this with pleasure, while remembering that Knox was Evelyn Waugh's mentor at Oxford. In the Baptist perspective, those moods are emotions directly shared with the resurrected Jesus, and that little raft is called soul competency. The Catholic disapproval cannot touch soul competency, the whole function of which is to negate Catholic doctrine. But my own questions, to which I now return, compel the further question: Are Mullins's formulations dialectical, or simply self-contradictory? The Baptist church historian B. J. Leonard tactfully notes that Mullins himself declined to see the contradiction in giving equal primacy to the authority of the Bible and the competency of the autonomous soul of the believer:

Southern Baptists sought to unite the objective authority of the Bible with the subjective experience of the individual, and they often wrote as if each was *the* most important single doctrine of their history. Mullins's appeals to both Scripture and conscience, for example, have led many to identify him with their particular side in the present denominational controversy: Dr. Mullins the inerrantist, and Dr. Mullins the prophet of soul liberty . . . Mullins himself apparently saw no contradiction in holding both doctrines simultaneously. He helped shape a denomination in which respective proponents could find common ground. Reconciliation over these Baptist distinctives now seems increasingly impossible. Rather than struggling for balance or allowing groups that emphasize the doctrines in different ways to coexist within the denominational house, each faction is forced to choose one doctrine over the other. (p. 76)

We are thus returned to the central enigma: What do Southern Baptists believe, and are their beliefs contradictory? A dialectic would have to be as subtle as that of Valentinus, the second-century Gnostic, to bring what he would have called the "spark" or *pneuma* of the individual and the true alien God so close together without collapsing them into a virtual identity. Sufficiently emphasized, soul competency brings the resurrected Jesus and the Mullinite or Moderate Southern Baptist so near to one another that two heresies unite. Creator and creature are indistinguishable, and the dualism of body and soul is abrogated, so that the Baptist mystic already *knows* what it is to have been resurrected. Here is Mullins in 1904, reviewing a book by the philosopher Borden P. Bowne (a William Jamesian personalist and pragmatist):

> If man is made in the image of God, then he has powers capable of rising to God. Philosophic agnosticism, which pronounces man's intellect incompetent in the realm of theology, really degrades man to a lower plane of being than the human. For the characteristic of man is that he is made in God's image and likeness. This kinship is the basis of intercourse and fellowship, intellectual and otherwise, between God and man. (*Review and Expositor*, July, 1904, p. 249)

Like all Gnostics, including the Kabbalists, Mullins needs to be read between the lines, since his religious writing frequently sounds much more conventional than it is. "Philosophic agnosticism" there is Mullins's personal term for Roman Catholicism. Thus, John Doe cites a remarkable sentence from the *Axioms of Religion*:

> Agnosticism, which denies the competency of the human intellect, is the Roman Catholicism of philosophy, and is a belated view of human ability in the intellectual sphere. (p. 66)

In the passage from the review of Bowne, a sly attack therefore is made against Roman Catholicism, which is seen as degrading the theomorphic qualities in man, his possession of "powers capable of rising to God." The kinship between the Baptist and Jesus is then celebrated with a subtle ambiguity as "the basis of intercourse and fellowship, intellectual and otherwise." That "otherwise" opens a wide gateway for a mystical interchange, so that soul competency begins to acquire a new range of reverberation. An unmediated fellowship with the resurrected Jesus returns one to the forty days experienced by the Disciples between Resurrection and Ascension, and allows for a true sense of Mullins's audacity, which nevertheless is hardly his alone but belongs to all Southern Baptists who can rise to it.

What place can the experience of reading Scripture assert in this unmediated fellowship with miracle? Mullins declines to confront the question, but he hints endlessly at the answer, which would obliterate mindless Fundamentalism. The awakened, indeed spiritually resurrected, Baptist will read the Bible by an inner light kindled by the experiential fellowship with Jesus. That reading, by the economic principle of soul competency, will be a justified interpretation, whether or not it accords with the inerrant dyslexia of prides of Texas Fundamentalist preachers. Having talked to Jesus, any Baptist whatsoever is at least as competent to interpret Scripture as the Reverend W. A. Criswell or the Reverend Bailey Smith, or even Judge Paul Pressler, the Pope of Houston. For the Spirit is immediate, and mediates the Bible, preventing the Bible from any possibility of being external to the Baptist. Reading in the Spirit will bring an inspiration not different in kind from that enjoyed by the biblical authors themselves.

The word "competency" doubtless came to Mullins from its nineteenth-century usage of economic self-sufficiency, but Mullins may have had in mind the Latin origin of the word in *competere*, "to seek together." Soul competency is a quest or seeking, but its togetherness is with Jesus and not with one's fellow denominationalists. Indeed, soul competency cannot belong to any particular sect or grouping. It is a purely individual attribute, and by definition is a universal human endowment, as applicable to Arjuna in his chariot with Krishna as to Saul of Tarsus on the road to Damascus. I would extend Mullins, but still (I think) stay within his spirit, if I myself personalized soul competency as the freedom from every form of overdetermination: societal, historical, economic, even psychological. Freedom, for Mullins, must be freedom from the Church also. John the Baptist is the prototype of soul competency, in that a Southern solitary, who has walked with and talked to Jesus, and who reads the Bible in that inspired light, does not need a Southern Baptist church in order to be justified for salvation. Mullins, always alert and agile in remembering that his authentic spiritual enemy is the Roman Catholic Church's insistence upon its mediating function, could not have denied my extreme instance of the absolutely unmediated soul. Competency is Mullins's pragmatic version of Emersonian self-reliance, and is the gateway into an authentically experiential belief.

The pattern for all Southern Baptists' experiential faith is set by what they famously call "the Roman Road," a narrative collation of half a dozen passages in Saint Paul's Epistle to the Romans. Here is the Roman Road:

But God commendeth his love toward us, in that, while we were yet sinners, Christ died for us. (5:8)

For all have sinned, and come short of the glory of God. (3:23)

As it is written, There is none righteous, no, not one. (3:10)

For the wages of sin is death; but the gift of God is eternal life through Jesus Christ our Lord. (6:23)

For whosoever shall call upon the name of the Lord shall be saved. (10:13)

That if thou shalt confess with thy mouth the Lord Jesus, and shalt believe in thine heart that God hath raised him from the dead, thou shalt be saved. (10:9)

No scholar has determined who first paved this Roman road, and it is not even certain that it is of Southern Baptist origin. But it has become the essence of the Southern Baptist faith, and presumably is meant to follow the model of Saint Paul's own conversionary experience. As a reading of Romans it is very selective indeed, and is pretty well refuted by Krister Stendahl's demonstration that Luther severely misread Paul, even as Augustine had. Wayne Meeks, summarizing Stendahl, remarks wryly that "Paul was not a Lutheran pietist nor an American revivalist. Paul did not reduce the gospel to the forgiveness of sins, let alone to the assuaging of guilt feelings." Yet it is fair to say that Mullins's Saint Paul, and the Saint Paul of all Southern Baptists, is very much an American revivalist. The six paces of the Roman Road do not exactly take us to Karl Barth's vision of the Epistle to the Romans:

God does not need us. Indeed, if He were not God, He would be ashamed of us . . . God is the unknown God, and, precisely because He is unknown, He bestows life and breath and all things. Therefore the power of God can be detected neither in the world of nature nor in the souls of men.

This is not the God of the Southern Baptists, though it may indeed have been the God of Saint Paul. But if you personalize the resurrected Jesus as Baptists do, then it is precisely in the souls of men that Jesus the God will be detected. Barth knows the difference between the Reformed faith and Gnosis, but this is a difference unacknowledged by the Baptists, whose faith overwhelmingly is a personal knowing of Jesus. If you strip Romans down to the Roman Road, then salvation is immensely simple, however inwardly felt. Triumphalism is the only mode in which Mullins and the Baptists read Romans. Like the Mormons, the Baptists do not need the Crucifixion, and show little interest in it. They pragmatically move from Incarnation to Resurrection, and are most at home at the end of Romans 8: "In all these things we are more than conquerors through him that loved us."

John Doe, sketching a Baptist exposition of Romans, follows Mullins in seeing the problem of sin as being solved "through Christian Experience," but then gently suggests that the Paul of Romans is a touch less optimistic than Mullins on the internal complexities of sin. Here Mullins was at his subtlest and most American, by distinguishing between the "historical significance" of the Baptists, and "the Baptist creed," which is close enough to that of other Evangelical denominations. A true Baptist in his distrust of all creeds, Baptist ones included, Mullins's preference for "historical significance" remains the center of Moderate Southern Baptism. Here is Mullins at his best, conveying what surpasses creed:

> The sufficient statement of the historical significance of the Baptists is this: The competency of the soul in religion. Of course this means a competency under God, not a competency in the sense of human self-sufficiency. There is no reference here to the question of sin and human ability in the moral and theological sense, nor in the sense of independence of the Scriptures. I am not here stating the Baptist creed . . .
> Observe then that the idea of the competency of the soul in religion excludes at once all human interference, such as episcopacy and infant baptism, and every form of religion by proxy. Religion is a personal matter between the soul and God . . . (*The Axioms of Religion*, pp. 53–54)

The consequences of religion consisting entirely in a personal relationship with Jesus are manifold, and in their ultimate effects wonderfully destructive of all churches, as Mullins was well aware. Mullins's enthusiasm for Roger Williams was lifelong, and it seems extraordinary to me that Mullins ever could have served as president of the Southern Baptist Convention, but that was in a happier time. An appearance by him now before the Convention might cause a riot, despite his peculiar position as the unique theologian (however belated) of the denomination. "Baptists have furnished to American civilization the most spiritual interpretation of Christianity the world has seen," according to Mullins (*Axioms*, p. 261), a declaration so audacious as to make one wonder again just how quietly outrageous Mullins knew himself to be. To institutionalize a piety as personal and spiritual as Mullins advocated is scarcely possible and returns one to the full enigma of Southern Baptist belief, to its oddly pragmatic sense that "Doctrine must be both walked and talked," a Baptist slogan that my friend the Reverend John Doe remembers having learned at college. Acreedal as they are, Southern Baptists are still overbelievers when compared to William James, but Doe seems to me accurate in finding affinities between Jamesian and Southern Baptist exaltations of religious experience. The Southern Baptist soul-initiative towards Jesus is most certainly a clear analogue to James's emphasis upon the purposeful will to believe. In a curious way, both Mullins and James exemplify the authentic meaning of Nietzsche's Will to Power, which is a receptive and interpretive drive. Jesus does not descend upon the passive Baptist soul, but is met by the eagerness and effort of the questing spirituality that Mullins nominates as the personal experience of religion. One sees why Mullins could assert, so surprisingly, that William James "explains the fact of regeneration in terms which are quite in harmony with those of the Pauline epistles." Initially, I blinked at encountering this, but the harmony is with Mullins, and not with Paul. Pragmatic, experiential, and American as he was, Mullins almost involuntarily translated Paul into Jamesian terms. The primacy of human feeling is not the dynamic of Paul's work, but it is of James's and of Mullins's. What then of regeneration? There is the crux: Is Baptist regeneration a kind of pragmatic spirituality, a function of effort, expectation, and desire? Mullins, as I interpret him (with Doe's aid), crosses the line into what I would have to call a mystical theurgy, a strengthening of Jesus through the soul's love for him and need of him. We have seen a theurgical element in Joseph Smith's vision of Celestial Marriage, and another one enters, rather more subtly, in the Moderate Southern Baptist vision of regeneration as seen by Edgar Mullins. In his *Christian Religion in Its Doctrinal Expression* (p. 378), Mullins defines regeneration as "the change wrought by the Spirit of God . . . in which the moral disposition of the soul is renewed in the image of Christ." In the *Axioms* (p. 33), this change is amplified and pragmatized as "an intelligent response to the revelation of truth from person to person," one of those persons being Jesus:

> This faith arouses the entire being, the intellect, the emotions, the will, and the moral nature. The intellect grasps truth, the emotions are drawn out by trust and affection, the will yields to the commanding will of another, and the moral nature by an intuition of right and wrong puts the stamp of its approval upon the soul's act. Christ is the object of the soul's trust, and he thus inducts it into the kingdom, and reveals to it God's fatherhood.
>
> Observe now that the first and immediate result or attendant circumstance of the act of faith is regeneration and redemption. The immanent Spirit of God employs the word of truth as instrument, and the soul, fully aroused in all its parts, is brought forth into a new life—is constituted spiritually a son of God, and translated into the ordered spiritual realm of God's kingdom. (*Axioms*, p. 33)

The quiet of this rhetoric conceals the extremity of this Enthusiastic regeneration. What Mullins describes is a falling in love with Jesus, in which we become what we behold, and achieve his relation to God. But what does Mullins have in mind: Is this conversion "as nurturing process" or "as dramatic event"? I take these terms from a very sensitive essay by Bill J. Leonard, "Getting Saved in America: Conversion Event in a Pluralistic Culture" (*The Review and Expositor*, Winter, 1985). Leonard again indicates the ambiguity of Southern Baptist belief, which seems to see conversion both as process and as event, in a considerable theological confusion. Mullins, I think, means a fiercely dramatic event, a sudden falling in love, rather than a process of nurturing into love. The erotic analogue is passional, not familial, and the pragmatic purpose again is a kind of theurgy. Mullins is a deceptively serene religious writer; the burden of his *Axioms* is a pragmatic mysticism, oxymoronic as that must seem.

As an Enthusiastic religion of American experience, Moderate Southern Baptism approaches the Emersonian Orphic paradigm that I sketched in my second chapter. Mullins could not resolve the most prevalent of Southern Baptist contradictions: a spiritual life of ever-growing inwardness was the supreme reality, empirically and emotionally overcoming even the doctrine of the Incarnation. Mullins's most startling single sentence is: "That which we know most indubitably are the facts of inner experience," a superb declaration, but one closer to Shakespeare's Macbeth than to the Saint Paul of Romans. Later in the same book (see *The Christian Religion*, p. 73 and p. 396), Mullins remembered that there were saving acts of God in history, but clearly these mattered to him only because they were directly addressed to our capacity for subjective experience. Late Romantic as he splendidly was, Mullins was subjectively an American Gnostic, and only secondarily a Protestant Christian. It ought to be clear that I venture this as praise, not blame. Mullins gave his spiritual allegiance to the Southern Baptist conversion experience as such, and there I must conclude by following him, if his version of faith is to be apprehended.

How does the authentic (read Moderate) Southern Baptist reconcile a fanatical emphasis upon the absolute necessity for a personal, experiential encounter of conversion with the resurrected Jesus with a total devotion to Scripture? Both these terms are experiential, and so they are not dialectical. You may have the experience, but what you know is your interpretation of the experience. You may read Scripture, but what you have is your interpretation of Scripture. I have said this earlier, but place it now at the center of the Southern Baptist enigma. The experience in each mode is purely inward; you talk to Jesus, you sense him, you receive emotional assurance, but unlike Joseph Smith you do not see Jesus or hear the sound of his voice. And yet you are saved, once and for all; you receive certainty. Even the early Mormons did not outdo Mullins in the assurance of freedom, and in the assignment of the achieved image of God to the arena of America:

A symbol of his progress toward his goal is a sculptor carving out of the marble his vision, rejoicing in it for a time, and then destroying it or setting it aside and beginning his work upon another block and making a better statue; forever achieving and yet repudiating his achievement until he achieves the image of God in himself through God's grace. All this and more is implicit in our view of the competency of the soul in religion. America is the arena which God has supplied for the free and full play of the principle, and from here it is destined to spread until it covers the earth. (*The Axioms of Religion*, p. 68)

George Bush, in his post–Gulf War victory speech to the Southern Baptist Convention, did not exactly promise to make the world safe for soul competency, but as an Episcopalian he presumably was not any more versed in the doctrine than were his triumphalist Fundamentalist hosts. Elsewhere in the *Axioms*, the mystical idealist Mullins went so far as to stress that Jesus makes his believers into kings. The profound point is again what Mullins so strangely shares with the prophet Joseph Smith, and what neither share with the mainline Reformed churches. Call it man-godhood, or theomorphism, or what you will, but both Mullins and Smith exalted the image of the human. Baptist freedom, like the freedom of the Mormons' Restored Gospel, is the freedom to come very close to the divinity as well as the manhood of Jesus. Smith offered himself as mediator; Mullins proudly and powerfully rejected all mediation, old or new.

The Moderate Southern Baptist, in what is taken (rightly or wrongly) as an imitation of Saul of Tarsus on the Damascus road, presses for his or her soul's encounter with Jesus. Mullins's soul competency is the banner that celebrates and helps enable the encounter, yet I suspect it is also the flag of the Baptist's disposition, of a participation in the Resurrection. No Southern Baptist, of any camp, will believe me when I tell them that they are subject and object of their own quest. This most aggressive of Protestantisms is no Protestantism at all, but a pure outflaring again of an ancient Gnosis. The Jesus who is sought is already both principle and particle in the soul that seeks him. Nothing that I have perceived of the American Religion is more persuasive than the image of the Southern Baptist alone in the garden with Jesus. Even if, as I have to believe, the Baptist ultimately is alone with herself, she knows the two truths of spirituality that are most worth knowing. She knows, beyond knowing, that she is no part of the Creation, and she possesses the other American knowledge also, the freedom that is wildness, total spiritual solitude.

14

The Controversy: Fundamentalism

IN his study, *Enthusiasm*, one of my starting-points for this book, Ronald Knox distinguished between two types of Enthusiasts, "mystical" and "evangelical":

> I would suggest a distinction between "mystical" and "evangelical" enthusiasm. One, taking its point of departure from the Incarnation, rather than the Atonement, by-passes the theology of grace and concentrates on the God within . . . The other, more acutely conscious of man's fallen state, thinks always in terms of redemption; to know, somehow, that your sins are forgiven, that you are a new creature in God's sight, is all that matters.

Knox himself preferred "ultrasupernaturalism" to "enthusiasm," since he thought that the real character of the Enthusiast was that "he expects more evident results from the grace of God than we others." I have suggested throughout that the American version of religious "Enthusiasm" has been so prevalent for two centuries now that it is identical with the American Religion itself, whether that manifests itself as the Mormons or the Methodists, Assemblies of God or the Baptists, conservative Protestants or liberal Protestants. But Knox's distinction between Mystical Enthusiasts and Evangelical Enthusiasts works very well for the two rather different tendencies in the American Religion, in whatever denomination or sect. The current split in the Southern Baptist Convention is between the majority Fundamentalists (Evangelical Enthusiasts) and the minority Moderates (Mystical Enthusiasts). Before examining that conflict, I suggest that Knox's terms be tested against the sociological terms employed by Robert Bellah and his associates in *Habits of the Heart: Individualism and Commitment in American Life* (1985). Bellah's "internal" is Knox's "mystical"; Bellah's "external" is Knox's "evangelical," but the sociological and theological analyses are very close, though *Habits of the Heart* uses a very different language from Knox's, as here:

> Radically individualistic religion, particularly when it takes the form of a belief in cosmic selfhood, may seem to be in a different world from conservative or fundamentalist religion. Yet these are the two poles that organize much of American religious life. To the first, God is simply the self magnified; to the second, God confronts man from outside the universe. One seeks a self that is finally identical with the world; the other seeks an external God who will provide order in the world. Both value personal experience as the basis of their belief.

Bellah's cosmic selves are Knox's Mystical Enthusiasts, while his conservatives or Fundamentalists are of course Evangelical Enthusiasts. Even so, the moderate minority of the Southern Baptist Convention descend from mystics of the Inner Light, who read the Bible in radically individualist ways, while the conservatives of the Convention insist that the Bible reads itself (as it were), requires no interpretation, declares its literal and unerring truth in every verse. We are close to the center of the American Religion when we contemplate this split between an isolate selfhood, itself already part and parcel of God, and those desperate to locate God's authority in a doctrinal reduction of the Protestant Bible.

Whatever else is said of this division, I think it important to note that it is not, despite appearances, a conflict between subjectivity and supposed objectivity. There is no authentic dialectic between what are necessarily two modes of deepest subjectivity, one an illumination streaming out from within the psyche, and the other a complex, immensely difficult, vast anthology of ancient texts, to which a single, narrow, self-contradictory and clearly inadequate interpretation has been applied. Baptist Moderates and Baptist Fundamentalists alike are Enthusiasts, extreme subjectivists, and their dispute has nothing to do with greater or lesser degrees of objectivity. The Moderates rightly affirm that Baptists have a creedless creed, while the Fundamentalists desperately seek to impose a creed.

"Inerrancy" in the Bible is the starting point for the Fundamentalist creed, and is a very difficult notion to grasp, since "Biblical Inerrancy" does not mean that Southern Baptist Fundamentalists are obsessive, sustained Bible readers. An examination of most published sermons by them shows an astonishing biblical illiteracy. Ellen M. Rosenberg, in *The Southern Baptists: A Subculture in Transition* (1989), gives an accurate general account of this peculiar situation:

> In the absence of a creed, or a set of interpretive rules by which new challenges might be evaluated, Southern Baptists can hold together only with a core belief structure of extraordinary generality and ambiguity. The Bible fills the need; it becomes a projective test, a protean Rorschach. As the code words have become "Biblical inerrancy," the Bible itself is less read than preached, less interpreted than brandished. Increasingly, pastors may drape a limply bound Book over the edges of the pulpit as they depart from it. Members of the congregation carry Bibles to church services; the pastor announces a long passage text for his sermon and waits for people to find it, then reads only the first verse of it before he takes off. The Book has become a talisman. (p. 134)

"Inerrancy" has become a synonym for Knox's "ultrasupernaturalism" and by a terrible irony Baptists, historical rebels against Catholic, Episcopalian, Methodist, and Presbyterian creeds, wave the Bible as a compendium of unread creeds. Here is W. A. Criswell, only recently retired from his decades as pastor of First Baptist Church in Dallas, the Fundamentalist Vatican, stating his faith in the virtual identity of the Bible and God:

> My brother, if the Bible is not also scientifically accurate, it is not, to me at least, the Word of God. I have a very plain reason

for that. The Lord God who made this world and all the scientific
marvels which we are now discovering in it—that same Lord
God knew all these things from the beginning . . . Now if the
Bible is the Word of God, and if God inspired it, then it cannot
contain any scientific mistakes because God knew every truth and
fact of science from the beginning. (quoted in *Baptist Battles*
[1990], by Nancy Tatom Ammerman, pp. 83–84)

This Criswellian notion of the Bible as the Word of God is not
so much Christian as Muslim, since it applies more to the Koran
than to the Bible. The Koran gives us one voice only, the voice of
God himself, who speaks the entire text aloud to his Messenger,
Muhammad. Something of the rocky strength of Southern Baptist
Fundamentalism is interestingly similar to Islamic Fundamentalism. "Inerrancy" for both movements is an unconscious metaphor
for the repression of all individuality. The set of mind involved
curiously resembles the rabblement of lemmings who now domi-
nate American campuses. For "biblical inerrancy" read "politically
correct" views, as opposites merge into one another. The largest
truth we can discover about the Fundamentalist war cry of "biblical
inerrancy" is that it has almost nothing to do with anyone's actual
experience of *reading the Bible*. Reading is a skill or at least an
activity, and few ventures are as disheartening as trying to get
through books on the Bible by Southern Baptist Fundamentalists,
such as Harold Lindsell's *The Battle for the Bible* (1976).
    What Fundamentalists cannot understand is that their attempted
literalization of Scripture is itself a giant metaphor: a conversion of
the Bible into a statue or an icon. It is in itself a restrictive interpretation, with not the slightest relation to the Bible's actual text. One
of the great ironies of Protestant history is that the exaltation
of Scripture, which in the seventeenth century endowed Baptists
and other Protestants with freedom from institutional constraints
and with spiritual autonomy, has become, as the twentieth century closes, the agency for depriving Baptists and other Protestants of their Christian Liberty, their soul competency to read and
interpret the Bible, each person by her own Inner Light. In the
Old Baptist Meeting House in Providence, Rhode Island, there
stands a lectern as huge as an altar. There the Baptists of colonial
America set their Bible as an emblem of spiritual freedom. Fundamentalism, in the America of the 1990s, is a frightening and

degrading betrayal of the seventeenth-century Baptist dream of human dignity and freedom in fellowship with Jesus, the Word of God.

The overwhelming urgency (and viciousness) of Southern Baptist Fundamentalism surpasses all other American instances of that errancy, and makes it shockingly similar to Iranian Shiite Fundamentalism or the worst excesses of the Neturei Karta in Israel. In a most grievous way, the strength and uniqueness of the Moderate Southern Baptist tradition, as codified by Mullins, involuntarily helped produce the furious anti-intellectualism of Criswell, Pressler, and the other representative leaders of the now dominant Fundamentalist faction of the Southern Baptist Convention. The mystical distrust of language in the Moderates, with its attendant repudiation of theology, is reduced by the Fundamentalists to a total devaluation of all language and all thought. Even as Fundamentalists insist upon the inerrancy of the Bible, they give up all actual reading of the Bible, since in fact its language is too remote and difficult for them to begin to understand. What is left is the Bible as physical object, limp and leather, a final icon or magical talisman. To *read* Criswell or any other Fundamentalist clergyman on the Bible is almost a literal impossibility, at least for me, because they are not writing about the text, in any sense whatsoever of text, or of that text. They write about their own dogmatic social, political, cultural, moral, and even economic convictions, and biblical texts simply are quoted, with frenetic abandon, whether or not they in any way illustrate or even approach the areas where the convictions center. They are quoted also as though they interpreted themselves and were perfectly transparent in their meanings.

It seems heartless to blame the Moderate Baptists for any aspect of this absurdity, but no Southern Baptist (as such) seems to be much at home with or in language. Theology depends upon analogies, arguments, metaphors, all of which enforce the difference between words and the realities they represent. Fundamentalist Baptists never even seem to realize that the Bible is in the first place language. But Moderate Baptists, being sincere and pragmatic Enthusiasts in their unmediated relationship to Jesus, tend to despair that the unmediated experience they have of Jesus ever can be represented in language. We thus have the paradox that the Fundamentalists resent or ignore language, while the Moderates at best are ambivalent towards it, and probably even fear it, since they do not wish it to mediate Jesus for them.

Christian Fundamentalism essentially is a North American phenomenon; except for the United States and Canada, it has had an indigenous life only in Ulster. Its other worldwide manifestations tend to be exported from the United States. Yet I cannot regard it as anything but a parody of what I have called the American Religion. Its spiritual content, to the religious critic, is difficult to locate. This was not always so; there were some serious intellects involved in later nineteenth- through earlier twentieth-century Fundamentalism. Today, there are none, and yet Fundamentalism threatens to become almost a synonym for Evangelicalism in contemporary America. Partly this is caused by media overreporting, and by the plain shock experienced by our upper-middle-class public each time they find themselves yet again allied with lower-middle-class Fundamentalists in the support of Reagan, Bush, and their party. The moral agenda of the Fundamentalists is rather drab, and, like Bush, generally reduces to waving the flag and the fetus at us as though these constituted a single entity.

Ernest Sandeen contended that Fundamentalism began as a form of Anglo-American millenarianism in the prewar years from 1875 to 1914. To Bruce Lawrence, this is not persuasive. He points out how ambiguous and belated a term "Fundamentalism" is, being a journalistic coinage of 1920. The Presbyterians, now hardly Fundamentalist (or much of anything, except debaters of sexual morality), adopted "five fundamentals" before the First World War, but these were only loosely adopted by what we now think of as *the* Fundamentalists. Lawrence therefore characterizes our Fundamentalism as a more general malaise:

Despite Sandeen's pioneering endeavor, fundamentalism cannot be inextricably linked to millenarian origins and directions. More than a mere social movement, fundamentalism is the direct consequence of neither doctrinal symbiosis nor sectarian disputation. It is, above all, a religious protest against modernism, embodying more strengths than millenarianism and combating more enemies than higher criticism. (*Defenders of God* [1989], pp. 168–69)

Aside from the curiosity of naming millenarianism as a strength, this definition is a touch too comprehensive, since there are a host of religious protests against modernism, whatever we take that to be, and many of them reject Fundamentalism. American Fundamentalism, professedly Protestant, is the central spillover of the American Religion into the Republican Party, the particular secularization of our faith, but into groups of Democrats as well. Here we had best consider the Fundamentals themselves. These Fundamentals of the faith have been variously expounded and expanded, but generally reduce to five:

1. The Bible is always right.
2. Jesus resulted from a Virgin Birth.
3. His Atonement substitutes for us.
4. He rose from the dead.
5. He will come again, in a refreshment of miracles, to govern over a final dispensation of a thousand years of peace upon earth, before the final Judgment.

Since 2, 3, and 4 all are ancient Christian doctrine, it is no surprise that Fundamentals 1 and 5 pragmatically matter most. The literal inerrancy of the Protestant Bible, and premillennialism, are the authentic stigmata of American Fundamentalism, the firm bedrock of their dogmatic anti-intellectualism. That the Bible does not interpret itself is scarcely their concern, while our entrance into the final decade of the twentieth century is now their truest preoccupation.

The best analyses of Fundamentalism have been by James Barr, starting with his book of that title in 1977, where the conclusion remains the last word on this subject. Barr begins, quite dryly, by observing:

For the church and theology as a whole, fundamentalism constitutes an ecumenical problem rather than an intellectual problem. (p. 338)

It is not an intellectual problem because it is no way an intellectual matter:

The ecumenical problem is constituted by the frightening alienation of fundamentalism from the main stream of church life and theology. The basis of this alienation is religious. The root of it is the fact that fundamentalists deal with the real difficulties of differences in faith and life by deeming non-Christian the bodies and the persons who do not agree with them. At the root of the problem there lies therefore a judgment that is more religious and existential than doctrinal or biblical: the problem is formed by the absolute and overweening certainty possessed by fundamentalists that their form of religion is absolutely and uniquely right. (p. 338)

As Barr adds, this anti-intellectualism necessarily leads to a simple inability to read:

Contrary to all that might be expected from polemic documents, conservatives often ignore the literal sense of the Bible, often minimize miracles and the supernatural, often postulate substantial corruptions in the text. (p. 341)

The principle of inerrancy means, in practice, that the literal sense is taken up or dropped where it either supports or might trouble the constant elements in all Fundamentalist "interpretation." As for "error," it is (as Barr points out) not a *critical* issue, but merely a Fundamentalist obsession. Obsessiveness has been the increasing signature of Southern Baptist Fundamentalists since the unsettling decade of the 1960s, and erupted clamorously in the Southern Baptist Convention of 1970 in Denver. It is rather arbitrary of me to take that as the starting point of the fierce controversy between Fundamentalists and Moderates in the Convention. One could just as well begin in 1925, when the Southern Baptists nearly split upon the evolution issue. But something new and sinister came into being around 1970 among Baptist Fundamentalists, nothing less than a successful conspiracy to take over the entire denomination in order to purge it of its "liberalism." What actually has been purged is the entire spiritual legacy of E. Y. Mullins, with consequences that are very likely to be fatal for everything that is uniquely valuable in this faith.

In the last twelve years, the Southern Baptist Convention has ceased to be a religious body, in any true sense, and has become a rather frightening American phenomenon, a more-than-Orwellian mechanism. Mullins both followed and broadened Baptist tradition by linking soul competency to the priesthood of the believer, every believer. The Convention has now repudiated everything that made Baptist faith distinctive and unique, and is at work literalizing Martin Marty's wry remark that it was "the Catholic Church of the South." The Fundamentalist pastors have been declared to have the authority of priests, while lay persons have been denounced for what amounts to soul incompetency in spiritual matters. It is not a joke to observe that Southern Baptists now may be said to be alone in the garden with Wally Amos Criswell, or free to walk and talk with Bailey Smith (who attracted national attention with his candid proclamation: "God does not hear the prayer of the Jew"). No American literary satirist, not even the Nathanael West of *A Cool Million* and *Miss Lonelyhearts*, could have had the audacity to write the Southern Baptist Convention's Resolution No. 5: On the Priesthood of the Believer, passed in 1988:

WHEREAS, The Priesthood of the Believer is a term which is subject to both misunderstanding and abuse; and

WHEREAS, The doctrine of the Priesthood of the Believer has been used to justify wrongly the attitude that a Christian may believe whatever he so chooses and still be considered a loyal Southern Baptist; and

WHEREAS, The doctrine of the Priesthood of the Believer can be used to justify the undermining of pastoral authority in the local church,

Be it therefore RESOLVED, That the Southern Baptist Convention . . . affirm its belief in the biblical doctrine of the Priesthood of the Believer (I Peter 2:9 and Revelation 1:6); and

Be it further RESOLVED, That we affirm that this doctrine in no way gives license to misinterpret, explain away, demythologize, or extrapolate out elements of the supernatural from the Bible; and

Be it further RESOLVED, That the doctrine of the Priesthood of the Believer in no way contradicts the biblical understanding of the role, responsibility, and authority of the pastor which is seen in the command to the local church in Hebrews 13:17, "Obey your leaders, and submit to them; for they keep watch over your souls, as those who will give an account," and

Be it finally RESOLVED, That we affirm the truth that elders, or pastors, are called of God to lead the local church (Acts 20:28).

This is hilarious if you are not a Southern Baptist Moderate, to whom it is the precise equivalent of the Roman Catholic Church suddenly announcing that every believer, woman and man, is a priest, and that actual priests have no more spiritual authority than their parishioners. But then, there is no single Baptist principle outlined in Mullins's *The Axioms of Religion* or his disciple Herschel H. Hobbs's *The Baptist Faith and Message* (1971), that has not been either twisted or abrogated by the Fundamentalist Convention. Hobbs began his book by reprinting a motion passed by the Southern Baptist Convention, meeting in 1962 in Sodom, or San Francisco, California (where the post-Fundamentalist Convention will certainly never convene again). The motion, near its conclusion, summed up its "living faith" with a Mullinsesque sentence that now aches with the pathos of a lost glory:

Baptists emphasize the soul's competency before God, freedom in religion, and the priesthood of the believer. (p. 4)

Baptists emphasize W. A. Criswell's competency before God, authority in religion, and the priesthood of Texas preachers.

The story of just how, in twelve bad years, the Southern Baptist Convention has been converted into an Orwellian nightmare has been told, with skill and discernment, by Nancy Tatom Ammerman in her *Baptist Battles* (1990) and by Ellen M. Rosenberg in her *The Southern Baptists: A Subculture in Transition* (1989). Ammerman is a sociologist of religion, and Rosenberg an anthropologist. Here I desire only to add whatever seems relevant to what I regard as religious criticism. The death of one of the two most vital and original versions of the American Religion is a somber subject, and the political, socioeconomic, and anthropological implications of so immense a demise are beyond my competence or my informed concern. Only spiritual loss becomes the theme of the remainder of this chapter, which is a modest lament for the vision of Edgar Young Mullins, an outlook that, after all, was also the stance of John Milton and of Roger Williams. If that vision abandons the United States forever, then more than our spiritual democracy will yet be threatened.

I return to a suggestion I made earlier in this book, that our Fundamentalists of the last two decades in America are not really

Fundamentalists at all, and ought to be called something else. American history provides the useful example of the bigoted nineteenth-century political party called the Know-Nothings, which is a highly appropriate name for the dominant reactionaries among the Southern Baptists. It is especially applicable because they know nothing at all, including the Bible, which they carry about but appear never to have read. Real Fundamentalists would find their archetype in the formidable J. Gresham Machen, a remarkable Presbyterian New Testament scholar at Princeton, who published a vehement defense of traditional Christianity in 1923, with the aggressive title *Christianity and Liberalism*. I have just read my way through this, with distaste and discomfort but with reluctant and growing admiration for Machen's mind. I have never seen a stronger case made for the argument that institutional Christianity must regard cultural liberalism as an enemy to faith. Machen reviewed E. Y. Mullins's *Christianity at the Cross Roads* (1924) with a rugged empirical attack on Mullins's characteristic personalism and mysticism. What remains the Moderate Southern Baptist vision of the Resurrection, an intensely emotional confrontation between the Baptist Soul and the resurrected Jesus, was decried by Machen as an evasion. Either Jesus was resurrected, as a bodily fact, or he was not. Termed by George M. Marsden a commonsense follower of Sir Francis Bacon, Machen also reminds me of the boldly realistic Dr. Samuel Johnson. One can see Machen refuting Mullins in the style of Johnson refuting Bishop Berkeley, with Machen rebounding from kicking the great stone rolled aside from the tomb of Jesus. But if Machen, a scholar and an intellect, is rightly called a Fundamentalist, then I must insist that Wally Amos Criswell and his swarm be called something else, and Know-Nothings will do very nicely.

The background of the Know-Nothing coup at the Southern Baptist Convention of 1979 goes back a very long way, but I will pick it up, in Marsden's wake, with arguments conducted in America a century before that, between premillennialists and postmillennialists. Postmillennialism had dominated the country until the end of the Civil War, and was particularly identified with our major theologian, Jonathan Edwards. Our age was fulfilling the prophecies of the Revelation of John the Divine, and at the end of our time would come the thousand years pervaded by the Holy Spirit, after which Jesus would return. But in the 1870s, a premillennialist drive began, with the growing sense of a new dispensationalism, which deprecated our era, denounced supposed progress, and reaffirmed ultrasupernaturalism. The dispensationalists, who became authentic Fundamentalists, first circulated the term "inerrancy" in regard to the Bible. The Know-Nothings of Nashville and Dallas have taken over the term, but originally it had a factual, indeed an empirical meaning. God had created both the cosmos and Scripture, so each would manifest a freedom from any error in design. The Bible, like the universe, would yield everything to a Baconian search of the facts. Gresham Machen inherited this argument, which he developed with great force. His dispensationalist or premillenarian condemnation of American culture as a Babylonish liberalism had a strong factual basis in the United States of the 1920s. Whatever we think of this today, we ought never to confuse it with the Know-Nothings who assert they are its heirs but are nothing of the kind. Marsden rightly insists that Fundamentalism was primarily a religious movement and only peripherally a social and political matter. But, as he added, that was Fundamentalism up to 1925, and not the movement of 1980, when his book was published. The tragedy of the Southern Baptist Convention is the result of a purely political and social conspiracy that still masquerades as a religious movement. Its reductive anti-intellectualism reminds one of the Spanish Fascism of Franco; the Know-Nothing Baptists are the heirs of Franco's crusade against the mind, and not the legatees of Gresham Machen. But Fascist has never domesticated itself as an American term, so I will continue to employ Know-Nothing as the accurate counter here.

The pietism or near mysticism of Southern Baptist experiential faith does not provide much worldly defense against a Know-Nothing crusade. No version of religion that stakes everything upon a personal friendship with Jesus is going to educate its followers against conspirators. Mullins was a remarkable religious writer, but no prophet; he did not foresee the authentic decline in American and Southern culture that made Criswell not only possible but inevitable. The Bible is the most difficult of all difficult books. The general decline in the ability to read nearly anything in the age of television has made the Bible almost impossible to read for all except an elite. Consider then the relief that the Baptist Know-Nothings brought with them as they stormed the Convention in 1979 and afterwards. You no longer had the burden of reading the

Bible for yourself. Criswell would do it for you, and would assure you that its prime meaning was its inerrancy. That required no interpretation, but only assent, an assent without grammar, understanding, or even coherence. Ellen Rosenberg, who is grimly and respectfully quite funny on this matter, quotes a Southern Baptist church bureaucrat as saying: "We hold together in the Spirit, not around words." There is the crux; if you listen to an audio tape by the venerable Criswell in which he purports to interpret a biblical text, you hear, not an exegete, but someone who has not yet realized that the Bible is written in words. The Southern Baptist distrust of language, disconcerting enough in Mullins, becomes a positive resentment, almost a hatred of language, in the Know-Nothings. The obscure, perhaps permanent, fear and dislike of language in so many working-class Southern Baptists makes them the inevitable victims of the Criswellite Texans. Their inerrant Bible, they are assured, was not so much written by God or by inspired prophets, as it was created by God. Creationism, I am now convinced, is only secondarily directed against the ghost of Charles Darwin. It is directed instead against all those who might deny that the Bible is a vast, solid object, like a cliff or a First Baptist Church in a Texas city. Neo-Fundamentalists want a densely substantial inerrancy, a truth beyond language, beyond ambiguity, beyond any possibility of refutation. Their ancestors were drenched in the Bible, twice-baptized with every immersion in its pages. Very few of them could pass the most elementary sort of Bible quiz, for the real meaning of "inerrant" is now "unread."

This results in an impossible situation for Moderate pastors attending a Southern Baptist Convention. How do you argue against Know-Nothing ministers, many of whom border upon functional illiteracy? Frustrated by eleven previous inerrant stampedes, most of the Moderates simply stayed away from the 1991 Convention, and are unlikely to return in their lifetimes. Once you eliminate the misleading word "Fundamentalism," the true dilemma of the Moderates is clarified. You can argue against dogmatism, which is the traditional enemy of the Southern Baptists in the shape of Roman Catholic doctrine. But how can you argue with an ignorance stubbornly proud of itself? Soul competency, religious liberty, the priesthood of the believer: what can these mean to a Texas inerrantist, whose true inheritance is dispensationalism or premillennialism? If you hold that the Kingdom of Jesus cannot be reached through the natural history of humankind, is ultrasupernatural, and totally out of continuity with the present age, then the Mullinsesque principles are beyond your understanding. But the dispensationalism of the Know-Nothings eliminates more of the Southern Baptist faith even than that; it shifts the focus from the resurrected Jesus to the sacrificed Jesus and the ascended Jesus. The vital genius of what made the Baptists spiritually unique is wrested away from them. The friend they have in Jesus ceases to differ very much from the Augustinian Jesus of the Roman Catholic Church. In yet another dark irony, the Catholic Church of the South has taken a further step towards its hereditary enemy.

Though many Moderates have blamed themselves for not being sufficiently wary, prevenient, unified, and combative, I do not think that any aspect of their catastrophe could have been evaded. There is a dreadful overdetermination in the pattern of the events that have ruined the Southern Baptist Convention between 1979 and 1991, and which have made it a perfect microcosm of the fall of America during these Reagan-Bush years. The emancipation of selfishness in every aspect of national life paradoxically destroyed the religion of the self. Ellen Rosenberg assigns the culprit's role to Southern culture, but as before I am skeptical of sociological or social anthropological accounts of overdetermination. Bill Leonard and Nancy Ammerman, themselves embattled Moderates, are much warier of theorizing about their defeat, perhaps because they need all their energies for continuing the struggle, though in other arenas, no longer in the lost Convention. As a total outsider, I only can report the deep sorrow, sometimes despair, of the young Southern Baptists, both clergy and lay persons, who study at the Yale Divinity School. To have one's denomination taken away from one by another, on the analogue of a hostile takeover in the corporate world, is clearly an extraordinary experience. I return to the complex question as to what it was in the spiritual stance of E. Y. Mullins and his co-religionists that exposed their tradition to this mindless assault, that made it vulnerable to the Know-Nothings within their own gates?

Sadly, it seems to have been the authentic and unique spiritual strengths of Southern Baptist piety that rendered the Moderates naked to their enemies. A religion of the Inner Light that rejected all mediation and all authority had built no hedge around its Torah, to appropriate a great phrase from a tractate of the Talmud. Ro-

mantic personalism pervades Mullins even as it informs the genius
of Faulkner. The exaltation of soul competency and the emphasis
upon the priesthood of the believer necessarily made for diffuse
organizational structures. When the Pressler-Criswell Know-Nothings plotted their takeover, they accurately counted upon very little
inherent organizational resistance. Where nearly all are acreedal, it
proved relatively easy to begin imposing creeds, while calling them
something else. Added to all this was the Convention's tradition of
affirming unity, at whatever cost, in order to avoid schism. Themselves the consequence of a schism with Northern Baptists, the
Southern Baptists had an ancient fear of the possible consequences
of dividing again.

Though the Moderates represented nearly half of the Convention's membership, they are very aware of how difficult it will be
to create an entirely new denomination. After their eighth consec-
utive defeat, in 1986, they formed a rather tentative grouping, the
Southern Baptist Alliance. In 1991, grimly cognizant that this was
insufficient, they tried again with the Cooperative Baptist Fellowship. Unless this links up, in time, with Northern Baptists (the
American Baptist churches) or with one of the African-American
Baptist groups, it may wane rather quickly. Leaving the Southern
Baptist Convention is an emotional wound, but presumably more
and more Moderates will come to realize that the Convention increasingly is being transformed into a wholly different faith from
the one set forth by Mullins. Since the Know-Nothings have inherited nothing from the tradition except for its triumphalism,
their obduracy, racism, antifeminism, anti-intellectualism, and
plutocratic politics will only increase, and will drive out many
more Moderates. But the dilemma of most Moderates will continue. They are Southerners and Southwesterners, a nation apart,
and uneasy at yielding up regional heritages. More crucially, their
mystical personalism has far more in common with African-American Baptists than with Northern Baptists. My surmise is that an
entire generation will have to pass before there is an enormous
exodus from the Southern Baptist Convention. And yet it must
come, even if it affects the children of the Moderates more fully
than the current Moderates themselves.

After the tragedy, the farce; one comes to prophesying the future
of the Know-Nothings themselves. Their crusade against abortion
will be victorious, fit recompense for their strenuous support of

Reagan and Bush. But crusades against the mind finally fail, since our society can afford them only at the most prosperous times. The Southern Baptist Convention, in following a trajectory from E. Y. Mullins straight down to W. A. Criswell, risks becoming a provo cation to the nation's laughter. I conclude with an anecdotal juxta-position. On December 27, 1989, the *New York Times* quoted our military commander in Panama, the endlessly shockable General Maxwell Thurman (surely a creation of Stanley Kubrick), as revealing that General Manuel Noriega had reacted to our invasion by phoning his mistress, not his wife, and that Noriega also wore red underwear in order to ward off the evil eye. Previously, Thurman had told us that Noriega sniffed cocaine while invoking the gods of voodoo. Surrounding the refuge provided for Noriega and his entourage of thugs by the Pope, Thurman strenuously conducted his siege with sound trucks blaring out rock, a barrage that induced the music-loving Papal Nuncio into persuading Noriega to depart. But all this ended (in the spiritual sense) on May 15, 1990, with Noriega's conversion, in his Florida incarceration, by two Southern Baptist preachers, whose exertions caused the Panamanian drug lord to yield up his mistress and his red underwear. This triumph for the Southern Baptist Convention was fit prelude to the June 1991 meeting, where Oliver North waved the flag and the fetus, followed by George Bush weeping and praying as he stood before his constituents. Of such is the premillennial kingdom, in this dispensation.

V

THE AMERICAN RELIGION: A PROPHECY

15

African-American Religion as Paradigm

SCHOLARS of African-American religion tend to agree that the Black Church generated what C. Eric Lincoln called the "black sacred cosmos," a spiritualized vision of the entire universe. Nothing could be further from a Gnostic view than such a black sacred cosmos, which is the antithesis of what the Gnostics called the *kenoma*, the cosmological emptiness through which we wander. To regard the Black Church as a paradigm for the future of the American Religion is another audacity on my part, except that African-American spirituality was the starting point, not just of Pentecostalism, but of some of the most distinctive elements of Baptist experience. Black Baptists in the South go back to the 1750s, and they inaugurated many of the strains that culminated in E. Y. Mullins a century and a half later, though he evidently was quite unaware of his indebtedness. The overt ideology of the Black Churches always has been communal, as Lincoln stresses, but there was also a highly individual relation to Jesus mixed into the communal aspiration. Two separate visions of spiritual freedom are endemic in the Black Church; I would call them freedom for the self, and freedom from the self. Such a contradictory double stance has existed elsewhere in Protestantism, but rarely with so much intensity invested in both modes of freedom as in African-

American religion. The full complexities of Black Church spirituality are obviously beyond my comprehension. But this chapter deals only with what might be regarded as a single dialectical element in that spirituality: the struggle for communal freedom in order to be free for God, and the subtler struggle for individual freedom, again in order to be free for God, but in a finer tone or in another sense. The novelist-essayist James Baldwin was the classical analyst of that second struggle, but it is necessarily the common theme of much African-American writing. It informs the work of the two strongest poets of this tradition, Jay Wright and Thylias Moss, and it is powerfully implicit in Ralph Ellison's *Invisible Man*, one of the indubitably canonical novels of all modern literature. I wish to analyze it here as a religious critic, not as a literary critic, and so I turn to just a few instances in the long history of the Black Church in America.

The study of slave religion never has settled its leading controversy: Was it formed inwardly by remnants of authentic African faiths, or did it arise only from the imposition of Christianity upon the desperate slaves? Eugene Genovese has argued that this matter cannot be resolved, for lack of adequate information. I am persuaded by Jon Butler's complex suggestion in his brilliant *Awash in a Sea of Faith*, where he synthesizes a three-part model for the spiritual *praxis* of the slaves:

1. 1680–1760: A systematic devastation was carried out by the English colonies (the Anglican Church included) of all the inherited African religious systems among the slaves, without quite expunging particular rituals.
2. 1760–1800: A rebirth of family life among the slaves allowed for the development of a Christianized collective religious life on the English model.
3. 1800 on: African-American distinctive religion develops, in conjunction with what Butler calls the Spiritual Hothouse of pre–Civil War nineteenth-century America.

I find that this confirms again my own intuition that the American Religion is born about 1800, and that African-American religion was a crucial element in this origin. The ecstasies of Cane Ridge tapped a mysterious current of sensation and perception that emanated from the slaves. Mechal Sobel, in *Trabelin' On: The Slave*

Journey to an Afro-Baptist Faith (1979), convincingly intimated that
what became the religion of the Southern Baptists relied unknowingly upon African spiritual formulations. Certainly, Sobel's suggestions are the only rational evidence that I have seen that can
account for the radical difference between British and New England Baptist beliefs and the turbulent experiential religion of
Southern Baptists. There is an African-American paradigm that
informs the emotional immediacy of unmediated Baptist encounters with Jesus. As we move from the second to the third phase of
Butler's model, there is a development from collective to highly
individual spiritual experience among the African-American Baptists. Since their vision of a sacred cosmos had been destroyed, it
was replaced by a relationship to an internalized Jesus.

On that pattern (purely speculative, and yet proleptic of many
lasting features of the Black Church in America), freedom from the
self in a collective identity yielded to a new, but purely internal
freedom for the self, to know and be known by a black Jesus. Both
freedoms were mocked by a Christianized slavery, and both possi
bilities to some extent today are still shadowed by many of the
surviving consequences of such sanctioned and sanctified bondage.
Eugene Genovese distinguishes between the principal Christian
churches in the South, and Christianity itself, which provided the
ideological basis for the abolitionists, at least in *their* interpretations
of the Bible. Palpably, the paradigm of African-American religion
is extraordinary displaced in a Southern Baptist context, or in the
context of guilt-obsessed American universities in the 1990s. Like
the post–Civil War Southern Baptists, and like the Mormons, African-American religious believers see themselves as another Chosen
People, yet once more on the ultimate pattern set forth by the
Hebrew Bible. Freedom has so many ambiguities in the context of
God's choice of an entire people, that all of us ought to become
very wary of any unequivocal account as to just what freedom for
or from the self might mean for members of such a people. In the
J Writer, the first Biblical author, freedom for the Israelites was
conceived ironically, as the freedom to die during forty years of
dreadful wandering in the wilderness. Freedom to suffer is a hor-
rible irony, the rejection of which has been the spiritual health of
African-American religion.

The African sacred cosmos has been studied very extensively,
but the fundamentals of its view of spirit still are best set forth, at

least for my purposes, by Geoffrey Parrinder in *West African Religion* (1961) and by Marcel Griaule in *Conversations with Ogotemmeli: An Introduction to Dogon Religious Ideas* (1965). Mechal Sobel, citing them as her authorities, uncovered in the African-American Baptist faith clear survivals of the West African vision of the spirit. Strangely parallel to aspects of ancient Gnosticism, in my own judgment, these survivals may well be the tap-root of concepts of the spirit in the American Religion. Parrinder describes a mythology (as we might want to call it) in which every person and every object has a double or twin, its spirit, or true self. According to Parrinder: "The African might say that '*in each thing is another thing*' and '*in every man there is a little man.*' " The "little man" was not born and does not die, and so is no part of nature. This radical, indeed Gnostic dualism clearly survived in African-American Baptist conversion experiences, as Sobel noted:

> American blacks, in talking and writing of their experiences in converting to Christianity, have handed down a tradition that, on first appraisal, appears highly parallel to the white conversion experience. However, there is one jarringly different element, found only in the black recitals and found there with great consistency. It is the reference to "the man in the man," "the little me in the big me," "the little Mary in the big Mary," "the little John in the big John." For blacks, there was a twofold spiritual participation in the actual conversion experience that was not known to whites and, in each case, it was the "little me" inside the "big me" who traveled to visit God in Heaven during the ecstatic vision experience. (p. xix)

Sobel shrewdly observes also that the shamanistic travel-trance among the slaves became an individuated rather than a communal phenomenon. I would think that the characteristic evangelical trauma in American religious experience, to this day, found its origin in precisely this African-American transformation:

> The trance became a far more private affair than it had been in Africa, notwithstanding its American revival function, and individual blacks heard their own drummers and shouts, often alone in the woods or in their cabins. More importantly, they were not

taken over or "mounted" by God, as an African is mounted or used as a mouthpiece by a divinity, but they met and talked with God who then came to be and remained in their hearts. (pp. xxii–iii)

This center of black Baptist spiritual experience became the unknowing paradigm for white Baptist conversionary life. The Dogon "true me" or "real me," what ancient Gnostics called the "spark" or *pneuma*, became indistinguishable from the Spirit in which St. Paul had been caught up and transported to the heavenly regions. What continued to mark a difference between black and white Baptist experience was the more radical dualism of the African-American sacred cosmos. Doubtless, much of the provocation for this difference ensued from bondage, but survivals of Dogon twinning or doubling had to exist in order to account for the wide prevalence of African-American reliance upon the reality of the "little man" within, which was transformed into the saving presence of an interior Jesus.

Dogon mythology, as expounded to Marcel Griaule by the elder Ogotemmeli, is as complex a Gnostic creation-fall as that elaborated by the second-century disciples of Valentinus, the Alexandrian founder of the crucial version of Gnostic religion. Amma is the ultimate God but is nearly as withdrawn as the Valentinian "alien God" or "stranger God." The God of most African religions was either detached or alienated from many aspects of daily existence. In the Dogon faith, Amma makes love to the earth, which first brings forth a jackal, who in turn indulges in an improper relationship with the earth, out of which mismatch all evil proceeds. But after the jackal, Amma begets a sequence of Nommos, the words of God's spirit, doubles and twins of his father. The seventh Nommo reorganizes the fallen universe by sacrificing himself. Such a seventh and final, demiurgical Adam was easily assimilated by the African-American Baptists to the Pauline Christ. Yet "assimilated" may be a misleading word for this process, since Paul, despite some Gnostic aspects, conceived of a radical distinction between the Old Adam and Jesus as the New Adam. The early African-American Baptists may have declined to distinguish between the little man or woman within each one of them and the figure of the resurrected Jesus. Out of this emerged the particular

African-American Baptist rhetoric of Jesus as friend, a rhetoric without which white Southern Baptist religion would not have been possible.

If you assumed, as the Africans did, that your spirit was the best and oldest part of you, then you valorized past time as authentic time, and you tended to identify fulfillment in the spirit not with the future, but with returning to the past. This profound nostalgia of African religion marks a limit of African-American spirituality as a paradigm for the American Religion. Here I have some difficulty with Mechal Sobel's formulations:

> In the new black Baptist Sacred Cosmos, belief was replaced by knowledge. The converted black had been to Heaven, and *knew* God and *knew* Jesus and *knew* himself saved. African time had become Afro-Christian time; past had become future. (p. 245)

I think that something like the reverse of this was true. Knowledge of the Spirit or "little man" was partly replaced by an Africanized version of Pauline belief. If the converted black Baptists knew Jesus through a heavenly journey, that was because he and she had followed the shamanistic past, and had journeyed as their African ancestors had quested. Afro-Christian time remained African time, in that the blacks would not yield to white versions of dispensationalism. When Pentecostalism first rose, led by the former Baptist preacher W. J. Seymour, an African-American, its palpably African elements were evaded or suppressed, so that they are now quite invisible even as Jimmy Swaggart shouts when the Spirit hits him, yes indeed. The core of African-American spirituality, of any denomination or sect, continues to be in the spirit's knowledge of God, which is not necessarily different from a knowledge of self. That returns me to what must have seemed mere wordplay, and yet it has everything to do with the cultural and religious stresses that particularly afflict African-Americans. Their vision asks them to be at once communal, or free of self, and isolated, or free for the self. African spirituality demanded both, American Christianity implores both, and human consciousness is scarcely able to bear both.

Albert J. Raboteau, towards the close of his *Slave Religion* (1978), stated this contradiction as an apparent dialectic, which held true certainly before Emancipation, but not I think today:

The conversion experience equipped the slave with a sense of individual value and a personal vocation which contradicted the devaluing and dehumanizing forces of slavery. In the prayer meetings, the sermons, prayers, and songs, when the Spirit started moving the congregation to shout, clap, and dance, the slaves enjoyed community and fellowship which transformed their individual sorrows. (p. 318)

When is one made free: in solitude, or in community? Necessity, throughout American history, has dictated the communal answer for African-Americans. Freedom to be alone with Jesus would have to be the Baptist answer, black or white, but with which Jesus? Jaroslav Pelikan, in *Jesus through the Centuries* (1985), remarks that Martin Luther King's version of Jesus the Liberator is "a love ethic that repudiated violence and went beyond individualism." It is that last phrase which may be problematic, for a love that goes "beyond individualism" may not be available to Americans, or its ethic to the American Religion. What Mechal Sobel terms "the coherent Afro-Christian world view," which is that "Nobody knows but Jesus," centers upon a love that scarcely is beyond individualism. The issue, made apocalyptically poignant by slavery, was identity, and the highly personal love of Jesus for the individual conferred identity. Jesus knows the person, knows indeed "the little me" within the person. W. E. B. DuBois made the classical formulation of this complexity when he wrote of African-American double consciousness as "two struggling souls within one dark body," a dialectical tension expounded by C. Eric Lincoln and Lawrence H. Mamiya in their recent study of the Black Church. The intensely personal conversion, to however black a Jesus, by an individual African-American, is a very different event from what Lincoln and Mamiya call "mass catharsis" or communal ecstasy. And yet this may be the very center of the American Religion, and of the Afri can-American prophecy as to the future of our national faith. No one could ask of African-Americans that they be able to resolve a conflict so prevalent among all who live a spiritual life in America. It is rather more than enough that the African-Americans express the conflict more openly than any others among us.

It may be that the African-American difference in the American Religion is particularly apparent because of contrasting senses of temporality. West African religion possessed an intense apprehension of the dynamism of present time, and an acute conviction that the past scarcely had gone by. New Testament eschatology was restored to something of its original force by African-Americans, by whom the Second Coming of Jesus could not be regarded as a far-off event. This must be why American Pentecostalism developed in an essentially black context, and why it continues to meet the spiritual expectations of those not willing to tarry for an eternity before Jesus returns. The indefinite future does not exist in West African spiritual consciousness, which aided African-Americans in their persistent interpretation of Psalm 68:31:

> Princes shall come out of Egypt, Ethiopia shall soon stretch out her hands unto God.

That "soon" has been crucial, and reverberates endlessly in African-American religious consciousness. One could speculate that the black freedom from infinitely postponed apocalyptic expectations has saved the Black Churches from the crippling controversies that rage on among white Baptists and other Protestants. The inability to sustain metaphor that makes for Fundamentalism is not an African-American affliction. Generations who have learned to interpret the Bible as a manual for survival are blessedly free from the nightmare of Inerrancy. The black Jesus of the great spirituals is an immediacy, and he is a rhetorician who teaches how to transmute survival into liberation. Since the "little me" always has survived, was not born, and cannot die, then the God of the "little me" has conquered death also, and can be reached soon, by a stretching out of the hands. It seems by now a touch baffling that African-American religion ever was regarded as being primarily Christian, in the European sense. It is not Augustinian religion, and does not exalt the Church, but holds on hard to the two realities, a "little me" that refuses bondage, and a Jesus who liberates.

Many exhorters have come forth in recent decades to insist that Christianity was an imposition upon African-Americans. Historical and institutional Christianity indeed was in many respects either irrelevant or hurtful to a people in bondage, but then it was also inadequate to the needs and situation of white dwellers on the frontier. Cane Ridge and its aftermaths began to bring about a more American kind of religion, in a process that unknowingly followed the eighteenth-century development of the black Baptists.

Even as today's Moderate Southern Baptists are belated legatees of an African-American faith of two centuries ago, so our current advocates of a "black theology" suffer the irony of falling out of their own authentic tradition. It is a major irony of American spiritual history that consciousness raising tends to become cheerleading, whether in matters of religion or gender relations or in education. West African religion exalted a distant God, while providing for a crowded intermediate realm where lesser gods mingled with the ongoing spirits of dead ancestors. This vibrant atmosphere of diffused power survives in African-American congregations until this day, and has much in common with rival magic world views that never quite abandoned American folk religion. The African difference appears to reside not so much in the relative quantity of power assigned to what is either within or beyond the individual's spirit, but rather in the relatively unmediated relation enjoyed by the spirit within to the spirits without. The gods of Africa were mostly destroyed by Christianity, but the slave's access to spirit was not. Since Episcopalianism was so rigorous a system of mediation, it made a hopeless version of Christianity for Africans trapped in bondage. The far greater appeal of the Baptists was their almost unmediated access to Jesus; the Africans removed that "almost," and by making Jesus unmediated they made him black. It may be the greatest irony of American religious history that the Southern Baptists, the heart of the Confederacy, came to worship an essentially black Jesus without ever knowing how he had been purified of his last elements of mediated or Catholic tradition.

Christianity, like Judaism before it, is not a biblical religion, despite all its assertions, since its theologies are Greek, not Hebrew, even as normative Judaism, a second century of the Common Era formulation, was compelled to rely upon Greek thought-forms. It is one of the oddities of the American Religion that it is much more of a biblical religion than its precursors were. This irony is enhanced in African-American religion, which is fundamentally biblical. Nat Turner, Baptist preacher, exhorter, and visionary, regarded his butcheries of men, women, children, and infants as altogether biblical, fulfilling God's command to destroy the oppressors so that a chosen people could be liberated. That is the unattractive extreme of biblical obsession, in absolute contrast to the extraordinary humanity of the African-American spirituals, still the most impressive body of folk poetry produced in this nation. The spirituals frequently manifest the West African attitude towards time, in which the future is a wave about to break over enslaved persons, who then will be carried back to an African and mythic past. On the African heritage of the slave spirituals, the best-balanced judgment still seems to belong to Alan Lomax:

> The main traditions of Afro-American song, especially those of the old-time congregational spiritual, are derived from the main African song style model. European song style did influence the African tradition in America in regard to melodic form and, of course, textual content. In most other respects, Afro-American song has hewed to the main dynamic line of the principal African tradition. (Quoted in Raboteau, pp. 340–41)

This still matters, since Lomax doubtless meant the Bible as the source of what he called "textual content," and it is important to observe that the spirituals curtail the biblical sense of the future. In the spirituals, the future is always rushing towards you, and you are about to be hit by it, because there is no other future beyond the next few months, at the most. How would it be to be singing this, and be intuitively convinced that it must come that soon?

> Yes one o' dese mornin's bout twelve o'clock
> Dis ol' worl' am gwinter reel and rock
>
> I want to be ready
> I want to be ready
> I want to be ready
> To walk in Jerusalem just like John
>
> Great day! Great day the righteous marching
> Great day! God's going to build up Zion's walls

Great day in the morning indeed, if it comes next morning, or the morning after that. There must have been an immediacy in the spirituals for the first black Baptists in America that we cannot comprehend today. Gayrand Wilmore, in *Last Things First* (1982) interprets this and other spirituals in the manner of John Mbiti, whose work on African religion has centered upon the problem of temporality. Mbiti, in his very useful *African Religions and Philosophy* (revised edition, 1990), understands all of African religion in the context of the African difference in the philosophy of time:

> In western or technological society, time is a commodity which must be utilized, sold, and bought, but in traditional African life, time has to be created or produced. Man is not a slave of time; instead, he "makes" as much time as he wants. When foreigners, especially from Europe and America, come to Africa and see people sitting down somewhere without, evidently, doing anything, they often remark, "These Africans waste their time by just sitting idle!" Another common cry is, "Oh, Africans, are always late!" It is easy to jump to such judgments, but they are judgments based on ignorance of what time means to African peoples. Those who are seen sitting down, are actually *not wasting* time, but either waiting for time or in the process of "producing" time.

I am a little skeptical as to this, as it conveys an Africa inhabited only by Sir John Falstaffs and Walt Whitmans. Yet Mbiti brings together a hoard of observations of African religion to reinforce his point. On such a basis, African-American eschatology, past and present, takes on a force that breaks through many of the restraining traditions of Christian theology. Liberation theology, the work of Gustavo Gutierrez and others, is clearly akin to African views of time and history. American millennialism, roughly outlined in my third chapter, looks very different from an African perspective. One can venture that only three groups among us have active visions of the Kingdom of God in America: the Mormons, Southern Baptist Fundamentalists, and many of the African-American churches. These three visions are not reconcilable, though the first two certainly are represented, indeed overrepresented, in the Reagan-Bush Kingdom, from which the African-Americans are massively shut out. Gayrand Wilmore presents African-Americans as "another eschatological people," which makes me think primarily of the Mormons in the context of our time and our country. Even though blacks now can hold the priesthood among the Mormons, everything about Mormonism and African-American religion suggests future conflict between them, in an America where politics and religion increasingly refuse separation from one another.

Mbiti tells the poignant story of particular African converts who decided that Jesus had changed his mind and never would return. Wilmore relates this to the continuing appeal of black Pentecostalism, which overcomes such anxiety by the immediate evidence that testifies to the Holy Spirit's actuality. To me, Mbiti's anecdote suggests instead a stimulus for the complex history of the Nation of Islam with its remarkable personalities: the mysterious Wali Fard, Elijah Muhammad, Malcolm X, Warith Deen Muhammad, and Louis Farrakhan. Over one hundred thousand followers of Elijah Muhammad's Nation followed his son Warith Deen Muhammad into Sunni Islam, which recognizes no distinction between blacks and whites. Farrakhan's twenty thousand or so diehards, the remnant of the former Black Muslims, are too small a sect to greatly influence the future course of African-American religion. But no meditation upon the American Religion, our homemade varieties of Gnosticism and Orphic Enthusiasm, should neglect the visions taught to Elijah Muhammad, who had the tenacity and the spiritual drive that might have made him a twentieth-century Joseph Smith, if not for the national changes brought about by the work and martyrdom of Martin Luther King, Jr.

In the beginning was a man of many names: Wali Fard, the Honorable Master Fard Muhammad, Wallace D. Fard Muhammad, Professor Ford, Mr. Wali Farrad, or just the Prophet. He appeared in the guise of an Arab peddler in black Detroit, midsummer 1930, and rapidly gathered a following, being a person of great charm and mysterious wisdom. So far as I know, there is still no certain identification for Fard, whether as to his nationality, race, background, education, or even his age. His prophetic ministry lasted just four years, after which he evidently vanished forever, handing his movement on to the disciple he named Elijah Muhammad. The new Elijah was an organizer of genius, but seems to have been accurate in ascribing his doctrine to his teacher Fard, clearly a major American visionary, whether one likes his work or not. Fard insisted that he had arrived from Mecca, the Holy City, in order to recover the "so-called Negro" for Islam, the ancestral faith. He indicated also that his full nature and status would be revealed only later, an epiphany that took place only after his permanent disappearance, when Elijah Muhammad proclaimed that his absent master had been Allah himself.

The most remarkable single document about Fard that I have

seen is by Wallace D. Muhammad, who was named after the Master, and who sought to demythologize his father's teacher and doctrine in a declaration of March 19, 1976, about a year after Elijah Muhammad's death. I give only a few excerpts from this document.

> The Honorable Master Elijah Muhammad taught very vaguely about the Honorable Master Fard Muhammad as a person. He said that he was a "saviour," he said that he was "God," and he said that he was "God in the person of Master Fard Muhammad" . . .
>
> Most of the church people were hating their own identity, and they didn't even know it . . . This is the condition in which Master Fard Muhammad found us in the early 1930s when he came to America . . . Master Fard Muhammad is not dead, brothers and sisters, he is physically alive and I talk to him whenever I get ready. I don't talk to him in any spooky way, I go to the telephone and dial his number.
>
> When he saw that our problem was that we were already too spiritual (too wrapped up in the Bible), he devised a plan. He knew he could not get us if he came at us with the Holy Scripture. Whatever anyone had come at us with, it would not have been any stronger than what we already had in the way of spiritual force . . .
>
> When you find a people completely dead, you do not come to them with the spirit. You can come to a society that is alive socially and economically by teaching them the spirit (the "heaven"), but you cannot teach the "heavens" to a society that has not yet been formed in the earth. You have to teach them the earth, first . . .
>
> Master Fard offered friendship because he knew that the only friend we identified with was the friend "Jesus." We identified with that friend because our suffering resembled his suffering. Master Fard began to take our minds off that Jesus because he realized that until we could see our own suffering, we would never be able to be serious about doing something to remove that suffering—so he began to tell us about our own suffering. (*Afro-American Religious History*, edited by Milton C. Sernett [1985], pp. 414–16)

Wallace D. Muhammad sums up Fard's achievement quite tersely: "He formed us physically and then put desire in us," an evident allusion to Fard's divine or semidivine status. All this is preamble to Wallace Muhammad's call for revision; the great work of Fard and Elijah is done: "The emphasis has to be taken off of revolution." With these words, the mass movement of the Black Muslims ended, and the greater part of those who had followed Fard and Elijah Muhammad were carried over to orthodox or Sunni Islam. Whites were admitted, the flag was displayed, and a revolution, one still associated with the name of Malcolm X, became American history, despite the rearguard media assaults of Louis Farrakhan. Perhaps Fard *was* still alive in 1976 as Wallace Muhammad said he was; it had been forty-two years since his disappearance, and no one knows what age Fard was in 1934. Perhaps the elusive Fard is alive somewhere today, though it seems most unlikely. There are ancient rumors that Fard died in 1934 as a voluntary ritual sacrifice, in order to begin the reign of Elijah, but that also is a rather baroque speculation. What matters is that Fard succeeded in his religious project; there are estimates now that Islam has nearly six million adherents in the United States, making Muslims more numerous than Jews or even Mormons (though their growth rate is small when compared to the Mormons' sustained burgeoning). Some surveys indicate that a million African-Americans, most of them males, are now Sunni Muslims, inspired to one degree or another by the American Muslim Mission of Imam Warith Deen Muhammad, as the movement and its leader are now called. Fard is certainly vindicated as a prophet, even if Elijah Muhammad's fierce version of his teachings matters now only to Farrakhan and his barely twenty thousand followers in the Nation of Islam.

Islam, whether orthodox Sunni or Shiite Fundamentalist, is hardly a variety of the American Religion and would form no part of my subject except for a particular strain in the doctrine of Fard and Elijah, a violent Gnosticism still prevalent in the flamboyant Farrakhan, but hardly expressed by him in a finer tone. He asserts that in 1985, a decade after Elijah Muhammad's death, he again met that prophet in a spaceship, in order to renew his spiritual relation to his Master. This is a religious statement, and doubtless deserves to be understood as such, but it lacks the homely spirit of Warid Deen Muhammad picking up the telephone to call Fard. What Farrakhan still maintains is Elijah's cosmological myth, which may have been Fard's teaching (though we will never know this) but has been discarded by the American Muslim Mission. The myth, rancid in itself, has the same parodistic relation to the American Religion as have the grotesque visions of Jehovah's Witnesses and the orange squash of the New Age, and deserves a glance on that basis, even if it is no part of what is likely to make African-American spirituality an ongoing paradigm for the nation.

As text, one takes Elijah Muhammad's *Message to the Blackman in America* (1965), a revision and expansion of his earlier *The Supreme Wisdom*. The villain of these writings is Yakub, father of all devils, and creator of the white race:

> The great archdeceivers (the white race) were taught by their father, Yakub, 6,000 years ago, how to teach that God is a spirit (spook) and not a man. In the grafting of his people (the white race), Mr. Yakub taught his people to contend with us over the reality of God by asking us of the whereabouts of that first One (God) who created the heavens and the earth, and that, Yakub said, we cannot do. Well, we all know that there was a God in the beginning that created all these things and do know that He does not exist today. But we know again that from that God the person of God continued until today in His people, and today a Supreme One (God) has appeared among us with the same infinite wisdom to bring about a complete change. (p. 9)

The Supreme One is Fard, to whose teaching Elijah ascribes the story of Yakub. Of Fard, Elijah tells us mysteriously (pp. 24–25), that he was persecuted, jailed in 1932, ordered out of Detroit in 1933, and subsequently jailed in Chicago. We are told nothing more of the fate of the Mahdi, who was God. What remains, at the center of the Supreme Wisdom, is the ghastly career of the devil Yakub, which defies summary. One can hardly speak of the highlights or achievements of Yakub, whose exploits in Elijah Muhammad's texts sometime remind me of the zany splendors of Christopher Marlowe's Barabas, the hero-villain of *The Jew of Malta*. Yakub, who begins in Mecca but ends his evil life of one hundred and fifty years on Saint John the Divine's isle of Patmos, has something of Barabas's superb daemonic vitality, which is oddly contagious and even informs Elijah's account of him:

Yakub was the founder of unlike attracts and like repels, though Mr. Yakub was a member of the black nation. He began school at the age of four. He had an unusual size head. When he had grown up, the others referred to him as the "big head scientist."

At the age of 18 he had finished all of the colleges and universities of his nation, and was seen preaching on the streets of Mecca, making converts . . .

He learned, from studying the germ of the black man, under the microscope, that there were two people in him, and that one was black, the other brown.

He said if he could successfully separate the one from the other he could graft the brown germ into its last stage, which would be white. With his wisdom, he could make the white, which he discovered was the weaker of the black germ (which would be unalike) rule the black nation for a time (until a greater one than Yakub was born). (p. 112)

Fard, if he was the origin of this weird tale, had an authentic religious imagination, of the kind out of which folk religion always has emanated. Yakub has an irksome memorability as a crude but pungent Gnostic Demiurge, marring to a false creation. His devils people Europe, producing all those Dead White European Males of Western culture, now so unacceptable to politically correct student non-students. Fard (or Elijah) pioneered by making one of the embryonic myths of our current academic rabblement who practice fashionable Resentment. One sees why, aside from his capacity for mischief, Farrakhan now finds a constituency upon our campuses. What is also apparent is the pragmatic wisdom of Walid Deen Muhammad, who has liberated his followers from the tales of Yakub.

I return to the long tradition of African-American religion serving a paradigmatic function for our generic spirituality, with the advantage of the contrast afforded by the rebellion against Afro-Baptist tradition by the Nation of Islam and its flowing-off into Sunni Islam. If I were asked where one could find an authentic devotional poetry in contemporary America, I would turn to the best of our current poets who have emerged from African-American culture, Jay Wright and Thylias Moss. I conclude this chapter by briefly meditating upon a poem by each, but I intend the meditation to be the work of a religious critic, not a literary one, and so I will try to expound only the spiritual interest, rather than the extraordinary aesthetic value that is involved. In the splendid "The Warmth of Hot Chocolate," to be found in her *Rainbow Remnants in Rock Bottom Ghetto Sky* (1991), Thylias Moss begins by establishing her status as an angel, with recently trimmed wings:

> Everybody thinks they grow out of the back, some people
> even assume shoulder blades are all that man has left
> of past glory, but my wings actually grow from my scalp,
> a heavy hair that stiffens for flight by the release
> of chemical secretions activated whenever I jump off a
> bridge. Many angels are discovered when people
> trying to commit suicide ride and tame the air. I was just
> such an accident. We're simply a different species,
> not intrinsically holy, just intrinsically airborne.

Irrefutably identified as an angel, Moss's speaker proceeds to theurgy, to the process of strengthening a God much in need of it, this late in a long tradition of a highly personal relationship of the angelic spirit, or "warmth of hot chocolate," with a humanized God who now perhaps needs to be saved from himself:

>   . . . He doesn't
> figure many possibilities are open to him. I think
> he's wise to bide his time although he pales in the
> moonlight to just a glow, just the warmth of hot
> chocolate spreading through the body like a subcu-
> taneous halo. But to trust him implicitly would
> be a mistake for he then would not have to maintain
> his worthiness to be God. Even the thinnest,
> flyweight modicum of doubt gives God the necessity
> to prove he's worthy of the implicit trust I can
> never give because I protect him from corruption,
> from the complacence that rises within him sometimes,
> a shadowy ever-descending brother.

This beautiful and imaginatively audacious revision of the African-American God is the antithesis of cheerleading, and is an authentic act of knowledge, worthy of the best American religious poetry, or rather of the poetry of the American Religion, the work of Walt Whitman, Emily Dickinson, Hart Crane. Thylias Moss subtly transfigures the intimate relation to God that has governed African-American tradition from the time of the first black Baptists on to Baldwin's *Go Tell It on the Mountain*. Knowing also how vexed our era is, Moss moves to protect her God from the corruption of complacence, the affliction of nearly all organized religion, mainline and Fundamentalist, in our country today. Spiritually as much as aesthetically, this seems to me a poem that we all of us need.

I close this chapter with one of the high chants of Jay Wright, the difficult and powerful poet who has founded so much of his art upon his own deep study of African religion. Dogon mythology in particular informs Wright's spirituality, as here in "The Eye of God, the Soul's First Vision" from his *Dimensions of History* (1976):

> Like the master of the spear,
> I cross my river now,
> always to return to one beginning,
> which may be one or no beginning,
> under the tightly bound arms
> and the spirit of masks,
> I return to you,
>   to name,
>   to own,
> to be possessed and named myself,
> following the movement of the eye of God,
> whose lids will close upon your greater claims.

The sad possibility that it may be "no beginning" or the closing of the lids of God's eye upon the largest assertions are alike instances of DuBois's "double consciousness," the division in the self that is part of the African-American cultural legacy. Wright's "I" and "you" are both aspects of the same self, and we return to the central dilemma of the African-American quest for freedom, which I think is the inevitable paradigm now for all similar American quests. Is the self to be made free of itself, or free of other selves? The goal is to be made free for God, however you interpret *that* freedom, but do you deny the self for a community, past or present, or do you affirm the self by evading community? Like DuBois,

Jay Wright clarifies the question, and abandons us to the process of finding an answer. "The Eye of God, the Soul's First Vision" closes instead with eloquent requestionings that evoke the full poignance of the relation of African Americans to their religious heritage:

> Who has burned this land?
> Who has sent me, shaven head,
> bleeding for my princes?
> Who has chosen me
> to reconstruct this eye of God,
> to understand the signs
>   of this dispossession?
> to slip, beyond this pain, this key in the lock
> to objectify this joy?

16
The Religion of Our Climate

WHAT would a purified and amalgamated form of the American Religion be? I have judged, in this book, that two of the most admirable versions of such a faith were the one left incomplete by Joseph Smith when he was killed, and the one worked out by Edgar Young Mullins at the turn of the nineteenth century into the twentieth. Joseph Smith's faith has been transmuted by the Mormon Church into its current compromise with American society; the Moderate Southern Baptists, fighting back against their Texas Fundamentalist overlords, are attempting to rescue their soul competency. Whatever comes in the future, these two very American modes of belief will maintain themselves, but respectively in dimmed and embattled forms. I have tried to show that both are very original hybrids, in which traditional Christian impulses have been intermixed with Gnostic, Enthusiastic, and American Orphic elements. I turn now to the hard question: Will there be, someday, what might be called the religion of our climate? To ask such a question is to enter upon a speculation that transcends history and yet suffers a nostalgia for it.

Religious criticism, even if it seeks to banish all nostalgia for belief, still falls into the experience of the spiritual, even as literary criticism cannot avoid the danger of falling into the text. Myself a Gnostic without hope, I am fascinated by the American Gnosis that will not abandon hope, even where the cost is Mormon fantastifaction or Moderate Southern Baptist solitude or the African-American double consciousness. Any movement from another kind of criticism to religious criticism invokes the shadows of revisionism, a movement of the mind that causes every one of us to ask: How can I attain an original or at least individual relationship to truth or God? How can I open the traditions of religion to my own experience? Very few of us will give the very radical answer of Joseph Smith, which is just as well, since even the United States scarcely could afford another Joseph Smith. Our nation, from 1800 until now, never lacks for new religions. We always will have too many of them, just as we will have an endless oversupply of evangelists, greedily seeking yet more revivals.

No other Western nation, as I remarked earlier in this study, matches our obsession with religion. The vast majority of us believe in some version of God, and nearly all of that majority actually do believe that God loves her or him, on a personal and individual basis. Very few of us believe that death closes all, and perhaps no nation ever has rejected death with an intensity comparable to ours. Death, in literature, is the mother of beauty; death, in life, is the father of religion. Those who would deny that formula might experiment with the question: If medicine someday could grant immortality (virtually, to those who could pay for it), you, of course, still would be religious, but what about your neighbor? The world, and Europe in particular, has a long and bad record of coercing people into faith; we have done better, until recently, anyway. When people frighten themselves into faith, as millions of Americans do, what ought religious criticism to do with that fright? Why is it that we have produced so few masterpieces of overtly religious literature? Devotional poetry or narrative or drama, of any aesthetic eminence, or of any profound spirituality, hardly exists among us. Fundamentalism, as I have shown, is viciously anti-intellectual, but so, alas, is most American religion, of whatever camp. Fear and mindlessness can engender parodies of religion, but what value is there in supposed faith that is essentially political? Few phrases are as ambiguous as "I believe in God" or "I love Jesus," since all they generally mean is that "I cannot function because I dread dying" or "My neighbor won't vote for me" or "If I don't get a Temple Recommend, I'll lose my job" (a Mormon anxiety).

Ancient Gnosticism, together with its Enthusiastic shadows, was the most elitist and negative of theologies. It is the dubious achievement of the darker versions of the American Religion that they have democratized Gnosticism. Fundamentalist Southern Baptists and many organization Mormons join Pentecostals, Adventists, Jehovah's Witnesses, and Christian Scientists in a revel of sparkless self that mocks what began at Cane Ridge. Since I am persuaded that much of what this book describes can be found also in Americanized Catholicism and Judaism, as well as in most mainline Protestantism, much of American religiosity clearly lacks spiritual content. The societal consequences of debasing the Gnostic self into selfishness, and the believer's freedom from others into the bondage of others, are to be seen everywhere, in our inner cities and in our agrarian wastelands.

And yet the fear of death does not ensue only from cowardice or self-intoxication, but can be provoked by an extraordinary vitality. The United States, as our best writers always have seen, remains alive beyond belief, and has the drive perpetually to seek the Blessing of Yahweh, or the Resurrection and the Life of Jesus. Joseph Smith's vision of men progressing so as to become gods, or the Baptists' experience of walking with the risen Jesus, has the human poignance and spiritual pathos that mark the American Religion as an inevitable expression of our Evening Land. African-American spirituality at its most intense is the most prophetic evocation of what may be the nation's religious future. The figure of Jesus is endlessly adaptable to nearly any conceivable communal or individual need or desire. Salvation, according to the fiercely anti-Jewish Gospel of John, is from the Jews, and much of the history of the American Religion, white and black, has seen a displacement of ancient Israel by the New World.

If there is, as I have surmised, the American Religion, then there must be something peculiarly different about the American God. Conceptions of God, throughout Western history, have varied very widely, not just between Judaism, Christianity, and Islam, but within those religions themselves. The anthropomorphic God of the Yahwist, the first major author in Hebrew, has very little in common with the God of the composite Torah, as put together by the Redactor in the time of Ezra the Scribe. Roman Catholics apprehend a God who has little in common with John Calvin's sense of the divine, and the Calvinist deity, first brought to America by the Puritans, has remarkably little in common with the versions of God now apprehended by what calls itself Protestantism in the United States.

The God of the American Religion is an experiential God, so radically *within* our own being as to become a virtual identity with what is most authentic (oldest and best) in the self. Much of early Emerson hovers near this vision of God:

It is by yourself without ambassador that God speaks to you . . .

It is God in you that responds to God without, or affirms his own words trembling on the lips of another.

Such recognitions have become commonplace in our kind of spirituality, and have provoked much criticism, of which the most distinguished is the lament of the martyred Dietrich Bonhoeffer: "God has granted American Christianity no Reformation." That seems essentially true to me, but I do not take it as a spur to grief. If the American Religion is now just two centuries old, from Cane Ridge to the present, then it seems too early for a Reformation. The issue is not self-worship; it is acquaintance with a God within the self. Not to know this God is to be asleep in the outward life, where all of North America perpetually dozes away. A neo-orthodox revival of Continental Reformed Protestantism is precisely what we do not need. It would return us to a more severe dualism than we have developed for ourselves already, and we are peculiarly unfitted for any more stringent dualism.

The late Ioan Couliano's *Tree of Gnosis* (1991) studies dualist trends in religion and culture, from ancient Gnosticism until today. Religion in America, let alone the American Religion, is not its concern, but Couliano's analysis of dualism has an inevitable relevance to my subject. Are our principal American religious thinkers essentially dualists? We have had only a few vital intellectual speculators in religion: Jonathan Edwards, Emerson, Horace Bushnell, William James, the Niebuhrs. Edwards lived and died before the American Religion came to its turbulent birth at Cane Ridge. All the others rather inconsistently courted moods of monism, yet

were profoundly dualistic, since they shared with the American
Religion of the populace the conviction that what was best and
oldest in them went back well before the creation of the world or
of people in anything like their present form. That is my sense of
dualism, but not quite Couliano's, who emphasizes the dualist's
stance as a sense of superiority either to the Cosmos or its Creator.
But Americans regard priority as superiority, doubtless because
we are the belated Western nation, the Evening Land of Western
culture.

American religious dualism seems at first not to be dualistic at
all, according to Couliano's criteria. Emerson and his descendants
do not believe that either the world or the body is evil, are not
ascetics, and generally eschew vegetarianism: one remembers the
meat pies prepared for Emerson's breakfasts by his "Asia," the
formidable second Mrs. Emerson. An amiable antinomianism,
however, is very Emersonian, as is the Orphic impulse that Couliano rightly posits as one of the sources of Western dualism. American or Emersonian Orphism again divests itself of the notion that
the body is evil, while finding the Cosmos to be not so much
wicked as merely inferior to the Adamic American. The dualism
of the American Religion is not therefore very dualistic; it devalues
context, perhaps in defiance of the Sublime expanses of American
space. American Religionists, whether Southern Baptists or Mormons, Pentecostals or Black Muslims, assign a singular prestige to
origins, as befits a religion whose principal anxiety is priority, or
the lack thereof. And *there* is the clue to American religious dualism: the origin of the occult self, the saved element in one's being,
goes back beyond nature to God, beyond the Creation to the Creator.

Gnosticism and Orphism alike therefore are somewhat inadequate analogues for the American Religion, though we are not
likely to discover closer ones. The American finds fault with nature, time, and history, but neither with God nor with herself or
himself. This is not wholly a bad thing, as assorted moralists would
have us believe, since it keeps us a republic of hope, at least in the
pure good of theory. I have ventured already that the American
Religion, as a gnosis, has much in common with the American
romance, a peculiar literary genre that includes narratives as
diverse as Hawthorne's *The Scarlet Letter* and Pynchon's *The Crying
of Lot 49*. The American Gnostic embarks upon a quest to find the

American Jesus, necessarily an internalized quest. Such a journey is bound to be more successful than the endless quests for the historical Jesus. The historical Jesus doubtless existed (though we have only Christian warrant for this, since I do not trust any of the passages attributed to the ancient Jewish historian Josephus, all of them appearing to be Christian interpolations). But beyond Jesus' existence, we know little we can rely upon, since everything available to us is so clearly tendentious. Saint Paul is central to the American Religion primarily because Jesus mattered to him not for how Jesus had lived, but only for his death and reputed resurrection. The risen Jesus, scarcely reported in the Gospels, or even in Acts, remains a mystery. What did he reveal of the Kingdom of Heaven in those forty days and nights in which he tarried with his disciples? Gnostic texts, mostly of the school of the highly imaginative Valentinus, attempted to answer the question. Reading a Valentinian work like *The Gospel of Philip*, *The Treatise on the Resurrection*, or *The Exegesis on the Soul*, we are carried back to the canonical New Testament's denunciation of highly imaginative notions that our Resurrection already has taken place:

> But shun profane and vain babblings: for they will increase unto more ungodliness.
> And their word will eat as doth a canker: of whom is Hymeneus and Philetus;
> Who concerning the truth have erred, saying that the resurrection is past already; and overthrow the faith of some. (2 Timothy 2:16–18)

Ibn Khaldun, who died in 1406, thus summarized the Lawgiver Muhammad on the Resurrection, and its connection to God's creative power:

> He causes our resurrection after death. This constitutes the final touch to His concern with the first creation. If created things were destined to disappear completely, their creation would have been frivolous. They are destined for eternal existence after death.

The Koran almost might be called the Book of the Resurrection, so certain was Muhammad that the Creation had not been frivolous. But the author of the original J text, the Yahwist, knew nothing of the doctrine, and indeed the Hebrew Bible knew nothing more of it until the apocalyptic Book of Daniel, the historical end of the Jewish Scripture. Moses and the great prophets were not obsessed with individual survival. There had been Enoch, taken up to become the angel Metatron, and Elijah, but they were not resurrected; they never died. There was a Hebrew Hades, Sheol, where you went if unburied, and where malcontents were swallowed up alive, if they rebelled against Moses in the Wilderness. Or you went there anyway, whoever you were, according to a lament of Job. But in Daniel, in the era of the Maccabean revolution, the need for an ultimate justice led to an un-Hebraic prophecy: "Many who sleep in earth's dust will awake, some to life eternal." This became the Pharisaic vision of the resurrection of the body, and the vision also of the Pharisee who became Saint Paul. Jesus, in the Gospel of Mark, also stands with the Pharisees, asserting that God is the God of the living, not of the dead, thus prompting Paul's faith that our animal body will be raised as a spiritual body. In an exalted passage directed to the Corinthians (I Corinthians 15:51–53), Paul unfolded a mystery:

We shall not all die [before the return of Christ], but we shall all be changed in a flash, in the twinkling of an eye, at the last trumpet call. For the trumpet will sound, and the dead will rise immortal, and we shall be changed. This perishable being must be clothed with the imperishable, and what is mortal must be clothed with immortality.

In *The City of God*, Augustine subtly interpreted Paul's idea of the "spiritual body" as being one's own body, but "subject to the spirit, readily offering total and wonderful obedience." On this view, immortality in the spirit is an issue of authority, of the human reluctance to obey God no longer being an impediment. Here (as elsewhere) Augustine was highly congenial to John Calvin and all who have followed him since, but as we have seen, the American Religion is not Calvinist. E. Y. Mullins, theologian of all true Baptists, favored a more mystical interpretation, as did Joseph Smith. Both these heroic spirits associated the resurrected Jesus, the resurrection of the spiritual body of all mankind, and America. In doing so, they joined a long tradition that never quite culminates, even in the severely modified Calvinism of Woodrow Wilson: "America had the infinite privilege of fulfilling her destiny and saving the world." George Bush's New World Order is a fresh shadowing of the image of American-led Resurrection, even if we all of us would be startled if our nonvisionary President were to utter the shocking Wilsonian sentence: "America was intended to be a spirit among the nations of the world."

Ancient Gnosticism was an elite religion, or quasi-religion; the oddity of our American Gnosis is that it is a mass phenomenon. There are tens of millions of Americans whose obsessive idea of spiritual freedom violates the normative basis of historical Christianity, though they are incapable of realizing how little they share of what once was considered Christian doctrine. Even the Mormons, who so clearly are as radical a departure from Christianity as is Islam, regard themselves as the legitimate Church of Jesus Christ. But at least the Mormons do recognize their own overt elitism; only *they* will progress to godhood. The more deeply I study the Mormons and meditate upon their peculiar appropriateness for the American spiritual climate, the more I become convinced that someday soon they will be the Established Church of the American West, even as the Baptists are the Catholic Church of our South. Independence, Missouri, according to Joseph Smith, was to be the site of Zion, or New Jerusalem, which would be built just before the Second Advent of Jesus. By a splendid irony, Independence is the Salt Lake City of the rival Reorganized Mormons, only about a fortieth the size of the Utah-centered Mormons. When Brigham Young led the trek west to the Great Salt Lake, Emma, the Prophet's wife, declined to join in. With her sons and a remnant of her husband's followers, she gradually moved to Independence, where Joseph Smith III became Prophet, Seer, and Revelator, and where descendants of the Prophet have presided ever since. If the New Jerusalem is ever built, amiably close to the not very biblical Kansas City, it will be surrounded by Reorganized Mormons who still follow Emma in her declarations that Joseph never practiced polygamy, never taught a plurality of gods, never advocated that the dead be baptized, or that we become gods.

The larger irony behind this is that the American Religion, which is nothing if not a *knowing*, does not know itself. Perhaps that is a permanent and general American irony, which would have been much appreciated by Nietzsche; we may be uniquely the nation where the knowers cannot know themselves. Our national epic and best poem is Walt Whitman's "Song of Myself," where my self indeed turns out to be unknowable, because it follows both the ancient Orphic and the African-American model, in which "the real me" or "me myself" (the Africans' "little me") stands apart and never can be known. Joseph Smith, in his King Follett discourse, sadly told his disciples and followers that they did not know him, because as he moved inexorably towards martyrdom, he was coming to understand how little he knew his own innermost spirit. The American Religion is neither a Christian "believing that" nor a Judaic "trusting in"; it is a knowing, and as such properly horrified the Protestant consciousness of D. H. Lawrence, who found such knowing obscene when he encountered it in such representative American Gnostics as Poe and Melville.

I surmise that a sense of cultural, historical, and religious belatedness, inevitable in the Evening Land of America, increases the appetite to know, rather than to believe or to trust. The urgency of our national drive to know renders European Protestantism inauthentic in our professedly Protestant culture, and has turned us towards Gnosis these last two centuries. Again, I marvel that this turn should have been so much more numerous than any elite could provide. A full generation before Emerson came to his spiritual maturity, the frontier people experienced their giant epiphany of Gnosis at Cane Ridge. Their ecstasy was no more communal than the rapture at Woodstock; each barking Kentuckian or prancing yippie barked and pranced for himself or herself alone. The American Orphic ecstasy never has been Dionysiac, for the Bacchic freedom is the freedom to merge into others. American ecstasy is solitary, even when it requires the presence of others as audience for the self's glory. Our father Walt Whitman, despite his self-advertisements and the dogmatic insistences of our contemporary gays, seems to have embraced only himself.

Humanly there is something quite cold about the religion of our climate. Our sacred frenzies are directed towards ourselves or towards the resurrected Jesus; the American Religion takes up the cross only as emblem of the risen God, not of the crucified man, if indeed it takes up the cross at all (the Mormons do not). Pentecostals and many other sectarians white and black experience a sacred violence as the Spirit hits them, but the violence assimilates very quickly to American secular violence, altogether as prevalent in the countryside as in the cities. The American Religion in itself is not violence, but confusion frequently attends both, and certainly our knowing is more often than not a violent knowing. A religion of the self is not likely to be a religion of peace, since the American self tends to define itself through its war against otherness. If your knowing ultimately tells you that you are beyond nature, having long preceded it, then your natural acts cannot sully you. No wonder, then, that salvation, once attained, cannot fall away from the American Religionist, no matter what he or she does. We export our culture abroad, low and high, and increasingly we export the American Religion as well. If Woodrow Wilson proves correct, and we were intended to be a spirit among the nations of the world, then the twenty-first century will mark a full-scale return to the wars of religion.

Coda: So Great a Cloud of Witnesses

THE late Walker Percy and his distinguished exegete Cleanth Brooks have seen Gnosticism as the curse of Protestant America. I am not of their judgment, as this book has made plain, though I am also not interested in arguing the reverse: that our peculiar mixture of Gnosticism, Enthusiasm, and Orphism in itself is of inestimable spiritual value. But then, celebrating our pervasive, expanding, and only partly covert national faith seems to me no more useful than deploring it. One basic axiom of religious criticism must be: *There are no accidents*. One generation after the American Revolution, the American Religion fiercely sprang into existence at Cane Ridge, and then for a full century afterwards exfoliated into its myriad forms. Though the denominations and sects I have examined here are confined to American originals— Mormons, Southern Baptists (both those on the Moderate or "creedless" side, and the Know-Nothing Fundamentalists), African-American faith in general, and the Pentecostals, Adventists, Witnesses, Christian Scientists—much of what I call the American Religion is as relevant to Methodists, Presbyterians, Congregationalists, Episcopalians, and other Mainline denominations as it is to Baptists and to Mormons. The fundamental convictions as to relations between the human and the divine are sometimes different among Catholics, Lutherans, and Jews in America, but nearly all else who are believers are American Religionists, whether they are capable of knowing it or not. Large unconscious assumptions have far more to do with belief than do overt doctrinal teachings, at least among our vast Protestant population, so great a cloud of witnesses whether they be or not.

A religion-mad country entering upon the final decade of the twentieth century is doomed to enjoy some very interesting times indeed before that decade, and century, pass into what is to come. The national election to be held in the year 2000 will reverberate with sanctified forebodings, perhaps more than ever before in American history. A millennial land from our start, we once had a George Bush who prophesied vast overturnings in society, but that was an amiable Swedenborgian of a hundred and fifty years ago, a man who read books. Reading is not an activity of the Age of Reagan and Bush, and Reagan's brief flirtation with the Falwellian Rapture does not make me wish that President Bush stay up nights to read the Revelation of Saint John the Divine. The American Religion, always millennial, will soon enough engage us all in fearful expectations of finality.

Our most authentic and ghastly millennial yearnings were post-Revolutionary, and have gone on now for more than two hundred years. Millenarianism has never been a pleasant matter, as a reading of Norman Cohn's *The Pursuit of the Millennium* (second edition, 1961) powerfully demonstrates. Sixteenth century Protestants, throughout Europe, believed that all of human history had been prophesied, obscurely but definitively, in the Book of Daniel and in Revelation. In the early seventeenth century, Protestant scholars returned to the faith held by the first Christians, which was that Christ would come again not just to end time, but initially to bring about the millennium, a golden age here, in this world, that would precede the apocalypse or final judgment. As the European Enlightenment spread, this Protestant expectation began to be identified with the idea of progress, an identification studied by Ernest Lee Tuveson's *Millennium and Utopia* (1949).

The Hebrew prophets had given Protestantism a series of visions of finality, of which the most crucial was taken to be Daniel 7:13–14, where "one like the Son of man" descends from heaven to rule over the earth in "an everlasting dominion, which shall not pass away." But the New Testament ventured upon a less lasting dominion, when Revelation predicted that Christ would bind the dragon only for a thousand years, after which the dragon would be free to fight at Armageddon, and to lose, thus ushering in the resurrection of the dead and the Last Judgment. A new heaven and a new earth, and a new Jerusalem as bride of the Lamb of God, would then replace fallen reality forever. Congenial as all this has been to the Protestant temperament, it was a peculiar problem for the Roman Catholic Church until Saint Augustine allegorized the millennium as the spiritual realm already instituted by the Resurrection of Jesus. This Augustinian solution removed the unhappy implication that Rome, named as the Whore Babylon in Revelation, would continue to play the part of Babylon, except in the visions of heretics. Yet heresies arose in plenty, until at last they triumphed in the Reformation.

It was not a heretic, but the learned Cistercian monk Joachim of Fiore who in the twelfth century rather dangerously employed Revelation as the basis of a new prophecy of three historical ages: the Father (from Adam to the Incarnation), the Son or the present era, and the future perfection when the Holy Spirit would reign. Joachim's disciples, after his demise, began to conceive of his Third Age as a cleansed spiritual kingdom, socially and politically redeemed and so free of the errors of the Roman Church itself. But Joachist stirrings, though they never have quite ceased, have never been enough to divert the Catholics into millenarian yearnings. That was left to heretic or Protestant tradition, from the Anabaptists in sixteenth-century Germany on through the Cromwellian Revolution in Britain, and then culminating in the American Revolution. New World prophecy, from Columbus through our contemporary New Age Enthusiasts, has identified America with the land of the Millennium. Columbus insisted to Ferdinand and Isabella that he had mapped his voyage in Isaiah (11:10–12), an assertion that the mariner makes again in Hart Crane's American epic, *The Bridge* (1930). Amerigo Vespucci, writing to Lorenzo de Medici, speaks of what will be named for him, America, as a New World. The largest implications of the American Newness did not receive a full intellectual statement before Emerson, but theologically and politically they were expressed by the millennial strain in the Protestant denominations that most strongly sided with the rebels in the American Revolution: Baptists, Congregationalists, and Presbyterians, rather than Anglicans, Quakers, Methodists, and Lutherans. Despite Luther and Calvin, who had sought to preserve Saint Augustine's appropriation of millenarianism for the established authorities, the left wing of the Cromwellian Revolution exalted the Inner Light of the individual Bible reader, and by that light Daniel and Revelation presaged a sectarian New Age in a New World.

The Great Awakening of the 1740s may well be a retrospective interpretive fiction of the historians, but something like it does seem to have focused American millennial expectations and may have helped spur the American Revolution. Jonathan Edwards, still our greatest theologian, invited the English evangelist George Whitefield to Northampton in 1740 with explicit hopes that the millennium would begin soon, most likely in America. Whatever revivalist links to the American Revolution can or cannot be proved, much of the rhetoric preceding the war in the 1770s was inevitably millennial in nature. And yet we cannot call it a religious war, since the American Religion proper still had not been born, perhaps never would have been born unless our democracy and republic came first. Our religious wars began with the Civil War and continue still, making our denominations and sects, who might have been so great a cloud of witnesses, something very different from what they go on hoping to be.

Some of them, though, have hopes that vary widely from those professed, at least to the rest of the nation. I ponder again, here at the end, the curious, at least tacit alliance between two powers spiritually opposed to one another: the majority Southern Baptist Fundamentalists who have seized the Convention, and the Mormon Church. Neither of these would acknowledge the alliance, but it is at the center of the loose but dangerously strong coalition of American Religionists that now guarantee the continued ascendancy of the Reagan-Bush dynasty. Even as I write, in mid-August of 1991, President Bush's Justice Department has associated itself with the militant (indeed violent) Operation Rescue mob that has been assaulting abortion clinics in Wichita, Kansas. It is true that President Bush has urged them to be kinder and gentler in their protests, but nevertheless his intervention (denounced by the Federal District Court judge whose order the mob defies) keeps faith with the American Religion, if not with the Constitution. Again

President Bush waves the flag and the fetus, and we are returned to some of the darker consequences of the Gnostic stance of the religion of our climate.

The Wichita protesters comprise the usual mix of Operation Rescue stalwarts: Pentecostals directly sent by the Holy Spirit, Catholic nuns and priests, assorted Fundamentalists, and followers of new and still obscure sects. A woman among them is quoted by the *New York Times* (August 12, 1991, p. 1) as saying: "I'm surprised God hasn't allowed another nation to take us over yet," as a divine judgment for our crimes against the fetus. These "warriors of prayer," whatever the sanctions of a Wichita federal court, know that President Bush, the nation's spiritual leader, stands with them. This is hardly my irony, since the Department of Justice has entered on their side, and that entry is the abiding significance of the Wichita protests. We are on the verge of being governed by a nationally established religion, an ultimate parody of the American Religion sketched in this book. The Established Church of the South and Southwest, the Southern Baptist Convention, and the burgeoning, soon-to-be Established Church of the West, the Mormons, are only two components of a multiform alliance that will transform our nation by the year 2000, under the leadership of a Republican Party that since 1979 has become the barely secular version of the American Religion. The crusade against abortion will accomplish its aims, against the will of sixty percent of us, through the instrument of a Reagan-Bush Supreme Court, but that may be only the opening triumph of the parodistic American Religion's militancy in the concluding decade of the twentieth century.

Why have so many Americans, particularly from 1980 through the present, voted against their own, quite palpable economic interests? There is of course patriotism, as manifested in our victories over Grenada and Libya under Reagan, and over Panama and Iraq under Bush. But the religious dimension of those campaigns was clear enough, and Bush's heroics in themselves would not have carried him to his present bad eminence. I am inclined to credit Secretary of State James Baker, the supreme strategist of the Republicans since 1979, with the shrewd insight that has now made the Presidential Republican party altogether invincible. Just after his fellow Texans managed their takeover of the Southern Baptist Convention, Baker observed the parallel fall of the Republican party to the Reaganites, whom he joined himself on to for the campaign of 1980. Authority, in the context of the American Religion, is another form of gnosis, another knowing, and what it knows is that it must replace the purely secular authority brought about by the American Revolution. If the American Religion, as I surmised, began a generation after the Revolution, then it is a dangerous irony that, two centuries later, a belated version of our national faith is moving to abrogate our secular origin; so great a cloud of witnesses we yet may be to the triumphalism of our politicized shamans.

Index